Kings College,
Cambridge.

Quasi una Fantasia

Quasi una Fantasia

Essays on Modern Music

THEODOR W. ADORNO

Translated by
Rodney Livingstone

VERSO

London · New York

First published as *Quasi una fantasia* by Suhrkamp Verlag 1963
This translation first published by Verso 1992
© Suhrkamp Verlag 1963
Translation © Rodney Livingstone 1992
All rights reserved

Verso
UK: 6 Meard Street, London W1V 3HR
USA: 29 West 35th Street, New York, NY 10001–2291

Verso is the imprint of New Left Books

ISBN 0–86091–360–0

British Library Cataloguing in Publication Data
A catalogue record for this book is available from the British Library

Library of Congress Cataloging-in-Publication Data
A catalogue record for this book is available from the Library of Congress

Typeset by Type Study, Scarborough
Printed in Great Britain by Bookcraft (Bath) Ltd

Contents

Translator's Note

I should like to express my gratitude to Eric Graebner of the Music Department of Southampton University for the help he has given me with this translation. He patiently answered all my queries and read through the entire draft, making countless suggestions and picking up numerous errors. Needless to say, any that remain are my responsibility alone.

Passages in square brackets are my additions. The footnotes too are mine, unless otherwise specified.

Rodney Livingstone

Music and Language: A Fragment

Music resembles a language. Expressions such as musical idiom, musical intonation, are not simply metaphors. But music is not identical with language. The resemblance points to something essential, but vague. Anyone who takes it literally will be seriously misled.

Music resembles language in the sense that it is a temporal sequence of articulated sounds which are more than just sounds. They say something, often something human. The better the music, the more forcefully they say it. The succession of sounds is like logic: it can be right or wrong. But what has been said cannot be detached from the music. Music creates no semiotic system.

The resemblance to language extends from the whole work, the organized linking of significant sounds, right down to the single sound, the note as the threshold of merest presence, the pure vehicle of expression. The analogy goes beyond the organized connection of sounds and extends materially to the structures. The traditional theory of form employs such terms as sentence, phrase, segment, ways of punctuating – question, exclamation and parenthesis. Subordinate phrases are ubiquitous, voices rise and fall, and all these terms of musical gesture are derived from speech. When Beethoven calls for one of the bagatelles in Opus 33 to be played 'parlando' he only makes explicit something that is a universal characteristic of music.

It is customary to distinguish between language and music by asserting that concepts are foreign to music. But music does contain things that come very close to the 'primitive concepts' found in epistemology. It makes use of recurring ciphers. These were established by tonality. If tonality does not quite generate concepts, it may at least be said to create lexical items. Among these we may start by singling out those chords which constantly reappear with an identical function, well-established sequences such as cadential progressions, and in many cases even stock melodic figures which are associated with the harmony. Such universal ciphers were always capable of entering into a particular context. They provided space for musical specificity just as concepts do for a particular reality, and at the same time, as with language, their abstractness was redeemed by the context in which they were located. The only difference is that the identity of these musical concepts lay in their own nature and not in a signified outside them.

Their unchanging identity has become sedimented like a second nature. This is why consciousness finds it so hard to bid farewell to tonality. But the new music rises up in rebellion against the illusion implicit in such a second nature. It dismisses as mechanical these congealed formulae and their function. However, it does not dissociate itself entirely from the analogy with language, but only from its reified version which degrades the particular into a token, into the superannuated signifier of fossilized subjective meanings. Subjectivism and reification go together in the sphere of music as elsewhere. But their correlation does not define music's similarity to language once and for all. In our day the relationship between music and language has become critical.

The language of music is quite different from the language of intentionality. It contains a theological dimension. What it has to say is simultaneously revealed and concealed. Its Idea is the divine Name which has been given shape. It is demythologized prayer, rid of efficacious magic. It is the human attempt, doomed as ever, to name the Name, not to communicate meanings.

Music aspires to be a language without intention. But the demarcation line between itself and the language of intentions is not absolute; we are not confronted by two wholly separate realms. There is a dialectic at work. Music is permeated through and through with intentionality. This does not just date from the *stile rappresentativo*, which deployed the rationalization of music in an effort to exploit its similarity to language. Music bereft of all intentionality, the merely phenomenal linking of sounds, would be an acoustic parallel to the kaleidoscope. On the other hand, as absolute intentionality it would cease to be music and would effect a false transformation into language. Intentions are central to music, but only intermittently. Music points to true language in the sense that content is apparent in it, but it does so at the cost of unambiguous meaning, which has migrated to the languages of intentionality. And as though Music, that most eloquent of all languages, needed consoling for the curse of ambiguity – its mythic aspect, intentions are poured into it. 'Look how it constantly indicates what it means and determines it.' But its intentions also remain hidden. It is not for nothing that Kafka, like no writer before him, should have assigned a place of honour to music in a number of memorable texts. He treated the meanings of spoken, intentional language as if they were those of music, parables broken off in mid-phrase. This contrasts sharply with the 'musical' language of Swinburne or Rilke, with their imitation of musical effects and their remoteness from true musicality. To be musical means to energize incipient intentions: to harness, not indulge them. This is how music becomes structure.

This points to the question of interpretation. Interpretation is essential to both music and language, but in different ways. To interpret language means: to understand language. To interpret music means: to make music. Musical interpretation is performance, which, as synthesis, retains the similarity to language, while obliterating every specific resemblance. This is why the idea of interpretation is not an accidental attribute of music, but an integral part of it. To play music correctly means first and foremost to speak its language properly. This calls for imitation of itself, not a deciphering process. Music only discloses itself in mimetic practice, which admittedly may take place silently in the imagination, on an analogy with silent reading; it never yields to a scrutiny which would interpret it independently of fulfilment. If we were to search for a comparable act in the languages of intention, it would have to be the act of transcribing a text, rather than decoding its meaning.

In contrast to philosophy and the sciences, which impart knowledge, the elements of art which come together for the purpose of knowledge never culminate in a decision. But is music really a non-decisive language? Of its various intentions one of the most urgent seems to be the assertion 'This is how it is', the decisive, even the magisterial confirmation of something that has not been explicitly stated. In the supreme moments of great music, and they are often the most violent moments – one instance is the beginning of the recapitulation in the first movement of the Ninth Symphony – this intention becomes eloquently unambiguous by virtue of the sheer power of its context. Its echo can be heard, in a parodied form, in trivial pieces of music. Musical form, the totality in which a musical context acquires authenticity, cannot really be separated from the attempt to graft the gesture of decision on to the non-decisive medium. On occasion this succeeds so well that the art stands on the brink of yielding to assault from the dominating impulse of logic.

This means that the distinction between music and language cannot be established simply by examining their particular features. It only works by considering them as totalities. Or rather, by looking at their direction, their 'tendency', in the sense of the 'telos' of music. Intentional language wants to mediate the absolute, and the absolute escapes language for every specific intention, leaves each one behind because each is limited. Music finds the absolute immediately, but at the moment of discovery it becomes obscured, just as too powerful a light dazzles the eyes, preventing them from seeing things which are perfectly visible.

Music shows a further resemblance to language in the fact that, as a medium facing shipwreck, it is sent like intentional language on an odyssey of unending mediation in order to bring the impossible back home. But its form of mediation and the mediation of intentional language unfold according to different laws: not in a system of mutually dependent meanings, but by their lethal absorption into a system of interconnections which can alone redeem the meanings it overrides in each individual instance. With music intentions are broken and scattered out of their own force and reassembled in the configuration of the Name.

In order to distinguish music from the mere succession of sensuous stimuli it has been termed a structured or meaningful totality. These terms may be acceptable in as much as nothing in music stands alone. Everything becomes what it is in memory and in expectation through its physical contiguity with its neighbour and its mental connection with what is distant from it. But the totality is different from the totality of meaning created by intentional language. Indeed it realizes itself in opposition to intentions, integrating them by the process of negating each individual, unspecifiable one. Music as a whole incorporates intentions not by diluting them into a still higher, more abstract intention, but by setting out to proclaim the non-intentioned at the moment when all intentions converge and are fused together. Thus music is almost the opposite of a meaningful totality, even when it seems to create one in contrast to mere sensuous existence. This is the source of the temptation it feels to abstain from all meaning from a sense of its own power, to act, in short, as if it were the direct expression of the Name.

Heinrich Schenker has cut the Gordian knot in the ancient controversy and declared his opposition to both expressive and formal aesthetics. Instead he endorsed the concept of musical content. In this respect he was not unlike Schoenberg, whose achievement he failed to his shame to recognize. Expressive aesthetics focuses on polyvalent, elusive individual intentions and confuses these with the intentionless content of the totality. Wagner's theory misses the mark because it conceives of the content of music as the expression of the totality of musical moments extended into infinity, whereas the statement made by the whole is qualitatively different from that of the individual intention. A consistent aesthetics of expression ends up by succumbing to the temptation to replace the objective reality with transitory and adventitious meanings. The opposing thesis, that of music as resounding, animated form, ends up with empty stimuli or with the mere fact of organized sound devoid of every connection between the aesthetic form and that non-aesthetic other which turns it into aesthetic form. Its simple-minded and therefore ever-popular critique of intentional language is paid for by the sacrifice of art.

Music is more than intentionality, but the opposite is no less true: there is no music which is wholly devoid of expressive elements. In music even non-expressiveness becomes expression. 'Resounding' and 'animated' are more or less the same thing in music and the concept of 'form' explains nothing of what lies beneath the surface, but merely pushes the question back a stage to what is represented in the 'resounding', 'animated' totality, in short to what goes beyond form. Form can only be the form of a content. The specific necessity, the immanent logic, evaporates: it becomes a mere game in which everything could literally be something else. In reality, however, musical content is the profusion of things which obey the rules of musical grammar and syntax. Every musical phenomenon points to something beyond itself by reminding us of something, contrasting itself with something or arousing our expectations. The summation of such a transcendence of particulars constitutes the 'content'; it is what happens in music. But if musical structure or form is to be more than a set of didactic systems, it does not just embrace the content from outside; it is the thought process by which content is defined. Music becomes meaningful the more perfectly it defines itself in this sense – and not because its particular elements express something symbolically. It is by distancing itself from language that its resemblance to language finds its fulfilment.

(1956)

PART 1

Improvisations

Motifs

Beethoven comments on the cadenza of the E-flat major Concerto, *'Non si fa una cadenza, ma s'attacca subito il seguente'*.[1]
Schoenberg uses 'free' as a binding expression mark. In this way
the exceptions prove the rules of their age. Whereas Beethoven
takes the cadenza, the last vestige of the freedom to improvise,
and subjects it to the composer's subjective intentions, freedom
nowadays is strictly required of the interpreter in order to soften
the strictness of the interpretation which is specified by the
freedom of the composition.

Nothing could be more revealing of the melancholy which lies at
the heart of all inwardly directed music than Schumann's direction, 'Im fröhlichen Ton'.[2] To name the cheerfulness is to deny
its reality, and the 'in', which presupposes that the cheerful tone
is both known and exists in the past, simultaneously proclaims
that it has vanished and attempts to conjure it up once more.

No revolution is to be feared from Stravinsky. He provides both
bomb-plot and life insurance on his own initiative and in the
same policy. Accompanied by 'sightseers'[3] he travels in the state
coach of the *ancien régime* to inspect the bomb-craters created the
previous day. And in no time at all the blue-bird is building its
peaceful nest in them.

---

1. Don't play a cadenza, but go immediately into the next section.
2. In a cheerful tone.
3. In English in the orignal.

9

The plight of organs is a sorry one indeed. The orchestral organs with their endless, arbitrary stops and their expressive mechanisms are losing credibility and it is not just the advocates of a musty inwardness who emerge as their resolute opponents. However, the archaic organs from the age of Buxtehude have also ceased to provide a welcome change. They will probably all have to fall silent.

Ravel's *Valse* seals the fate of the waltz as such. To be a revenant means that you have first to have died.

The meaning of foreign words in operettas merits investigation. Originally, no doubt, they were meant to distinguish the banal, bourgeois world, which defines the imaginative horizon of the operetta, from the pathos of the romantic opera, which employs consecrated language and boycotts all mundane expressions. The romantic opera and the banal, bourgeois world constituted a coherent whole. The operetta invokes both. In the 1880s the foreign word acted as an index of the ironically accentuated lowlands to which art feels superior. Subsequently it became the isolated theatre-prop of a cultivated style of conversation which has ceased to exist in reality.

(1927)[4]

What Kant and Beethoven have in common is defined neither by the reliable moral principles nor by the long-since vanished pathos of the great personality, of which Kant once remarked that it was nothing to write home about and which is completely negated by the alienated constructs of the late Beethoven. It is doubtless true that only a forceful personality is capable of such acts of creation in isolation from his social context. However, the constructive plan soon squeezes the personality out of works whose temperature falls so dramatically. Yet there is something here which is common to both Kant and Beethoven and unites them in the same historical space. In the hierarchy of the Kantian

---

4. The dates refer to the year of publication of the preceding aphorisms.

system the narrow realm of the synthetic a priori judgements contrives to preserve the outlines of a vanishing ontology in diminished form, freely creating it once more in order to salvage it. And this act of creation both succeeds and perishes at the vanishing point of the subjective and objective. In the same way, in Beethoven's works, the images of long-since vanished forms arise from the abyss of an abandoned mankind and illuminate him. Beethoven's pathos is the gesture of the hand which lights the torch. His success is the depth of shadow in which the mourner hides from the end of the light. His suffering is enacted in the stony glance that catches the fading light as if to preserve it to the end of time. His joy resembles the flickering reflections on walls that are closing in.

The use of old, formal concepts to explain the new music might be acceptable if only the old categories were employed to demonstrate the difficulty of expressing the strangeness of the new in terms of the familiar. Thus the concept of tonality may indeed be applied to the later Schoenberg; but not so as to show that he too composes tonally – for in the final analysis what music might not be described in terms of the diatonic system? Indeed what music might not be described in terms of the twelve-note row? Instead, the concept should be used to show that he does not compose tonally; and that the use of a tonal scheme is an incomparably more complicated way of grasping what is actually happening than a more adequate system. However, the customary explanations are not in fact attempts to reduce music to schematic systems of representation. Instead the old descriptive modes are credited with a natural dignity. Thus to explain something in terms of the old modes of description means to ground the music in a dehistoricized nature. Hence at a stroke a descriptive system is transformed into a yardstick which gives good marks to what fits in easily and bad marks to whatever causes trouble. Thus the very attempt to understand the new music historically ends up by obscuring its genuine historical features. One is almost tempted to believe that in the absence of a newly discovered technique every explanation of music in terms of a static, material principle suppresses the best and distorts the work by forcing it into the straitjacket of an antiquated framework.

There is a lot of talk about *serenitas* nowadays. It is said to be the coming thing, along with its comrade-in-arms, the New Sobriety. If only we knew why we were suddenly all supposed to be more cheerful. Have we really only forsaken the dying Tristan in order to urge him to 'keep smiling'[5] and twist a face distorted with pain into a grimace of pleasure? If expression in music has become a dubious matter why must this expressionlessness, whose purpose lies shrouded in mystery, force itself to assume a mask of gaiety? Would it not be both harder and more important to make this expressionlessness a reality? When it comes down to it, it may turn out that this *serenitas* was hastily invented to persuade people that emptiness is the most sacred characteristic of their community. Or could it be the case that *serenitas* is supposed to prevent them from inquiring too closely into the nature of their community? There is an authentic serenade in our time: it is by Schoenberg. There is nothing very cheerful about it.

Many a music critic may be adequately characterized by his use of the genitive of the indefinite article before an author's name. 'The impressionism of a Debussy.' Such critics devalue the concrete *œuvre* which they have failed to comprehend by reducing it to the example of a type which does not exist. Culture is what mediates between the two.

Among the most infamous of the phrases used to defeat changes in musical consciousness is that of the 'trendsetting or pioneering work'. A work of art legitimates itself historically only by virtue of its uniqueness and intrinsic validity. Only works which have truth and consistency can impinge on the historical process. The specific work can never be reconstructed or deduced from the historical totality; on the contrary, the totality is contained within its most minute cell. But by substituting a connection with the

---

5. In English in the original.

presumed course of history for insight into that unique concrete artefact the critic defects from the work and escapes into a future which, as often as not, turns out to be the past. If a work points in new directions it raises the hope that it will not be necessary to expend too much effort on it, since it is nothing but a stopping point along the track which will surely lead into the Grand Central Station of the great platitudes. Thus Schoenberg has been consistently reduced to the status of a scout or precursor. It is as if he had composed the *Erwartung* purely for the sake of the Handel renaissance and the Latin Oedipus,[6] whereas the truth is that such enterprises have their origins in the fear of having one day to compose music as real, truthful and enduring as the *Erwartung*.

The problematic nature of music criticism may well be aggravated by the fact that for a long time the phenomenon of the collector was really unknown in music. The only way to collect music was to lock it up in cupboards. The connoisseurship of the non-specialists is always tied to the actual performance of music and hardly ever possesses the concrete familiarity of the hand that passes over the sheet of graphic art. For this reason the dilettante is to be found on the margins of music and the way to the centre is normally barred to him. The dilettantes are unable to establish any standards, whereas in the other arts it is often they who create a genuine critical distance. The fact that music, unlike pictures and books, cannot be physically owned has meant that, for all its popularity with the bourgeoisie, it has always remained esoteric.

The child trying to pick out a melody on the piano provides the paradigm of all true composition. In the same tentative, uncertain manner, but with a precise memory, the composer looks for what may always have been there and what he must now rediscover on the undiscriminating black and white keys of the keyboard from which he must make his choice.

---

6. The reference is to Stravinsky's *Oedipus Rex*.

Someone should write a musical aesthetics dealing with the art of omission. There are composers, and indeed whole genres, which are more accurately defined by what does not occur than by the positive events that take place in them. Abundance is not the only sign of a composer's imaginative powers; no less important is the force with which his intentions blast a void into all the possibles with which they are concerned. The power of an original musical intuition traces figures in the fine dust of discarded opportunities and it is these which often have to be deciphered if the nature of the composition is to be revealed. Of the more recent composers Debussy is the pre-eminent master of such discarded opportunities.

Many a contemporary composer is praised for his 'dynamism'. In the world of machines, which we insult when we compare that sort of music with it, it is a matter of moving masses of material or people. But musical dynamism is ideologically a law unto itself: nothing is moved and why the only visible purpose, that of the work of art, should be achieved by means of movement for its own sake, remains a mystery. For this reason it is inevitable that movement should soon turn out to be mere pseudo-motion in the static structure of this 'dynamic' music in which nothing that occurs is forced to change. They are all running on the spot like soldiers on the parade-ground. If you really want to dismantle humanity, you should at least try to find more intelligent excuses.

It's touching. Where do they get it from? Where did the Germans suddenly discover this powerful drive towards a new objectivity, a drive which is preparing itself to eliminate all individualism and *décadence*, subversiveness and aestheticism, and all this shoulder to shoulder with the Youth Movement and in tune with the pithy utterances of secondary-school teachers? Where did all this collective healthiness spring from all of a sudden? In music, at any rate, the example has been set by Stravinsky and Cocteau, the advanced exponents of a big bourgeoisie to whom the sphere of the individual and the particular has no new sensation left to offer. It is evident that their sense of chic conflicts with any desire to be an individual at all. Instead, they now enjoy, for the sake of the sensation, the laws of an existing collective, or rather of a collective that does not yet exist. In their eyes it exerts an indeterminate charm that lies somewhere between sport and neo-Thomism, and they unhesitatingly reach out for every social cement that promises to steady their nerves. In this respect the reconstruction being undertaken under these highly implausible auspices is not without a real foundation. Not indeed in terms of its unimpeachable intellectual and spiritual resources, but on the economic plane, which, even if they have gambled away their own interests, they have every reason to persuade others to accept as a God-given order and an unimpaired reality . And here they meet with astounding success. Petty bourgeois who cannot afford psychology are provided with the pretext to outgrow it before they have properly understood what it actually is. This is the road that runs from Raymond Radiguet to the musicians' guild. 'It's a long way to Tipperary.'[7]

There is one sphere in which the previous generation has failed us after all: musical pornography. Tristan's ecstasies between night and day, the complex and resonant soul of Princess Salome and, lastly, the cosmic utterances of Alexander Scriabin – however exalted their aspirations may have been, their goal ultimately was always the musical representation of a consummated sexual intercourse. But this they were unable to achieve. Notwithstanding Schreker's notable experiments and Skriabin's valiant efforts, the orchestral euphoria remains paltry when compared with the ecstasies of physical intercourse. The fate of that idea of unattainable joy inaugurated by romantic music is now sealed. It is not simply that it has lost the idealistic Divine Spark which it had ostensibly been striving for. Even worse, the actual bodily pleasure which was its real focus was denied it. So the belief that the erotic music of the nineteenth century was impotent is more than just psychologically valid and the state prosecutors who left it in peace had good reason to do so.

---

7. In English in the original. Raymond Radiguet (1902–23) was known for two brilliant novels of psychological analysis, *Le Diable au corps* and *Le Bal du Comte d'Orgel*).

Every great, authentic piece of musical kitsch – and this holds good even more for the sentimental than for the jaunty variety – is capable of acting as the accompaniment to imaginary catastrophes. Beneath the bright, shining deck the water is flooding into the ship's hold and threatens disaster. Where the tap-dancing is at its most assured, the boiler threatens to explode. Even on the basses of *Gern hab ich die Frau'n geküßt* [How I've liked kissing women], the listing *Titanic* presses down like a shadow from which there is no escape. The ship exploding against the backcloth of the lurid red evening skies, the burning house, an inferno literally engulfed in flames reaching up to the sky; the bridge breaking in two and crashing down into the Mississippi, taking with it the thundering train belonging to the Pacific Railway – all these images of unmitigated despair, which we have retained from our childhood, from illustrated books and our fears of falling asleep, rise up again as a warning in musical kitsch and illuminate the night sky as constellations of horror.

(1928)

Cavalleria Rusticana: migrants who go to the Argentine from Southern Italy return home rich and build themselves villas as white as Circe's palace, poised above the azure of the eternal sea; temples adorned with columned halls, scattered randomly around the historic landscape, a gloriously radiant barbarism. These buildings, financed by profiteering on potatoes, are more easily tolerated than their gentler sisters on the Ligurian coast. With its shapes and colours the volcanic soil's ever-present threat to destroy everything on it encroaches up to the very edge of the architecture and justifies for a moment the illusion which it kindles in those superannuated forms. For this illusion is founded on death. For the brief space of their life these buildings may borrow the mythological images which are invoked by the proximity of death. The transitory nature of the landscape immortalizes the brittle glaze with which men clothe it. In the same way the superficial, precarious and half-dilettantish music of *Cavalleria Rusticana* derives a luminosity from its proximity to death and so cannot be understood in terms of the antithesis between culture and kitsch. It is an improvised island upon which the mythical passions, however distorted, are abruptly elevated above the historical world, only to sink back at once and vanish again. How else to explain how this dusty framework, as small as a memento, can positively teem with all kinds of ordinary people, and seem to twitch with wild excrescences when it is violently shaken.

Chopin's form is no more concerned with the development of the whole through a series of minute transitions than with the representation of a single free-standing thematic complex. It is as remote from Wagner's dynamic thrust as from the landscape of Schubert. For all that it still contains the inherent contradiction that dominates the whole of the nineteenth century, the contradiction, namely, between the concrete specificity of the parts and their abstract, subjectively posited totality. He masters this contradiction by removing himself, as it were, from the flow of the composition and directing it from outside. He does not high-handedly create the form, nor does he allow it to crumple before the onslaught of the themes. Rather, he conducts the themes in their passage through time. The aristocratic nature of his music may reside less in the psychological tone than in the gesture of knightly melancholy with which subjectivity renounces the attempt to impose its dynamism and carry it through. With eyes averted, like a bride, the objective theme is safely guided through the dark forest of the self, through the torrential river of the passions. Nowhere more beautifully than in the A-flat major ballade, where the creative idea [*Einfall*], once it has made its appearance like a Schubert melody, is taken by the hand and conducted through an infinite vista of inwardness and over abysses of expressive harmonics where it finds its way to its second confirming appearance. In Chopin paraphrase and doubtless every kind of associated virtuosity is the resigned expression of historical tact.

What Debussy's music, the very epitome of Impressionism, means in the technical history of music, and what its relationship is to contemporary painting, became evident once its topicality disappeared. Something of its secret is revealed by a remarkable passage in Maupassant's novel *Mont-Oriol*, which illuminates the impressionism to which it belonged in more ways than one. In a description of the small spa we find the following:

> They came to the park which was lit up by lanterns suspended from the branches of the trees. The 'casino' orchestra played a slow, classical aria, which sounded as if it were limping, so full of gaps and pauses was it. The same four artists played it, wearily, without interruption, morning and evening, playing in this solitude only for the foliage and the stream, in an effort to create the impression of twenty instruments.

The gaps and pauses in such nineteenth-century music have grown longer since then. But it was Debussy who composed the music which strove to cover them up with the dense yet loose texture of its cells. It serves the same function: the shrubbery and the dream are to be consoled for their isolation, for being completely cut off from mankind. Hence the music absorbs their disappearing reflex into itself. Subjectivity produces the bright glow of the shrunken objects in order to salvage it in an image. The wretched piano, which has imprisoned the objects in the meshes of its strings, has to resound like an orchestra, so that the gardens in the rain will imagine that they are being serenaded by twenty musicians, whereas in reality only one is mourning for them.

I once heard, in the great Galleria in Naples, cinema music coming from outside. It was not the jumble of posters that revealed the fact that it was coming from a cinema: it was evident in itself. Not simply from the crude medley of tunes, but from the peculiar feeling that it was an accompaniment, even in the voices bearing the melody, a feeling that could not be explained in precise technical terms. This is how music sounds from which something is missing. But since it was not specially composed for the film, its interpretation turns towards the film. Confronted with the film, the melodies taken from exhausted operas are so drained of their force that they can only serve as background music. This is why they cannot exist for the listener as music, but exist musically only for the film. The music comes to the film because the latter is silent and it rocks the film gently into the darkness of the audience, even when it makes the gesture of passion. It is not meant for the audience. The listener only notices it when the film passes him by at a distance, separated from him by an abyss of empty space.

The resolute specificity of pieces of music based on folklore is justly punished by the abstract similarity which they all have with each other. Confronted by the present state of consciousness, the musical structures which deny its existence all draw closer to each other. What previously was supposed to bind each of them uniquely to a particular landscape, now binds them uniformly to each other. In Hungary as in Spain the monody of earlier centuries suppresses the more recently developed dimension of harmony. The ritual repetition of one and the same motif becomes an unconvincing means of creating form, once the motifs themselves have become interchangeable. Listening to them from the standpoint of the rational tonality of European music whose subsequent modifications they appear to be, even though they may be older in fact, it becomes difficult to distinguish their primitive keys from each other. Indeed, the motifs themselves converge in a remarkable manner. In this way the very music which aimed to preserve the distinguishing marks of its origins now falls under the same dominance of the universal which, as the music of the people, it revolves around, now that its substance has withered away. Nowadays the only music which can achieve concrete specificity is music which traverses the entire realm of reason right to its very end, preserving in it anything natural that has survived the experience.

The more specifically an instrumental work is written with an eye to the potential of the instruments which are to be deployed, the easier it is to transpose it into a completely different instrumental sound, to 'arrange' it. And the less closely it is tied to its original medium, the more problematic it is in any other. It is well known how much of Strauss's fresco-like conception still remains intact in the piano score. Mahler, on the other hand, in the interests of thematic clarity, 'orchestrates' more than Strauss, and is less influenced by timbre as such. Yet his music often sounds distorted on the piano. It is no less striking that Debussy and Ravel are infallible in their use of instrumental *peinture*, in their ability to remain faithful to the French origins of the 'arrangement'. Thus pieces like *Le Tombeau de Couperin* display the same perfection whether played orchestrally or on the piano. What this means is that only the truly concretizing work is capable of the transformations which it adds to the historical repertoire. Only when the instrumental tone has been precisely imagined and realized can it be rethought through. The transposing imagination is given a firm lead by a clearly defined structure, whereas it can never orientate itself among the vague possibilities of a general tone.

Nowhere is the struggle against the expert, which Mechtilde Lichnowsky[8] called for, more necessary than in music. For nowhere is the power of the dilettante greater. But expert and dilettante mutually complement each other. The dilettante feels he has been raised to a higher plane as soon as he understands the expert, whom he thereby elevates in his turn. The expert needs the dilettante in order to prove to himself that he isn't one. Together they form the twin poles of a middlebrow musical life whose hour has now struck. This is why it is so essential for the critic to extend his immanent listening as far as possible, while at the same time approaching music radically from the outside. To think about twelve-note technique at the same time as remembering that childhood experience of *Madama Butterfly* on the gramophone – that is the task facing every serious attempt to understand music today.

(1929)

---

8. Princess Mechtilde Lichnowsky (1879–1958) was a well-known writer of novels, plays, poems and essays. In her novels she took her subjects from the life of the aristocracy. Following her second marriage in 1937 she settled in London. Her works are now neglected.

That closing section in the finale of Mozart's A major Piano Concerto: a mechanically varied accompaniment figure between tonic and dominant over a pedal-point, with a melody which really only advances like the ticking of the second hand and then, without changing direction, suddenly breaks up into the most minute motifs; that conclusion whose dense texture brings the whole development and dynamism of the rest of the movement to an end, as if the framework wished to take prisoner the time that had flowed freely earlier on. What a close resemblance to the clock which the seventeenth-century philosophers imagined to be the nature of the universe. This was the clock which a Divine Mechanic had originally set in motion and then left to its own devices, trusting in the efficiency of the mechanism. It is a magic mechanism. While controlling time itself, by incarcerating it, it displays the time to an unknown observer outside. Inside, everything remains the same. The world is the dream of its sleeping Maker. But when the clock of Mozart's closing section, the coda, starts up for the third time, it is as if the Maker had suddenly remembered His half-forgotten work, as if He had intervened and broken the spell. Time takes control of the clock and, reconciled, plays its epilogue to itself before falling silent.

The emotion expressed in Schubert's music is humility [*Ergebung*], not resignation. Resignation (and indeed defiance) are attitudes typical of men faced with death. If a man insists on preserving his own nature, he will end by capitulating in resignation before the overwhelming power of nature, without guilt, indeed, but without hope. Schubert's humility, however, is not under the spell of nature; death is not its last word but its most gentle transition. 'I am no savage', is the message of his allegory of death; it is the mythic image of an already demythicized reality. The model of such a transition is the act of falling asleep. What Kierkegaard wished for the Christian could be said of Schubert: 'Blessed is he who does not grow angry, but who has faith – like a child who is taught to repeat certain words to lull it to sleep. The child says, "I believe in Him", and then falls asleep. Yes, he is blessed because he is not dead, but merely asleep.' Thus it is in the middle section of the slow movement of the E-flat major Trio. It fades away after the development and then holds fast to the last cadential motif and repeats it, becoming ever fainter. To the point where it falls asleep, where music forfeits its rights together with all human speech. A forte summons them back again.[9]

The landscape of Mendelssohn's *Auf Flügeln des Gesanges* is that of one of the earlier botanical gardens. At the time the song was composed botanical gardens had become quite common in Europe. A landscape roofed over and surrounded by glass: the tropics in confinement, miniaturized, a restricted area within the city of stone, but with genuine palm trees and a steamy warmth. Full of that exoticism of the interior – an interior of which potted cactuses have become the last survival now that the drawing-room palm is a thing of the past. An exoticism which is painful because it became quite unattainable through being brought too close to us. But this closeness has a magic power. Daughters with brown eyes, practising the song at the piano, are transformed by it into frail, mournful gazelles who utter a greeting to a beloved woman whom they would have liked to become. This is why the song remains so sad.

Beethoven and Kant really do meet up in Schiller. But in a more specific way than simply under the umbrella of a formal ethical idealism. In the 'Ode to Joy' Beethoven composed, programmatically, the Kantian postulate of the Categorical Imperative. In the line '*muß ein lieber Vater wohnen*', he emphasized the '*muß*'.[10] Thus God becomes in his eyes a mere postulate of the autonomous ego, which makes an appeal beyond the starry heaven above us to something which did not seem to be fully contained in the moral law.[11] But joy fails to respond to such an appeal, joy,

---

9. The middle section is apparently mm 41 (or thereabouts) to around m 80. The forte occurs at m 67. [Note by Eric Graebner.]

10. 'There must dwell a loving father.'

11. Adorno alludes here to the conclusion of the *Critique of Pure Reason*, in which Kant asserts: 'Two things fill the mind with ever new and increasing wonder and awe, the more often and the more seriously reflection concentrates upon them: the starry heaven above me and the moral law within me.'

which the ego impotently chooses, instead of its rising above him like a star.

(1930)

There is music from the nineteenth century which is so unbearably solemn that it can only be used to introduce waltzes. If it were left as it is, people listening to it would fall into a despair beside which every other musical emotion would pale. All the feelings of great tragedy would surely overwhelm them and they would have to veil their heads with gestures that have fallen out of use since time immemorial. This music no longer possesses a form with which to clothe its minor key. Chords are struck alternating with plangent tunes, and each stands on its own so that the listener is exposed to them in their naked immediacy. Only the excess of pain helps which springs from the certainty that things cannot go on like this. The double attack of F in the violins, the dominant of B-flat minor – a pathetic remnant of sadness together with a tiny E grace note, which a moment later will drive on the waltz melody in sharp, jolly spasms, always staccato and always in the train of the E. Nowadays such music thrives for the most part only in the band music played in zoos or in the small orchestras in provincial spas. Children are its greatest fans. It sounds best when heard at a fair distance, where the sighing flute is made to depend entirely on the passage of the great drum roll.

Very brief musical passages quoted out of context often seem banal, particularly in the case of older vocal music to which monothematicism is an unknown concept. I still remember from my earliest studies of music history how I would be overwhelmed by feelings of disdain when I was confronted with certain ostensibly expressive phrases from Josquin or Senfl and even Schütz. Nor could anyone work through *Lohengrin* in detail without being made to feel claustrophobic by the countless chords in minims in which feeling is stretched to the limits, even though they would scarcely attract attention on stage. And why?

23

The less securely the musical phenomenon is embedded in the context in which the constructive imagination has placed it, the more conspicuous is its basic material. Whenever the compositional technique is unable to govern it, the material finds itself refuted by technique and stands convicted of banality. Hence the most stringent test of any music is to see whether its smallest components make sense, and whether they can be quoted in their own right. This is only possible where nature itself finds expression in the technique, as in Schubert, or where the composer's freedom is able to grasp and shape the material down to the individual note, as in Schoenberg. Between these two extremes lies the realm of the 'creative idea' [*Einfall*]. But in the banality of the singular the mythical illusion of surface totalities stand revealed: it is of these that blind nature gains control.

Composers who distrusted and shunned each other in the light of day often come together in secret: Wagner and Offenbach in the crimson salon of a God-forsaken love. In the passage following the Rome narrative, when the degenerate Tannhäuser goes on living without hope and then enters the luminous sphere of Venus for the second time, 'To thee, Lady Venus, I return once more / to the sweet night of thy enchantments' – doesn't the artificial, Winter-Garden-like transparency of the music recall Offenbach, Helena's waltz and Hoffmann's stories in *The Tales of Hoffmann*? On the word 'sweet' [*hold*] the anticipated tonic under the first inversion of the leading-note triad, the diminished seventh and the triplet flourish in the vocal part could all come from Dapertutto's Mirror Aria which helps to cajole Giulietta's second victim. How thin is the crust which separates the upper world from the menace beneath and which just manages to protect the world of order above. In Offenbach the different spheres merge in parodic ecstasy without either gaining the upper hand. In Wagner the lively sense of horror just contrives to retain a hope of salvation in which even Wolfram does not truly believe as he begins to tremble in his fear of lust. But what would have become of the nineteenth-century opera if Offenbach and Wagner had been serious about liberating the underworlds of their singers, Orpheus and Tannhäuser? The turning point would only really have come if they had been able to gain entry there. If Elisabeth had followed Tannhäuser into the Venusberg with the gesture which she finds at the end of Act II, then he would have ended by expelling the Landgrave and his family and banishing them to the empty heavens.

It is an oddity that many of the most perfect melodies sound like quotations. Not like quotations from other pieces of music, but rather as if they had been taken from a secret musical language from which the ear picks out snatches here and there, which it does not even understand, but which present themselves forcefully and with the most patent authority. Instances of melodies with such authority are occasional creative ideas [*Einfälle*] of Schubert's, subsidiary ideas – never main themes – in Chopin and a few things of Beethoven's. The most extreme example is also one of the most familiar: the major mode refrain '*L'amour est enfant de Bohème*' from Carmen's Habanera, a primeval quotation which sounds familiar to everyone hearing it for the first time. Only the profundity of such memories can justify such banalities. Our music, produced as it is in isolation, has long since forgotten how to conjure up such quotations. The only composers who still know something about it, albeit without ever being able to achieve it, are the operetta composers. When countless hit songs narrate the prehistory of their own refrain in melodically unstriking couplets, their aim is to make them quotable by ensuring that they first appear as a quotation, a quotation from the banal sphere behind whose banality the banality of primal images lies buried. One is almost tempted to believe that this was the reason for inventing the refrain in the first place.

For all the respect due to Handel the time is surely ripe to do away with that ludicrous coupling which still joins his name to Bach's. It originates in that infamous *juste milieu* which can no more tolerate one of its great men on his own, without his heavenly twin, than the morning prayer on the wall can dispense with the evening prayer. It pairs its classics off like opponents in a gladiatorial contest. For counting off your artists in a military rhythm, one two, one two, releases you from the gravest obligation of the work of art, that of its uniqueness. Of course, even dinosaurs may feel some inhibitions when talking of Goethe and Schiller in a single breath. But musicologists do not hesitate to yoke the homophonic Handel and the polyphonic Bach to the crude plough of stylistic history. It is not necessary to deny the greatness of Handel's late works and many a fulfilled moment in the earlier ones, or to fail to recognize the purity of many individual melodies, to admit that according to very specific and reliable technical criteria the musical quality of the overwhelming majority of Handel's works cannot justify their performance nowadays. Whereas in Bach's case, even in the plethora of cantatas there is scarcely a single one which would not repay performance with a host of fresh insights. Behind the official, pharisaically emphatic admiration for Handel's expressive power, simplicity and objectivity what lies concealed is resentment and the inability to judge the music as composition. The essential lesson that Handel has to teach is one of economy of means. The best part of this was assimilated into the bare, austere power of Beethoven's *œuvre*. All that remains today is the hieratic gesture, which no longer suffices.

(1932)

The significance of the pastoral tone in Offenbach's music has not been the subject of much reflection – that Arcadian landscape that lives in the memory of the Prince, but also in the song of Paris, the shepherd on Mount Ida, and especially in the sound of Offenbach's woodwinds above translucent pedal-points. Offenbach's idyll is as remote from the pastoral images of the eighteenth century as only the nineteenth century can be. The awakening creature no longer shyly plays the melody of freedom. Instead the liberated creature recognizes that its freedom, bourgeois freedom, is an illusion and its pleasure is converted into an infernal joy, as if in a hall of distorting mirrors. Its melody is transformed into a phantasmagoria, its dream branded with the stigmata of illusion. The shepherds whose oboes resound here so innocently are girls in boys' clothing. They are playing in front of the gates of Orpheus' underworld. Their sweet severity lures us ambiguously into Pharaoh's realm where they all cheat: '*évohé! que ces déesses / pour enjôler les garçons, / ont de drôles de façons!*'[12] Meanwhile the woodwinds and the shepherds reveal their true nature to the prisoners in the salon landscape by dancing the cancan.

Ever since the title of doctor lost its alchemical aura and its humanist dignity it has been left to the operetta to salvage it and its magic. Not in its images, but as resplendent script which displays the name of the industrious magician together with the humbug. There they are in all their glory, the graduates of the faculties of law and philosophy, whose education qualifies them to order the Three Musketeers around once more, or to sell the Pompadour yet again. Their *risqué* verses probe the flesh of the chorus girls, just as in olden days those sinister magicians, the genuine doctors, carved up bodies in the anatomy class.

The true subject of *Der Freischütz* is nowhere better revealed than in Max's statement '*Abends bracht' ich reiche Beute*'.[13] The true action, an archaic one, lies at a deeper level than the superficial Fate tragedy. The power of Fate that leads Max to cast the magic bullets with Kaspar in order to win his bride stems from the time when the man was a hunter who had to bring food for his loved ones, or even to buy their freedom. But what keeps the hunter from his spoils is not demonism, as the characters imagine and as the authors may well intend. It is the very secret Christian objection to the heathen right of plunder which insists that a person who has incurred guilt can only be bought free at the price of another living person. Max sings of his beloved (whose saintly name is anything but fortuitous), '*Drohend wohl dem Mörder, freute / sich Agathes Liebesblick*'.[14] But for her to experience joy, her threat has first to be fulfilled. This happens dialectically,

---

12. 'Eheu! These goddesses have strange ways of captivating boys.'
13. 'In the evenings I brought back a rich bag.'
14. 'Threatening though it would be to a murderer, Agathe's loving gaze rejoiced.'

27

thanks to the same forces whose ancient rights are to be broken. The nature gods of the dim and distant past, banished from a world in which the hunters are being domesticated as foresters, return once more as demons and strive to destroy man by recalling him to the obsolete spell of the right to plunder. This is why it is a good omen, not a bad one, that right to the end Max is unable to fire a decisive shot. And the year's probation before he can be appointed as forest ranger only means that, thanks to his fate, the nature demons are both reconciled and deprived of their powers. The Freeshooter is the last huntsman. With the stray bullet he has actually shot himself free from both the bride-purchase and the blood law. But the fear which always grips the audience at the Huntsmen's Chorus is the fear of the image of a historical myth as eternal recurrence. Dressed in the costumes of the Thirty Years War, each resembling the other, they crowd in on the wounded man like the obsessive figures of repetition itself.

It is Weber's music which first sheds light on the structure of the action. It had often been observed that the clarinet passage in the overture, the theme of hope, rises up like a constellation in the Wolf's Glen to the words, '*Ha! Furchtbar gähnt der düstre Abgrund!*'[15] But no star appears in the pitch-black heavens and Max brings no joyous news – unless it be the news that is to be found in the chasm itself: that the demons which have conspired against him to deny him happiness, or, by granting his wish, will drag him down to their inferno, are destroying themselves, since they demonstrate their impotence in the Christian world and are unable to fulfil their side of the bargain. This is why Kaspar dies cursing the devil as well as God. Max's voice over the chasm is just the echo of the devil's self-destruction which, rising up to the heights, turns into hope.

The route from the archaic action to a Christian drama, which amounts to a Christianization of the plot, is marked by Kind with

---

15. 'Fearful yawns the gloomy chasm.' This constellation is in fact a pair of themes that starts at m 96 with the theme later used for the verse quoted by Adorno and which leads eventually to the so-called 'hope theme' in m 123. The clarinet is present throughout the whole section ending in m 146.   [Note by Eric Graebner.]

a saying from the language of childhood which, like signposts in the forest, name origin and goal, the overgrown depths and the open field. With their music they can be quoted for ever. '*Ja, Liebe pflegt mit Kummer / stets Hand in Hand zu gehn.*' '*Er war von je ein Bösewicht, / ihn traf des Himmels Strafgericht.*'[16] With such sayings the opera creates a game between time and eternity, and Kaspar, the villain, speaks in the dog Latin of gingerbread rhymes: '*Ohne dies Trifolium / Gibt's kein wahres Gaudium / Seit dem ersten Übel.*'[17] The memory of this he bequeathes to children as a plaything for the Sunday matinée performance.

Whatever doubts may be raised about the authenticity of Wagnerian mythology, one figure at least seems to have sprung directly from the prehistoric world: the horse. '*Was ruht dort schlummernd / im schattigen Tann? / Ein Roß ist's, rastend im tiefen Schlaf!*'[18] Played in the most extreme piannissimo, with the Valkyrie theme quoted over the low, stagnant chords, this sounds more archaic than the hero's sword and the Valhalla of the gods. It seems as old as memory itself. Apart from the occasion when Tristan awakens to the sound of the shepherd's pipe there is no other scene where Wagner masters so completely the stratum of the dream-world, which elsewhere the trombones vainly strive to capture. For the horse knows more about heroes than they do themselves. Horses are survivors from the age of heroes: they appear as if the very first words had been addressed to them, so that those who have been made victims might struggle free from the condition of muteness. It is the only animal for which we feel no disgust, and hence the only one we should not eat, if we do not wish to regress to a pre-linguistic age. And this is why in Wagner the horse is seen eating and is given the Christian epithet 'blessed': '*Dort seh ich Grane, / mein selig Roß: wie weidet munter, / der*

---

16. 'Yes, love goes hand in hand with sorrow.' 'He always was a wicked rogue, Heaven's punishment has struck him down.' Friedrich Kind (1768–1843) was Weber's librettist.

17. 'Without this trifolium / There's been no true gaudium / Since man's first fall.'

18. 'What lies there slumbering in the shadow of the pines? A steed, sunk deep in sleep.' (*Siegfried*, Act III, Scene 3, mm 50–56)

mit mir schlief! / Mit mir hat ihn Siegfried erweckt.'[19] The grazing horse and the talking man – together they form the trope of awakening. Wagner has inscribed this trope with music which stands out from the rest of the *Ring*, as if it were surrounded by an aura of grace.

The infinite difficulty of satisfying the formal laws of opera – no form, whether the strictest or the most daring is so helplessly exposed to failure as opera – stems from the fact that it cries out to be disrupted, and disruption can only be tolerated by the most potent of forms. Opera does not replicate the stage action in order to elevate it to a loftier or symbolic plane, as the cliché would have it. Instead the music cuts in on the action as if to proclaim that the strictness of its causal motivation shares a frontier with freedom. Just as Orpheus' playing rouses the dead from their imprisonment in the cave, so opera rescues its characters from fate by singing about them.

'All opera is Orpheus.' But as proof of this it must transcend itself. It must insert into its own musical foundations the caesura which creates the form by destroying it. Thus when Mozart's *Don Giovanni* pauses in midstream to recall *Figaro*, this is no Romantic Irony, but something central to Mozart's conception. And when all genuine opera makes intermittent use, in however sublimated a way, of the elements of stage music, it is only following the innermost laws of its own nature. The protest of the fanfare in the prison scene [in *Fidelio*] is not just a dramatic moment, it is the operatic moment *par excellence*. The young Wagner remains true to this insight when he consistently plays off the gestures of what seems from the compositional point of view a formless, melodically unarticulated stage music against the immanent presence of the orchestra. And the later Wagner remains true to this insight, as we see when he shatters the dense chromatic structure by diatonic means. This may perhaps explain why Brahms, the master of a self-contained form which would brook no concessions, wrote no operas. He would never have been able to

---

19. 'I see Grane there, my blessed steed: how happily he grazes, he who was asleep with me! Siegfried awoke him along with me.'

bring himself to write the two bars too many which are essential to give the opera its full complement. The most sublime example of this is to be found in the finale of *Figaro*, in the ensemble which follows the brief reconciliation scene. Alban Berg, the planning architect of opera, has shown himself to be something more than that by keeping faith with this intention. With the enigmatic repeat of the crescendo B after the murder scene in *Wozzeck* and with the quotation from the beginning of *Wozzeck* in *Lulu*, he lets his victims return from the shadowy world of their images, over the narrow bridge which lies beyond their form.[20]

The bourgeois concert: before dismissing it, we should listen to the speeches in its defence, which explain whence it came and how it developed to its present state. It came from the lower depths, like the society that gave it birth. We could read about it in E. T. A. Hoffmann, but also in the great Wilhelm Hauff, whose horror story, *The Singer*,[21] can tell us a few things about it. It tells of child prodigies who appear to have been destined to lead a life of suffering from birth, and the inhuman beauty of their voices is the product entirely of their inhuman treatment:

> He tormented me for days on end and drummed into me the most difficult pieces by Mozart, Gluck and Spontini, which I then sang to great applause on Sunday evenings. Poor Schepperl – this was how my name Giuseppa was abbreviated – became one of those unhappy child prodigies whom Nature has given a wonderful talent to their great misfortune. The cruel man made me sing every day, he whipped me and gave me nothing to eat for days on end.

---

20. Adorno's text is confusing here. First, it is not clear why the repeated B should be puzzling, since the whole scene is based on the obsessive repetition of this pitch class. Second, if 'the beginning' of the murder scene is taken to be the point where the moon rises (3 bars after 95), rather than the beginning of Act III, Scene 2, literally, according to the text, the passage referred to in *Lulu* would be at bar 605 (Act II, Scene 1), accompanying the final words of Dr Schön whom Lulu has just shot. The similarity of the passages, although not obvious in the scores, since precise pitch identities are not in question, is actually quite striking and involves gestures, tempo, rhythm and contour in a general way.   [Note by Eric Graebner.]

21. Wilhelm Hauff (1802–27) is known for *Lichtenstein*, a historical novel in the manner of Scott and also for fairy tales with a tendency towards the grotesque and the satirical.

Having tamed and trained her in this way, her stepfather, as her first impresario, sold her to a house of musical pleasures in which the runs of the coloratura soprano glitter over the gaming table. With gold in her throat she resembles that other gold of which the singer had previously noted, 'It was my purchase price'. The carriage stopped in front of a large, brightly lit house:

> The following evening I was clad in splendid clothes. I was then led into the drawing-room. The twelve girls, all beautifully dressed, sat at gaming tables, on sofas or at the piano. . . . The master of the house led me to the piano. I had to sing. My performance was generously applauded.

It is the birth of the concert ticket as the genuine billet-doux:

> I was struck by one thing, however. One evening, when I chanced to walk past the stairs, I noticed that the gentlemen who visited us gave the porter money in return for which they received blue or red cards, which they then handed to a servant before entering the drawing-room.

Such coloured tickets no longer reveal that once upon a time a dandy produced one 'with a tender gaze'. But what of the fourteen-year-old boy who is allowed to attend his first concert and who passes through the double doors into the brightly lit house, entitled to enter because he is in possession of a blue or red card? A porter and a servant show him the way to the promised land. He listens entranced to the singer, his gaze fixed on her deep *décolletage*, a singer who surrenders to him more brazenly with her hired song than the ballet dancers of his morning dreams. He recognizes the unknown singer again as the ambassadress of the great brothels. Their entertainments paved the way for the public concerts, and it is the ritual memory of them that momentarily reappears in the radiance of the chandeliers.

(1937)

Percussion: Mahler occasionally calls for the cymbals to be attached to the bass drum, as used to be the custom in military bands and doubtless too with travelling musicians. Both instruments were played by the same person. This thrifty procedure prepares us for poor people's music. It is as utterly incompatible with the autonomy of either instrument and their freedom to fulfil their own artistic aims as is the mechanical nostalgia of the harmonica. In this primitive way of playing the delight in regression is mingled with poverty and childhood dreams. For the remembered promise of childhood glistens from the broken piece of glass picked up in the street. And the percussion has both the poverty of the brittle sound which has barely risen above mere noise and the promise of what has never been, which is inseparable from the traces of the very oldest things. The bass drum grumbles menacingly and says, 'Children, today something's going to happen.' And it has salvaged this double meaning and carried it over into great music.

The clash of cymbals: from way beyond the peaks of music a Horn of Plenty opens and gold trickles, streams and cascades down, vanishing into the most secret nooks and crannies. An image of happiness from the nineteenth century.

Side drum: three soft, rapid beats on the one instrument awaken the feeling of a mass of people marching in the distance. In this way we are reminded that all music, even the loneliest, is intended for the many whose gestures are preserved in its sound.

Flourish on the triangle: a woman becomes conscious of her body and shakes her locks. But it is just the sound of the triangle. A shaft of light falls on the instruments, making strings and brass gleam as if they had been illuminated not by the sun, but merely by the highlights of a painter untouched by taste.

Xylophone: bleached bones make the most colourful music.

The zoo used to contain not just the animals, but also a music pavilion and, occasionally, exhibitions of exotic tribes, Samoans and Senegalese. But the only sound that penetrated to them from the distant pavilion was the sound of the kettledrum. Whether it be the memory of this, or simply the condensation of what has long been forgotten – even today, when I hear the kettledrum it brings back the memory of Tamasese, the tribal chief. And at the same time I recall that the heads of Tamasese's prisoners were used as drums, or perhaps they were the cauldrons in which the savages cooked human flesh. Is the drum the successor of human sacrifice or does it still sound the command to kill? In our music it resounds as an archaic survival. It is the legacy of violence in art, the violence which lies at the base of all art's order. While as a spiritualized activity art strips violence of its power, it continues to practise it. Freedom and domination commingle inseparably in art. Its integral form, the triumph of its autonomy, is what also casts a spell on the listener, leaves no one out and subjects everyone to its speechless performance. It is only necessary to listen to the humane Beethoven from outside, from a sufficiently great distance, and nothing remains but the terror aroused by Tamasese. But perhaps all humaneness does is to keep the consciousness of terror alive, the consciousness of all that can never be made good.

(1951)

From my childhood I retain very clear impressions of the associations aroused in my mind by the name of Richard Strauss. I recall the moment when, shrill and very new, it first entered my consciousness where Schubert's Rondo and the *Kreutzer* Sonata had long since enjoyed a secure place. As had even Chopin's Nocturnes, which I really only knew about from the composers' version of Happy Families, which I especially loved and to which I owed my knowledge of Spohr's works. To me the name of Richard Strauss suggested music that was loud, dangerous and generally bright, rather like industry, or rather what I then imagined factories to look like. It was the child's image of modernity that was set alight by his name. What attracted me were the stories about the rumbustious plays he had composed which my parents and my aunt had heard. I was attracted even more strongly by their painful refusal to tell me the content of those operas which anyway I was still too young to understand – I

34

had been persuaded that the head in *Salome* belonged to a calf, and similarly, they had tried to convince me that all the excitement in *Otello* was about a handkerchief that had been mislaid.

But more than all this my imagination was kindled by the word *Elektra*. This word was explosive and full of artificial, seductively evil smells, like a large chemical works close to the town where we lived, whose name sounded very similar. The word glittered cold and white, like electricity, after which it appeared to have been named; a piece of gleaming electrical machinery that poured out chlorine and which only adults could enter, something luminous, mechanical and unhealthy. When, at the age of fifteen, I got to know some of Strauss's music, it had hardly any connection with that old sense of excitement I had felt and which was comparable to the prospect of an excursion to the Eastern docks. By then I knew about Berlioz, Liszt and Wagner, and was studying the theories of instrumentation. The description of a bass clarinet, an English horn or even the obsolete serpent gave me the same thrill as the self-contained machinery of the mysterious *Elektra* had done in the past. And in *Don Juan* and *Ein Heldenleben*, which I knew directly, I sought only to identify those instruments. Only much later did I notice that the images generated by my imagination in advance of any knowledge actually fitted the music far better than the verification procedures I subsequently conducted. Thus the latent content of a work of art may well be transmitted uniquely in the aura you enter when you touch it, without any real knowledge, whereas it is too encapsulated in the solid kernel of its form to reveal itself to us until that form is shattered. But that aura is created as an emission of rays; it hovers before us as a sign of the material which our eye is doubtless able to perceive in the form of fluid particles, but not in a solid mass. It is extinguished and then flares up finally once more, once our mind has penetrated to its core. No work is truer to its aura, and more deceptive in its form than that of Strauss, and it would scarcely be going too far to maintain that you only know it, if you know it by hearsay, rather than by hearing it.

A similar phenomenon may be observed on a journey through

places in which you have never stayed, but whose towns and cities are familiar. Even when you are no expert in the geography of the regions you are travelling through, you can guess the sequence of the stations simply from the atmosphere of each place name, which seems to suggest how close it is to, or distant from, other places in the same region. Fulda: the next station has to be Erfurt, since its aura suggests that it lies between Hesse-Cassel and Thuringia. You then expect Weimar, which does indeed lie in the fantasy realm of Thuringia, but, unlike Halle, is far from being so clearly located in a state with a Saxon dialect. If you then stop over in Halle and Erfurt these differences may easily shrink and the people and cities may turn out to be very similar. Only when you have looked at the map and constructed the constellation which all these towns form together does the original picture reimpose itself. What is needed is a precise overview of the Straussian province. Even more, you have to have left it behind you in order to discover once again the chemical, highly industrialized and neon-lit character of his Art Nouveau that was once advertised by the name *Elektra*.

(1929)

Commodity Music Analysed

1

Gounod's *Ave Maria*: an Englishman has proposed this formula for music hall: *Put three half-naked girls on a revolving stage. Then play the organ.*[1] This recipe is foreshadowed in the *Méditation.*[2] It is a piece of sacred pop music featuring one of those Magdalenes notable equally for their penitence and their seductiveness. Overcome with remorse, they reveal all. Thus saccharined religion becomes the bourgeois cloak for a tolerated pornography. You say Bach, but you mean Gounod. You have the rigorous prelude, but what you really respond to is the soulful melody. On the organ for preference, but with the violin obligato in the vocal part. It is the birth of the Wurlitzer from the spirit of Faust: archetypal cinema music.

Its basic gesture is supplication in pious self-abandonment. The soul delivers itself into the hands of the Almighty with uplifted skirt. This is how Henny Porten pleaded for mercy.[3] One of her earliest films was *The Parson's Daughter*. It ended in death.

The music rides roughshod over the words. Where they are felt to be inadequate, they are repeated. There is no proper place

---

1. In English in the original.
2. I.e., the *Méditation sur le Prélude de Bach.*
3. Henny Porten (1890–1960) was an actress of the German silent screen, celebrated for her portrayals of injured innocence.

for the 'fructus ventris tui'. It acquires that dubious imitative quality which the words 'blessed be the fruit of thy womb' had in childhood. But there is one word the music penetrates to its core. It is 'peccatoribus'. If the soaring note of redemption is prepared for by the restraint of the 'Ora pro nobis', so that you can hear well in advance just how high it has to go, then the Latin ablative ending is the springboard that propels the sinners into the next world. It is on 'peccatoribus' that the skirt-raising gesture falls. The dress that bears her aloft reveals her thigh. But the upward sweep is so overwhelming that even the moment of our death is powerless before it. The climax comes, God alone knows why, with the 'hora'; once the 'peccatoribus' have experienced their moment of bliss, it is irrelevant to ask where they have been transported to. The upward surge carries the 'hora mortis' along with it and, without letting you catch your breath for even a moment, it culminates joyously in the superfluous 'Amen'. Since the image of utopian happiness has vanished from great music, it is preserved only by inferior music, but in caricatured form, perfect illusion[4] as prayer.

Rachmaninov's Prelude in C-sharp minor: there are passages familiar from pieces for children and from school concerts which are marked 'grandioso'. Tiny hands execute the gesture of strength. Children imitate grown-ups, perhaps even the virtuosi who have been swotting up their Liszt. It sounds tremendously difficult and at all events very loud. But it is comfortingly easy to play: the child knows that the colossal effect cannot misfire and that he is assured in advance of a triumph that has been achieved without effort. The Prelude preserves this triumph for infantile adults. It owes its popularity to listeners who identify with the performer. They know they could do it just as well. As they marvel at the power which forces the four-stave systems into a fourfold fortissimo, they marvel at themselves. In their mind's eye they can see their lion's paws growing. Psychoanalysts have discovered the Nero complex. The Prelude gratifies this from

---

4. *Schein* means both illusion and appearance.

the outset. It allows the megalomaniac free play, without pinning him down to anything definite. No one can blame the thundering chords for turning the dilettante who churns them out so immaculately into a conqueror of the world. Risk and security are fused in one of the boldest instances of musical daydreaming ever created. The excitement rises to fever-pitch if, as a bonus, the piece is played in a three-quarters darkened hall. The sombre mood of destruction which the Slav idiom of the piece simultaneously threatens and glorifies, arouses in every listener the certainty that in the foreboding gloom he too could easily smash the piano to pieces. He is assisted in this not just by the conjunction of heavy artillery and easy playability, but by the design of the entire colossal bagatelle. Almost all tonal music, especially that of the pre-Classical era, provides the contemporary amateur with the opportunity to make his own gesture of power in the final cadence. This is an affirmative statement which says: so be it. It is an affirmation as such, whatever has gone before. Hence the ritardando. Its function is to underline and its strength enables the performer to measure his own by restraining himself and reining in his own impetuosity. Even if this gestural meaning of the final cadence may only date from the Romantic movement, it can be said that in the course of its post-Romantic debasement Rachmaninov emptied it of all content, freed it of every genuine musical event and threw it on to the market as a commodity.

The Prelude is just one long final cadence; it could be described as a single, long, insatiable, repetitive ritardando. It parodies the passacaglia progression by taking three cadence-forming bass notes which can conclude the theme of a passacaglia, and presents them, as it were, as a passacaglia theme. Repetition insists on the point with ruthless self-advertisement. The phrases are so short-winded that even the most insensitive ear can scarcely go wrong. Moreover, the motif-forming melodic counter-voice merely paraphrases the cadence. All the music does say is: so be it. The fact that we don't know what is to be is what constitutes the essence of its Russian mysticism. In the middle it breaks into a run with a cheap series of triplets and creates the illusion of fluent virtuosity. But in vain. It is only the motivic counter-voice. Fate remains fate and insists that things are so and not otherwise. And when at the end it explodes with all the primal force of conventionality, it can be assured of the gratitude of all those who have always known this and could see it coming.

Dvorak's *Humoresque*: at one time there used to be a craze for a certain type of puzzle in the entertainment and theatre section of the daily newspapers. They were called picture-puzzles. A caption might read: Can you find the burglar? The picture showed an empty street without any people. A long ladder is leaning against a house, but it too has no one on it. Dark spots of rain are shown falling on the white houses. There is no sign of a burglar. The trick was to turn the page this way and that, sideways or upside down, until you discovered that the lines signifying rain, when taken with a bulky chimney, formed a grimacing gaze which could be arrested. The memory of these picture-puzzles is preserved by Dvorak's *Humoresque* (Opus 101). Where is the humour hidden? For its consumption of art the bourgeois household has devised the idea of the sensitive person. It signifies an attitude towards art that has parallels with that of the collector. The sensitivity of the sensitive person resembles that of the man who is able to decipher the watermarks on stamps. It implies an intimate understanding of the work itself. But that can be deceptive. The sensitive person is not really a collector. Unlike the latter he does not really open up the work for inspection. He simply responds with the gaze of the solitary to what everyone else has already appreciated. The watermarks he reads are the clichés of fame. Those who like the *Humoresque* are sensitive people of this kind. The world is full of them.

In this instance the cliché of fame is the title itself. It is here that the humour has found refuge and the connoisseur simply adds his approving smile. You have to be quite exceptionally sensitive to discern any humour even in the rhythm of the initial melody. Admittedly, its dotted theme hops along, with a dragging attack which then speeds up in an improvised way. It is a mournful hop, a hopping amidst tears, for the sensitive listener. When the melody returns it changes, towards its end, with a sobbing ascending sixth, into an intermittent minor. On Kubelik's violin it sounded just like Moissi in the role of Fedya, when he says, 'Look, the sunset!'[5] And in general the piece is full of sunset. Its fame is not adequately explained either by the title or the hopping. The secret lies in the broad Bohemian thirds. It's wonderful to be able to wallow in them. You sink right in; it is here perhaps, that the affinity with the burglar is most evident.

The thirds are Bohemian, the middle movement is Slav through and through. It begins darkly, with passion. It could turn into a dance. Instead, nothing happens. The passion is as brief as a tunnel; you can already see the sunset at the other end. There is no need to become excited and, with the faithful recapitulation, you are rewarded with a mood of cheerful resignation as a bonus. This is what life is like: always the same. There is nothing to be done about it.

The sentimentality which is common to all remains unaware of its universality. For this reason it thinks itself refined, really posh. Rather quaintly, the piece was composed somewhere in America and a monument has been erected to it at the site. But the *Humoresque* itself survives as a monument to that knowing twitch at the corner of the mouth which denotes the willingness to show understanding for every form of hegemonic nastiness, so as to be the better able to forgive it.

The slow movement of Tchaikovsky's E minor Symphony: a bright, moonlit night in the Crimea. The general's garden, bright clouds, a bench surrounded by roses. The pictures are tinted green. A well-built young officer with the noble, but also chubby face of the tenor, in full-dress uniform. Simply covered with medals on which the camera dwells. From time to time a star flashes on his chest. The scent he is wearing and his passionate courtship are conveyed by the melody on the horn. He is

---

5. The actor Alexander Moissi (1880–1935). Fedya, the tragic hero of Tolstoy's *The Live Corpse*, was his most famous role.

answered by the chaste and tender voice of a girl. It is the oboe, the general's daughter. The two have evidently already reached an understanding; there is no resistance. The officer falls on his knees before her. 'I shall sacrifice everything for you – career, fame and even life and honour.' He buries his head in her lap. A voice from the woodwinds, perhaps the South Russian nightingale, Tatiana by name, executes a mournful arabesque. The uniform with the medals is now photographed against the girl's white dress. She has just returned from a Swiss boarding-school. They are brutally interrupted by the sounds of war. It is the Imperial Guard, the old general at its head. Implacably he demands an explanation from the young officer. The officer stands silently, his head bowed, deeply wounded, but with dignity. There is a long silence. A bright, moonlit night in the Crimea. The general's garden, a young officer, the nightingale, the Imperial Guard. But this time the hero is shot down by the Guard. He then repeats, 'I shall sacrifice everything for you – career, fame, life and honour'. It is doubtless true that towards the close of the nineteenth century the music that swept people off their feet did so because it combined drastic ideas with conventionality. In so doing it satisfied the demands of the cinema before the cinema was invented. It applied the techniques of cinema down to the very last details of its self-indulgent, butterfly mode of perception. Thus Tchaikovsky's backwardness, when compared with Wagner, proves to be in advance of its time because it was part of the culture industry, even before the real consumers of the culture industry had come into existence.[6] Nevertheless, such an audience does receive a reward for its receptiveness, a moment of reconciliation that dates back to their childhood. Even though these symphonies resemble films, they are not like the pretentious films that you have to see right through because you have paid so much to see

---

6. 'Culture industry' is a term used by Adorno and Max Horkheimer in their *Dialectic of Enlightenment* to refer to modern popular culture and indeed all the products of the electronic media. Since the culture industry represents 'the triumph of invested capital' it was regarded as the antithesis of all true culture whose function is to negate the existing social order.

them. Their form is rather that of the cinema long since past, where you came in in the middle and didn't fully understand what was going on, although all was clear. In such films the whole dissolved into familiar names and gestures – and how convincingly Tchaikovsky has found the appropriate melodies for them. And after the catastrophe, the beginning of the film that had been missed, returns, just as if nothing had happened, and without anyone's venturing to turn out the patient viewer for whom all the riddles were now resolved. Kitsch contains as much hope as is able to turn the clock back. It is the depraved reflection of that epiphany which is vouchsafed only to the greatest works of art. Kitsch only forfeits its right to exist when it enters into a parasitical relationship to history, mimics its verdicts and finds itself forbidden to reverse them. The mass art of today is inferior to the andante, its model, because it no longer permits anything comparable to the re-entry of the horn melody after the tragic general pause. The remnant of clumsy naivety, which is where Tchaikovsky has the advantage over the greater sophistication of mass art, was the refuge of what art must refuse and which is still art's sole *raison d'être*.

2

Especially for you:[7] Kark Kraus made it his special task to make the descent into the abyss of language. Once there he was able to discover the intention to appeal to specific human needs, those of the purchaser, as a justification of commodities which owed their existence exclusively to the profit motive. The aim of such a justification was to gear such goods more effectively to the market. But the truth is that the person for whom something is specially produced is actually no more than a customer and his particular needs are no more than the interchangeable representatives of universal needs themselves generated by the product. The devastating quotations in which Kraus fastened on

---

7. In English in the original.

the word 'especially' reveal that the character of the commodity infects the very individuality with which it curries favour. Individuals and individualistic communities are no better than the commodities which are purveyed in their name: 'Such a nation especially can never perish.' On the contrary, a nation that allows itself to be addressed as 'special' is already doomed. The products of the American pop music industry shed some light on this abyss. The sheer idiocy of a mass product created especially for you assumes the character of a ghastly necessity. Individual needs have been so ruthlessly eliminated from the product that they have to be invoked like magic formulae to prevent the customer from becoming aware of the murderous ritual of which he is the victim. The entire life of a lover is proclaimed to have been produced specially for the first person who happens to pass by. '*Especially for you* that's all I live for / *Especially for you* that's all I'm here for.' The consummate banality of the commonplace tune provides an instant refutation of the claim being made. The language leaves no doubt as to its authoritativeness in the sphere of commerce. It evokes the world of bank accounts: 'Can't you see what love has done to me / Just on account of *Especially for you*'. The swindle is so transparent that it cynically admits it and transfers the special to realms where it loses all meaning. The addressee of such assurances can only feel mocked by them, and doubtless that is the intention. '*Especially for you* the birds are singin', / *Especially for you* the bells are ringin'.' We are even told that mass-produced goods can explain the sun, moon and stars: '*Especially for you* that's what a moon's for / *Especially for you* that's what a June's for.' The cynicism has a precise function. By telling the consumer that he has no influence over the product and that the producer takes no more cognisance of his needs than the moon takes of the dog that barks at it, he is meant to realize that he is being mocked. He is made to feel that he is not expected to take the idea of something special seriously, let alone believe in it. But this frankness serves only to render him completely contemptible, in his own eyes and in those of the product. The laughter we hear is familiar to us from the radio where the announcer not only laughs, but laughs at his own laughter, defrauding the listener of the very deception which is being perpetrated against him. The customer knows full well that his wisest course is to acquiesce in this institutional laughter. He realizes that, whatever he does, he has no choice but to conform, whether as buyer, singer, lover or as a simple member of what is gradually turning into an organization of cosmic proportions. The truth is made explicit in the first instance by a warning prominently placed beneath the title of the hit song: 'Any copying of the words or music of this song or any portion thereof, makes the infringer liable to criminal prosecution under the U.S. copyright law.'[8] After reading this, anyone who had harboured the illusion that an object existed especially for him, and who had bought it on that assumption, will dismiss the idea that it actually belonged to him. He belongs to the product and not the product to him. If he wished to change this situation he would be locked up, if he weren't locked up already.

In an eighteenth-century drawing-room. What about Mozart?[9] His music neither provides readily marketable emotions, nor does it attempt through any pomp, forcefulness or power of rhythmic command to induce in the consumer the obedience the latter longs for.

Nevertheless, Salzburg is not without its attractions to the tourist. A series of falsifications contrives to tailor Mozart to contemporary taste. To begin with he is assigned to the Rococo age, whose limits he had just burst asunder. It is a chocolate-box rococo which has been degraded to stylized women with their hair in a bun, playing the harpsichord by candlelight and complete with silhouette. The Mozartian minuet was little more than the painted ribbon that bound human beings like Figaro, Cherubino, Susanna and Zerlina to the conventions of their age. Nowadays, history has converted Mozart into the inventor of the minuet. But the transformation of the humanist into a stylish puppet is assisted by his subjective content. The voice that reverberates with feeling is debased into a dainty lament for the

---

8. In English in the original.   9. In English in the original.

ancien régime. The expressiveness of the Werther decade appears as the sentimental reaction of the barbarian to a past dominated by form. Hit tunes are an aspect of that barbarism. They exploit the C major Sonata, a children's piece that was a fitting choice. Its simplicity matches the growing infantilism of the listener and its *étude*-like scales allow modern barbarians to laugh at the past for which they yearn and to pride themselves on how far they have advanced beyond Mozart.

The sonatina is gripped by a faith in progress that has now become moronic. Four bars introduction, a ludicrous pastiche of an old-fashioned mechanical style, then eight bars of an original Mozart melody but reharmonized with a turn toward the subdominant. The change has no function; even the most commonplace needs of pop music scarcely render it necessary. It arises from the sheer pleasure of touching what is forbidden. Nothing in the whole of world history can pass through Tin Pan Alley unscathed. The more you wish to pay homage to the past, the more you reward yourself for so doing, since you have it in your power to rule supreme over the supreme achievements of the past and manipulate them for the greater glory of comfort. There follows the Mozartian scale which culminates in a sharp blow on the head. Not one blow, but three. In fact it is KO'd, and the last two bars provide a pastiche of the gavotte that is supposed to represent the minuet that was − or rather wasn't − true to Mozart. This is the basis of the middle movement, genuine Raymond Scott. The recapitulation is preceded by a repeat of the four idiotic introductory bars. But they are described as an 'optional interlude'. The editor is, as it were, built into the composition. In the text the Rococo is projected into a timeless past in which an old book, inherited from an ancestor neverthe- less points to a model salon polished to a high gloss. 'I found in an old musty book, / long lost in some forgotten nook! In the book a faded picture, / and the scent of faint perfume, / two old- fashioned lovers in an eighteenth-century drawing-room.'[10] The gavotte extracts from the archaic drawing-room the consolation

---

10. In English in the original.

that nothing new can ever happen again. If things don't get any better now, you at least have the comforting thought that they were no worse even then. 'Nothing is ever new, / ever since love began, / see her two eyes of blue, / flirting behind her fan. / Look at his silk and lace, / isn't he debonair? / And the smile on his face / tells of the love they share.'[11] The recapitulation concentrates on the seminal moment. Regarding itself as a picture seen through the wrong end of some opera glasses, it finally gives expression to a yearning which, even though it is retrospective, has to be made completely abstract so as not to become too noticeable. The yearning for paradise has degenerated into the yearning for the hit song which itself feeds on that very yearning. 'Hear their two hearts softly beat, / one moment more and their lips will meet. / What a sweet and charming picture, / love in glory, love in bloom, / don't you wish that we were in an eighteenth-century drawing-room?'[12] No.

Penny Serenade: on the cover there is a picture of a crooked Southern street, depicted in ad-man's Cubism, all in turquoise, a white moon and a white façade. In the foreground the singer with a beribboned guitar, sombrero and cowboy trousers. He is standing so deep in the shadows that it is uncertain whether he is a troubadour or the Lone Ranger. The lady does not show herself. Instead, on the right, Guy Lombardo gapes at the scene, looking like King Kong in a dinner-jacket. Guy's hair is all slicked down, the gleam in his eye expresses a low humour, his teeth are as white as the moon. He is pleased with himself. He was the first to introduce the song and now he looks on at its thriving career.

But his pride is not really justified. The song comes from England and has turned its back on its origins. It is a nothing which obsessively points to its nothingness. It does not have any verses which narrate the story of the chorus;[13] in fact there is scarcely any verse and chorus to speak of. It is a hit song which simply invokes itself. The verse and the refrain bear more or less

---

11. In English in the original.   12. In English in the original.
13. Adorno uses the English words 'verse' and 'chorus' throughout this passage.

the same weight. Both are quite short, the verses some four beats longer, the refrain, advertised as a 'serenade', is only an eight-bar phrase. It sounds tiny and shrivelled, like something distantly remembered. It is not so much a commodity as just a trademark. This is why it calls itself everything at once: tango, foxtrot and ballad.

Thinly, but not without grace, the verse puts on display its three introductory sounds; an impressionistic ninth chord is shoved in and at once reversed into the principal key, so that you shouldn't have to take it seriously. Over the dominant, when the trademark is first quoted, a plagal syncopation provides a pretty, casually mournful inflection. The miniature refrain is really only a motif which occurs twice. It divides into 'Si, si, si' and 'You can hear it for a penny'. But even 'a penny' is no more than a direct inversion of the 'Si, si, si'. The whole thing, verse and chorus, is repeated; the usual hit-song practice of varying the refrain and dropping the verse is, as it were, cheated of its material. It has become so very unassuming that the mechanism has nothing to get a grip on.

In contrast to the main section there is also a trio in the tonic minor taken from an inverted motival remnant of the refrain. The trio, too, only lasts for eight bars. It carries its seconds like a helmet of invisibility, you scarcely see it. The fifth with which it closes is tacked on to the verse which faithfully follows for the third time: its minims match those that appear at the main focus of the verse. Then the refrain returns once more, followed by a coda to fade out with. The text begins with the obligatory love story: 'Once I stray'd near the window of a lovely, lovely lady'. While she is still smiling she is already forgotten in favour of what brought her into being in the first place: the commodity token itself. The name of the song might have come from *The Threepenny Opera*. But instead of just inviting the poor, it publicly declares its own poverty. The Italian syllables, which come not from Naples but from the slums – just as the street music of Southern Italy has migrated to the unemployed of Soho and the immigrants in the States – shake their heads like an old beggar; they are certainly not affirmative. The serenade's only content is that it can be heard for a penny: 'Just a Penny Serenade'. It is true that the 'Lovely Lady' is dragged in and the penny serenade is sentimentalized into a lovers' serenade.[14] But that is just non-sense, and no more is made of them than of the victory of the police in a thriller. As the new abracadabra, the penny serenade frightens off the phantoms of humanity.

The musical fetish comes into its own. If exchange-value really gazes out from the capital letters of the hit song like an idol, it is redeemed once the word 'penny' falls. Its magic is broken, like that of the Medusa when Perseus confronts her with her own reflection. Where the possibility of happiness is no longer conceivable, where it is replaced by naked numbers, dream finds its hiding-place, rather as it does on Thurn and Taxis stamps.[15] Who has never been overwhelmed with blasphemous envy at the sight of the most appalling homes of the poor, and by the realization that extreme poverty is more valuable than the usurpatory happiness of an order whose power is at least circumscribed by that poverty? The song preserves the traces of that envy. It has thrown in its lot with the commodity world which always promised more than it gave, but ultimately can promise more than is given by the world which is its home.

3

The belief of the popular social psychologists that the film is a dream-machine and the happy end[16] a wish-fulfilment misses the point. The shop girl does not directly identify herself with the glamour girl[17] dressed up as a private secretary who marries the boss. But when faced with this good fortune, and overwhelmed by its mere possibility, she ventures to admit to herself what the

---

14. In English in the original.
15. For centuries the family of Thurn and Taxis enjoyed a monopoly of postal services in the Holy Roman Empire. It was brought to an end in 1806 in Austria and 1866 in Prussia.
16. Adorno used the English phrase.
17. In English in the original.

entire organization of life normally prevents her from admitting: that this good fortune will not be hers. What is taken for the wish-fulfilment is the meagre liberation which consists in the realization that you do not have to deny yourself the most minimal degree of happiness, namely the knowledge that happiness is not for you, although it might be. The shop girl's experience is like that of the old mother who sheds tears at someone else's wedding, blissfully conscious of the happiness she herself has missed. Even the most stupid people have long since ceased to be fooled by the belief that everyone will win the big prize. The positive element of kitsch lies in the fact that it sets free for a moment the glimmering realization that you have wasted your life.

All this applies to music with even greater force. Most people listen emotionally: everything is heard in terms of the categories of late Romanticism and of the commodities derived from it, which are already tailored to emotional listening. Their listening is the more abstract the more emotional it is: music really only enables them to have a good cry. This is why they love the expression of longing more than happiness itself. The function, for instance, of the standardized Slav melancholy in the musical consumption of the masses is incomparably greater than that of the greatest moments of fulfilment in Mozart or the young Beethoven. The leverage of music – what they call its liberating aspect – is the opportunity to feel something, anything at all. But the content of the feeling is always that of privation. Music has come to resemble the mother who says, 'Come and have a good cry, my child'. In a sense it is a kind of psychoanalysis for the masses, but one which makes them, if anything, even more dependent than before.

This is no longer quite so easy, not even in music. The more closely you scrutinize jazz enthusiasts, the more you begin to suspect that it is not enough to have perceived that their behaviour is a mere reflex. They are not the mindlessly fascinated people they are claimed to be, and which they see themselves as. A particular act of will is required to submit to an ordained pleasure. You decide to go wild with excitement, just as you decide to have 'a good time'.[18] The identification with the agency which ordains the pleasure functions like this: as ego, you yourself issue the command to enjoy yourself and then produce the official instinctive reaction only as a rationalization. The model of this behaviour is the child who declares, 'Today I am going to be naughty', or the adolescent girl who writes in her diary that she will now get a crush on a particular teacher. The mimetic element in the behaviour of all fans,[19] their eagerness to imitate, probably originates in this kind of decision which takes place quite close to the threshold of consciousness. It is the same with humour. The jitterbug[20] is not able to believe in his own excitement, because he has himself turned it on and evades the conflict with the aid of ambiguity. The mechanism of rage plays its part here. Anyone who has decided to become excited simply has to screw up his eyes and clench his teeth.

Such reflections, like many of those with a direct bearing on society, seriously raise the question of how far the psychoanalytical distinction between the conscious and unconscious is really appropriate anymore. It assumes that the individual possesses a monadological density and autonomy which have simply ceased to exist: in order to repress anything you must start by having an ego. The present mass reactions, for which musical reactions stand as the model, are only separated from consciousness by a thin veil. This veil should be broken through, but this is the very thing which is almost impossible to achieve. In fact, subjectively, the truth is no longer so completely unconscious. The position is comparable to that of ideology, which objective praxis is beginning to replace with lies. This would require a modification of the thesis that spontaneity was being ousted by the blind acceptance of whatever is being forced on you. Even the belief that nowadays people behave like insects, transforming themselves into mere centres of obedience, is still just part of the façade. Such a notion is grist to the mill of all those who talk a lot of nonsense about the revival of myth. We should say rather that spontaneity is being

---

18. In English in the original. 19. Adorno used the English word.
20. Adorno used the English word.

eroded by the enormous efforts which are imposed on people by their very acquiescence in what is imposed, just because the veil which surrounds that imposition has become so thin. In order to be a jitterbug and to become enthusiastic about what is forced upon you it is by no means enough to surrender yourself and toe the line passively. For people to be transformed into insects they require as much energy as might well suffice to transform them into human beings.

(1934–40)

Fantasia sopra *Carmen*

For Thomas Mann on his eightieth birthday, in warmest admiration

Everyone on the stage knows from the outset that Carmen is the heroine. It is as if they had already seen the opera. The assembled youths all ask after her when the girls from the cigarette factory come out for lunch. Surrounded by the crowd of carefree girls, they lie in wait for her alone. However, she wants nothing to do with love on this particular day, from a pure desire for freedom, the antithesis of virtue. Right from the start we see the operatic convention at work which clearly distinguishes the main characters from the lesser ones – just as the chronicler of a heroic life comforts himself and his readers for light losses in battle with the thought that only minor figures have been killed. Here, quite innocently and, as it were, for reasons of greater dramatic convenience undisturbed by metaphysical preconceptions, the convention highlights the hierarchy of appearance and essence which normally is carefully blurred. Only in the heaven of ideas that lies beyond the deep azure of the actual sky is Carmencita more important than her friends who otherwise resemble her.

Of course, she does not take her incognito too seriously. Among the conspicuous crowd she is the most conspicuous of all, a white hind among the rest of the wild game. Under interrogation she sings instead of answering, and has only the easygoing conventions of opera to thank if this fails to give rise to a scandal. Her darting and whistling cheekiness has added the archaic pride of the simple young girl to the bourgeois repertoire, and even today a time-honoured custom requires that Carmen should raise her skirts provocatively in front of the hapless sergeant – mainly at the expense of her gracefulness, which is a no less vital requirement of the role. Our attention is drawn to her as an outcast, as a woman who has not been completely domesticated, and we may doubtless accept the ensemble's judgement that 'Carmen began the quarrel', the childish, anarchic bout of fighting, the destructive outburst which sets in motion the events which already seem to preclude a happy end. For Carmen is a gypsy.

Initially, not too much is made of this, apart from her ability to sing and dance better than the native population of Seville and the fact that her indifference goes to the head of the sergeant at whom she directed her wild gaze. Similarly, the gypsy scene in Act II remains within the operatic convention which ever since the days of *Preciosa*[1] has delighted in gypsy choruses and cannot do enough to express its envy of the colourful and unfettered lives of those who are outlawed from the bourgeois world of work, condemned to hunger and rags and suspected of possessing all the happiness which the bourgeois world denies itself in its irrational rationality. *Carmen* too is one of these operas of exogamy which begin with *La Juive* and *L'Africaine*[2] and proceed via *Aida, Lakmé,* and *Butterfly* to Berg's *Lulu.* All of them celebrate eruptions from civilization into the unknown. This is how Nietzsche understood *Carmen.*

> And how comforting we find the Moorish dance! How even our insatiable desire finds itself satisfied by its lascivious melancholy! – Love at last, love translated back into nature! And not the love of a 'more exalted Virgin'.

And without defining it explicitly, he put his finger on what separates him and Bizet most profoundly from their antipode, from the Wagnerian world of incest and the Grail community.

---

1. A play with music by Weber, first produced in 1821.
2. By Halévy and Meyerbeer respectively.

For in that world love loves only what is like itself, in fact only loves itself and hence does not really love at all. Hence it sacrifices nature to the inferno of society which is both invoked symbolically and glorified.

The gypsy costumery is only given an image in Act III, as the tragedy draws to its close, after Carmen has refused to be reconciled to her dissatisfied lover whom she has dragged off into a den of thieves. Upon his asking whether she no longer cares for him she replies with a Latinate precision that sharpens each of her sentences, as if for some wholly unknown courtroom record. So much is certain, she declares, that she loves him a lot less than before and that their relationship would be at an end if he refused to allow her the freedom to do as she pleased. The consequences would be of no concern to her. The conversation has scarcely ended when her two gypsy colleagues and fellow-smugglers produce the cards and all three set about telling each other's fortunes. The music wastes no time at all. Where the *Ring* laboriously unfolds dark oracles about the rolling wheel,[3] the music here starts to roll in an allegretto on the strings as if it were a roulette wheel and without a single word by way of commentary. Having reached A minor the music describes a magic circle and emphasizes it with a few piercing accents, like tricks in a card game. It knows that what the cards and cutting remarks have in common is that provocation of destiny which is nothing other than the Wheel of Fortune, the blindness of Fate itself. All this proceeds without a break, on the model of the *perpetuum mobile*, and only the chromatic basses ominously underscore the aimless hurly-burly.

This is countered by the refrain of the two Fate-like sisters in F major. They sing, not like the Norns, but like vaudeville characters and Nietzsche doubtless had them in mind when he said of the music he had praised as 'evil, stylish and fatalistic', that 'it nevertheless remains popular – it has the stylishness of a race, not an individual'. If anything he understated the stylishness of Bizet's masterpiece. For where *Carmen* becomes entangled in the

---

3. See *Siegfried*, Act III, Scene 1.

world of operetta, without ever, be it noted, forgetting the need for a certain compositional selectivity, its act of condescension takes place in the name of style, as the foil to a gravity that has no need of exaggeration because the slightest change of tone towards the frivolous alters the horizon of the music. It is presumably this procedure and not the influence of more modern composers that inspired Adrian Leverkühn[4] in his belief that dissonance should express the exalted and the spiritual, while hell is reserved for the banal and commonplace world of harmony and tonality:

> The sounds of French Impressionism, extended to the point of caricature, bourgeois salon music, Tchaikovsky, Music Hall, the syncopations and rhythmic somersaults of jazz – it all whirls round with the glitter of a circus act: but it moves above the basic language of the main part of the orchestra which asserts the intellectual standing of the work, grave, obscure and difficult, with radical rigour.

Of course, there is as little of the 'insipid exuberance of hell' in Bizet as there is of the obscure and the difficult. In contrast to atonality, which calls for the most violent contrasts, he can content himself with invoking the cliché 'song and dance' to set the higher music off against the more trivial. His shrewdness paid dividends; Fate sounds not like Fate, but reminds us instead of the little girl in the red dress with the tambourine at the Shrovetide carnival children's party. Fate is expressionless, it is as cold and alien as the stars into whose galactic configurations men project the entanglements which they subconsciously create themselves. Fate is reification to the nth degree and any music that borrows its voice must transform itself into a thing instead of behaving like the human essence before whose claims fate must retreat. Just as Frasquita and Mercedes warble soullessly when, as the French text claims, they clamour to hear news of the future, as if it were to be found in the tabloid press, so too is Adrian lacking in soul when he turns himself into a victim by imitating

---

4. The hero of Thomas Mann's novel *Dr. Faustus*, from which the following quotation is taken.

the voice which is not God's. And when, finally, the two mythic supporting figures in Act IV vainly warn the heroine of impending doom, the music achieves a climax of sensual impassiveness with the aid of a pair of flutes playing in thirds of the kind so sparingly used by the later Wagner, an extreme antithesis to that magnificently evocative dissonance with which the Rhine maidens give Siegfried his last chance, likewise in vain.

The opera *Carmen* contains a stratum where brightness and destruction meet, where an emphatic superficial gloss coincides with the subliminal. The spiritual [*geistig*] complexity of this stratum is scarcely ever matched by the much greater technical complexity of [Wagner's] expressive music. The theme of the great ballet music and above all the enigmatic intermezzo after Act II can be assigned to this stratum. This quality of profound frivolity, of illusion which is none, may have its roots in the fact that Fate itself, the myth, is merely an illusion, as ephemeral as the power of the Sphinx which plunges into the abyss on hearing the name of man.

Such subtlety calls for extreme accuracy on the composer's part. Nietzsche alludes to this in his panegyric on the music of *Carmen*: 'It constructs, organizes and reaches a conclusion. It thereby forms a contrast to that musical polyp, the "unending melody".' The value of such musical precision is demonstrated by its consequences, the fact that whatever takes place, leaves traces, has after-effects. Only through this logic, through keeping a firm hold on the identical, does music become capable of its opposite, of that otherness-in-identity which possesses a historical dimension. It was this that Wagner denied himself. For all his consistency there is no real compositional logic: everything flows, but nothing changes. In *Carmen*, on the other hand, once fate has cast its shadow over the stage, the action has difficulty in freeing itself of parody. Even after the card scene, it continues to have an effect in that ensemble [quintet and chorus] where the gypsy women act as if they had not peeked at the cards over which they have no control anyway, and had let their fantasies run wild at the thought of the customs officers who are all sinners and whom they are able to captivate until their contraband has been taken to safety. But first, during the fortune-telling itself, after the nice music has given the wheel one more turn, they continue with their parody, and now they make a direct assault on the soul. The inevitable is so alien to them that they do not even take it seriously, but through it mock themselves. The music wisely adapts itself to the disposition of the superstitious who never quite believe what they claim to believe and who are the more completely ensnared, the more vigorously they deny their delusions. The women sing a half-courtly, half-bourgeois ballad, which promises one of them a bandit as Prince Charming and another a wealthy old man.[5] He will die, leaving her to inherit his wealth: the same Horn of Plenty disburses both money and fate. But the ballad, in 6/8 time, openly makes fun of Schumann's young man's noblesse, much as Nietzsche did himself. This must be how the German dream sounded to Parisian ears in the Paris of the *Lost Illusions* and of the bosom friends, Pons and Schmucke: lovable and comic at the same time.[6] Frasquita acts out the dream with false pathos, Mercedes breaks in eagerly in answering phrases; she has her eye on the main chance, her husband-to-be is a suitable marriage partner, quite within her reach, but her down-to-earth imagination demolishes the mountains and steeds and castles of the other girls. She ends with a mock-operatic climax, and the laughter of the two girls culminates in the [F major] vaudeville refrain, with the roulette wheel as postlude.

Then it is Carmen's turn. Although she is not without forebodings, she is in no hurry. What remains for her, she asks calmly, over some hollow-sounding minims, very like the ones which erected the arch of the future for Frasquita and Mercedes. She lays out the cards to a diminished seventh and to the so-called Fate motif based on the gypsy mode. This is followed on both occasions by a chromatic run in shocked-rigid octaves, as she reads first of her own and, then, his death. A chord strikes heavily

---

5. This refers once more to the Card Trio.

6. *Lost Illusions* is a novel by Balzac. Schmucke and Pons appear in the same author's *Cousin Pons*.

above the tritone, and then a threnodic C – these are doubtless the tragic accents which Nietzsche meant when he said that more painful sounds have never been heard on the stage: 'And how they have been achieved! Without the trace of a grimace! Without any counterfeiting! Without the mendacity of the grand style!' And in fact their effectiveness arises from their concentration on essentials, from a parsimony which sets down the minimum, without repeating it and so expanding it into a style. Hence they represent only what they are; they are neither toned down nor mediated by any architecture and yet, thanks to that parsimony, they merge seamlessly with the form.

Following this suggestively elaborated recitative, which conveys an extreme emotion, as it were by leaving the outcome open and calling on the listener to complete it, Carmen begins to sing. Her aria is no song of Fate, but the individual subject's response to Fate and as such it is the first expressive passage in the whole trio. Despite such lyrical expressiveness there is scarcely anything in opera with such classical grandeur, not so much according to the yardsticks of neo-Classicism and culture, but in words and gestures which are as substantial today as ever. Classical grandeur survives even today in the Romance nations in an almost physical way; it has migrated into the objective spirit of their peoples. Their experience of the menacing forces at work in the world is so great that they could allow themselves to be Christianized without abandoning that paganism which consisted of a synthesis of mythology and scepticism. They possess μεσότης, that moderation of expression in which the anti-mimetic imperative of civilization joined forces with a sullen despair which has ceased to look to the expression of suffering to provide any easing of the pain and which does justice to pain, to an irreversible enslavement by nature, only through such a renunciation. It is this moderation that can be learnt from the gypsy song whose mere existence tells us more about the wisdom of Aristotle and the Stoics than the *Summae* of High Scholasticism and the proud systems of philosophy. 'Semplice e ben misurato', is how she begins, as naturally as Nature herself, who is preserved in her Mediterranean civilization. At the same time, it is as measured as if in time with Fate itself. She sings sadly of the ineluctable, not the smallest gleam of light lights up her voice, not even the 'hope beyond hopelessness, the transcendence of despair'. The gloom of the minor and the minor ninth chord, the sustained F pedal-point allows of no escape, nor any breakout.

But absorbed in herself though she is, she still distinguishes between possibility and reality. If the cards had turned out in her favour, she would have shuffled them undaunted, just as it is now all pain when they point to her death. And this possibility is indicated as the harmonies cheer up towards a cadence in the major [A flat], but still with such restraint and such absence of exuberance as if good fortune were something to be meted out like death itself. To Carmen's myth-ridden mind they are the two pans on the scales and no premonition promises her that luck could be part of a different scheme of things. However, this helps the singer's staying-power: only now does the lament intensify, led by a chromatic middle part and extremely slowly, in fits and starts which, like a controlled sexuality, recoil from any premature climax. Only with the second phrase does a crescendo begin leading to a fortissimo on the inversion of the subdominant, but without much ostentation and harmonic illumination, just following where the voice leads, and then breaking down swiftly. There is no reprise, instead, after the tonic F has been reached again, a kind of shoulder-shrugging coda, there is a series of brief, confirmatory interjections, together with ornamental appogiaturas, which treat Fate as if nothing more were involved than the interplay of diamonds and spades.

No sooner has Carmen fallen silent than we experience one of the greatest moments in all dramatic music, one of those for whose sake the entire opera form might have been invented, a moment that rivals in dignity the epilogue following the Countess's words of forgiveness in *Figaro* and the *Fidelio* fanfare which can penetrate even prison dungeons. But in the disenchanted world which in *Carmen* suddenly reveals its elective affinity with the myth, which is not discussed in so many words, this moment forms the extreme antithesis to the caesura set by the humane. Announced by no more than a dominant preparation of two bars, the two operetta Norns cut off their sister's dirge and strike up their unproblematic refrain. The immanence of Fate, which subdues the outburst of pain and refuses to grant it an outlet, becomes an immanence of form – a rondo, a round, the circle in which beginning and end are one. Carmen does not stand aloof, and she sings of her own death in the low register of her mezzo-soprano. However, she does not sing in antiphonally contrasting phrases, as Gilda does when she eavesdrops in the quartet in *Rigoletto*, but purely as an addition to the part-writing, a complicit counterpoint. In myth death enters the same realm as the living, without any claim to distinctiveness. The music then sets off once more, the three of them come together harmoniously, the leit-motif disappears discreetly in the bass and the scene ends with the most ordinary F major in the world, an F major without cadential force, which is reached by a plagal inflection which frivolously rubs shoulders with the minor origins of the piece.

In the Card Trio, as in *Carmen* as a whole, there is an absence of transcendence and meaning. Indeed, both are ruled out by an overall conception which could be called positivistic, with much the same validity as the term would have if it were applied to *Madame Bovary*. The Fate which rules and which nothing can halt is the primeval and pre-intellectual force of sexuality itself. Human beings are presented as pure creatures of nature, determined by something quite foreign and external. Since they are just mere existence, they are quite alien and incomprehensible to themselves. At the end Don José, the culprit, literally does not know what he has done. Nietzsche undoubtedly had an ear for the 'love which was translated back into Nature' in *Carmen*:

> Love as Fate, as fatality, cynical, innocent and cruel – and natural for that very reason! Love, whose methods are those of war and whose basis is the mortal hatred between the sexes! – I know of no instance where the tragic wit which constitutes the nature of love is so sternly expressed, where its horror is so succinctly formulated, as in Don José's last cry, the cry with which the play closes, 'Yes, I have killed her, / I – my adored Carmen!'

The contrast with Wagner, which according to the trite opinion induced Nietzsche to champion Bizet, is truly perfect. In Wagner everything, every sentence, every gesture, every motif and the overall interconnections – all are charged with meaning. In Bizet the inhumanity and hardness, even the violence of the form, has been used to obliterate the last token of meaning, so as to forestall any illusion that anything in life could have any meaning over and above its obvious one. According to the idea of good fortune [*Glück*] which is sacred to his music, the cardinal sin would be the lie that good fortune, happiness, is available here and now. In this respect *Carmen*, which cannot be accused of harbouring ascetic ideals, is more ascetic than any of Wagner's renunciation, and the *limpidezza*, the clean transparent air which so delighted Nietzsche, that refreshing absence of every ornamental excess, is the fruit of that asceticism.

But not the only fruit. While *Carmen* insists on confining itself strictly to the realm of natural life and a non-expressive action, the very fatalism which drew such vigorous praise from Nietzsche ensures that the opera's ultimate objective is freedom. It is a genuine product of the Enlightenment: it rejects the fetish of 'mankind' for the sake of mankind's emancipation. It is not for nothing that freedom is the only idea to which explicit appeal is made in the work, and it is in the name of freedom that the heroine dies. The absence of even the semblance of meaning, the uncomplaining acceptance of the fulfilment of the mythic spell, elevates the opera beyond that spell by which it seems hypnotized. By duplicating the myth, the opera robs it of its power; it is as if the Gorgon were to catch sight of herself in the mirror.

Works of art which create a totality of meaning do not allow the listener to escape for a single second, any more than they would give licence to a single note. While such a totality conjures up a vision of redemption, the work exerts an unrelenting compulsion which belies the redemptive message and for that reason necessarily unites redemption and death in an ambiguous and murky synthesis. In *Carmen*, which appropriates nature for itself without any sacral aura, one can breathe freely. The unsentimental, undiluted depiction of natural passion achieves what the inclusion of any consoling meaning would deny to the work. When passion is reflected in an aesthetic image, an appeal is made to an external court, one in which the work is enacted, just as the universal process is played out before an audience of Epicurean gods. This court of appeal has the power to call a halt to the inexorable progress of Fate – a hope infinitely more remote, but a little more cogent than any positive meaning claimed by a work of art itself. For in the aesthetic refraction of passion subjectivity becomes conscious of itself as nature, and abandons the illusion that it is autonomous mind [*Geist*].

That illusion is lodged at the heart of the sublime love which has no place in *Carmen*. 'On the whole,' Nietzsche maintains,

> artists make no better job of it than anyone else, indeed they often do worse – they misunderstand love. Wagner too misunderstood it. They imagine they are acting selflessly because they desire the wellbeing of another, often to their own detriment. But in exchange they wish to possess that other person. . . . Even God is no exception to this rule. He is far from thinking 'If I do love you, what concern is it of yours?'[7] – and he becomes terrible if His love is not reciprocated. *L'amour* – and this saying holds good for both gods and men – *est de tous les sentiments le plus égoiste, et par conséquent, lorsqu'il est blessé, le moins généreux.*[8]

Carmen corrects this misunderstanding of love: she confesses to this egoism. Her generosity of soul is not to lay claim to any and therefore not to desire to possess or keep anything, in this world or the next. Carmen's fatalism, this gesture of alienation, the sacrifice of every assertion of the right to dominate, is one of those figures of reconciliation which have been vouchsafed to humanity. It is a promise of finite liberty. The prohibition on transcendence destroys the illusion that nature is anything more than mortal. This is the precise function of music in *Carmen*.

Psychoanalytic theory thinks of music as a defence against paranoia and of the latter as a permanent dream which engulfs

---

7. This was the much-admired attitude of Philine in Goethe's *Wilhelm Meister's Apprenticeship*.

8. Of all the passions love is the most egotistical and therefore the least magnanimous when it is affronted.

everything. If this were the case, then music could be interpreted as the attempt to wake up, and the alarm-call would be its primal phenomenon [*Urphänomen*]. Through sound the anxious dreamer makes the demons resemble himself, just as if he were to don a cult mask which would put them to flight. The only people who can enjoy ghost stories are those who have overcome their superstitious fears, and the music of *Carmen* provides a comparable cure for the events that take place on the stage. Through the disappearance of the demonic illusion nature, by reflecting on itself, emerges from the circle of destruction which had been created by the violence of its blind self-creation. It returns itself to itself. This is the enigmatic character of the non-expressive Fate melodies and flute figures. As the merciless constellation of the laws of nature, they are also the echo of an ineffable sense of spiritual peace, like being on the threshold of sleep. What Nietzsche ironically says of a *Carmen* stripped of its magic applies quite without irony and without reference to that spiritual command which induced him to choose Bizet as the anti-pope to Wagner: 'This work, too, redeems'.

(1955)

The Natural History of the Theatre

In memory of my mother, Maria Calvelli-Adorno

APPLAUSE

Applause is the last vestige of objective communication between music and listener. Whatever goes on in the listener as he hears the music remains his private affair. The music plays on unaffected by it. The activation of the listener during the performance is an illusion; only in the blind act of applauding do the two meet. This act may be the distant descendant of ancient, long-forgotten ritual sacrifices. Men and women, our ancestors, may well have clapped their hands when the priest slaughtered the sacrificial animals. Music is no longer concerned with such practices. The audience are separated from it by the platform; that is to say, they are separated from a commodity which can be bought. Only the rhythm of the clapping evokes the memory of the origins of music in myth, something which ordinarily is carefully enclosed within its cells.

This explains why truly authentic applause is much more independent of the pleasure or displeasure of the audience than it imagines. It is at its best on great social occasions, celebratory performances or as a response to the heroes of music. It is at its most convincing when it is the expression not of a personal response, but of a ceremonial function. There is always a grain of doubt intermingled with the applause with which the connoisseur greets chamber music. It stems from the element of choice and hence, for all its benevolence, it is in conflict with the magic nature of applause.

This can be seen from a comparison with hissing and booing. If the act of applauding were the product of a free decision, booing would be on a par with cheering. But even when a play displeases us we always react involuntarily to booing with an indignation in which the mythic attachment to ritual has taken refuge.

It is the virtuoso above all who merits our applause, because it is he who most clearly preserves the features of the priest performing a sacrifice. Provincial critics who talk of the 'gifts' which are liberally bestowed in a solemn, consecrated hour, are actually on the right track without knowing it. Like the matador, who even today dedicates the bull to a saint or ruler before entering into combat, the virtuoso slaughters the piece of music in the name of the spellbound community as an act of atonement. In exchange he has to bear the risks of missing his aim and being gored on the horns of the *Études transcendentes*. But long practice and strict conventions enable him to disembowel the dead piece and set it ablaze in honour of unknown gods. In the process juicy titbits can be garnered by the listener. Even before the virtuoso begins his performance the audience is in no doubt about his talent. It goes wild and, in its insatiable craving for encores, its enthusiasm can turn to bloodlust. Of course, in a concert, as in our dreams, the actors in the rite may exchange their roles. Frequently we may no longer know who is being sacrificed: the work, the virtuoso or ourselves.

As a ritual act applause places a magic circle around both artist and audience from which neither can escape. This barrier can only be understood from outside. It is instructive, therefore, when in a play the actors applaud on stage. Such applause, coming from a distance, is disconcerting; the applauding actors on the stage appear to be ghosts from mythical times. It is as if, in the midst of the horrors of the sacrifice, they suddenly confront us, the detached spectators, with the masks of some primitive cult, repelling us with enigmatic expressions that appear to grin at us. But for a moment we sense how frequently we ourselves turn into such masks without realizing it. The radio completes the disenchantment of applause. On the radio applause sounds like the fire that flares up with a loud hiss from the sacrificial pyre.

THE GALLERY

Where today we have the gallery – uncertainly curtailed by the nearby wall, and somehow vaguely extended, as if the vertical order of the circles had lost its validity – the sky used to peer in on the theatre, and the play of the drifting clouds dreamily made contact with the human theatre beneath. Those who sat there were the spokesmen of the clouds in the trial of the stage action taking place below; the legitimacy of that action could be weakened or broken by their objections. It was here that Ibykus' cranes were summoned as witnesses, and here that the chorus of the Furies received their answer.[1] The dome has long since closed over the theatre and now reflects the sounds coming from the stage, barring a view of the sky. But those who sit nearest to it, for a small sum of money, and at the furthest remove from the stage, know that the roof is not firmly fixed above them and wait to see whether it won't burst open one day and bring about that reunification of stage and reality which is reflected for us in an image composed equally of memory and hope. Today, when the stage is bound by the text and the audience by bourgeois conventions, the gallery is the only part of the theatre which is open to true improvisation. It has entrenched itself at the outermost end of the auditorium and from the wood of the folding seats it builds its barricades.

The natural history of the gallery only reveals itself fully in the South. You have to have experienced the wild excitement of the

---

1. Adorno alludes here to Schiller's ballad 'Die Kraniche des Ibykus', which tells how the poet Ibykus was murdered on his way to the Olympic Games in Corinth. The only witness to the crime is a flight of cranes to whom the dying man directs his appeal for help. Subsequently, at a performance of a tragedy in which the idea of Nemesis is prominent, a flight of cranes hovers above the amphitheatre, and the murderers, unsettled by the play and shocked by the apparent return of the witnesses of their crime, unwittingly reveal their guilt.

bullfight, the foam on the waves of enthusiasm which splash up from the gallery towards the open horizon. I found traces of this in a music hall in Marseilles. There, right up above, at home nowhere else, surrounded by a thick fug of smoke, with girls, caps and drink, the harbour people had settled from the long evening voyage; faces confiscated from elsewhere and which would have looked better on any stage than in the auditorium. As they shouted, clapped and joined in the performance with encouraging remarks, over the heads of respectable citizens, it was as if the masquerade on the stage and the mummers in the gallery were conspiring to join forces against those in between, either by invading the stage from above or through a liberation of the entire auditorium by a stage full of eccentrics.

All this is much less visible in Germany where it is only ever brought to light by scandal. But even here the possibility of improvisation is created by the tension between these poles. In the gallery we find the irrepressible enthusiast, naively worshipping the tenor from the land of smiles, sitting next to the starving expert who unremittingly follows the inner parts in the score of *Tristan*. Both stand outside the ranks of the average opera-goer who feels offended by intimate knowledge and excessive emotion in equal measure. But if one day these two mutually exclusive extremes – enthusiasm and expertise – were to meet; if the enthusiasm were to be embedded in a process which had ceased to be veiled from the listener by the mysteries of a craft, then the singer who sings for the gallery would just about be able to satisfy the most stringent criteria of his craft and the now vacated stalls would become available for the action. Brecht spoke of the 'smokers' theatre' of the future.

The anecdotes told in Australia or the Wild West reveal the truth about the gallery. People understood it in that legendary bar where they attempted to counter it with the formula: 'Don't shoot the piano player, he's doing his best'.[2] The gallery and with it the stage can only be redeemed by the shot fired from the

---

2. In English in the original.

gallery which enters the heart of the actor playing the villain as if he were a figure in a shooting-gallery.

THE STALLS

The stalls are the home of the bourgeoisie in the theatre. It assembles here with the busy hum of the *agora*. All are seated on the same raked floor, carefully separated from one another by the arm of the chair. Their freedom is that of free competition, the freedom, namely, to disturb one's neighbour and to deprive him of the best view of the stage. Their fraternity stems from the long rows in which one seat is identical with the next; but all together are fixed immovably in the order of things. Limits are set to their equality by the hierarchy of seats and prices. But this hierarchy is invisible: the seats in the front stalls and back stalls do not differ from each other.

The seats fold up. With their red coverings they evoke the memory of the boxes. For the occupants of the stalls were advancing to become the class which ruled the world. But since they can be lifted up in order to make room for someone who is denied entry to the boxes, they are deprived of the dignity which attached to the conception of an immovable throne towering above the orchestra pit. Secretly they are really just chairs. Inside they are quaking, as becomes evident to the people as a whole when the seat-skeletons all clatter at once.

In the well-ordered, rationally laid-out stalls, in which everyone is allotted a precise place, adventures have ceased to exist. Only the eye may still experience some. It can close and thereby open to the ear the space between the orchestra pit and roof. Or, like an Odysseus sailing over a sea of human heads, and like him, anonymous, it can embark on the daring voyage to the stage. But first, it must escape from the prison of a Calypso in the shape of a fat woman whose hair-do blocks his escape from the cave. It twists and turns past Scylla and Charybdis, who lean towards each other and then spring apart, crushing everything between them. It skirts the Isle of Sirens in the shape of a girl's soft neck at the noonday of her fair hair. The Phaeacian with the bald head in the front row is no longer a threat. Ecstatic with joy, Odysseus' gaze lands on the knees of the coloratura soubrette, as if they were the shores of Ithaca.

How strange are the side-exits from the stalls. They open on to the passage that leads to the boxes. From there you cannot gain entry to the stalls. The middle classes may only take off their coats in the crush of the cloakroom belonging to the stalls. But you can leave the stalls through these doors and they are in fact the quickest way to the foyer. Coming from this direction it looks as if you have come from the boxes. So short and unprepossessing is the way which enables you to enter as self-assured burgher and leave as proud charlatan.

The most anxious concern of the stalls is to conceal their origins in the arena. They have successfully accomplished this. The play was banished as a spectacle to the stage and the arena was filled with chairs so that nothing could move in it. It is peopled by a domesticated public. But one thing was forgotten. That was the main aisles leading to the stalls. As they rise steeply, unsighted between the apron and the wall of the audience, they evoke the true circus. You feel there should always be sawdust scattered there. And doesn't the orchestra pit itself resemble the animal barrier which has been displaced from the centre of the arena to the edge. In our nightmares animal games are reintroduced into our respectable theatres and Bengal tigers break out triumphantly from their cloakroom-cages and go on the rampage in the aisles.

BOXES

The boxes are inhabited by ghosts. They have been living there ever since 1880, when the Ring Theatre in Vienna burnt down. They have not bought any tickets, but are the owners of prehistoric subscriptions, yellowing patents of nobility inherited from God knows whom. As authentic ghosts they are bound to this particular place. They may not sit anywhere else. Either they remain here or they must disappear for ever. They are cut off from all living beings in the theatre. But a concealed door leads from them to the machinery in the bowels of the earth behind the stage. Sometimes the ghosts provide champagne suppers for the great coloratura soprano in the intervals, and no one sees. True boxes are shrouded in darkness.

The true boxes: these are surely just the boxes in the proscenium which have been immortalized by Gaston Leroux. They are related to the outsiders' boxes (*Fremdenlogen*) – after all, what do outsiders want with a box if they have no invitation to the inner sanctum? – as coaches with curtains closed and drawn by white horses are related to hackney carriages. If the outsiders' boxes are occupied it is possible for people in the stalls to converse with them across the apron. They are barely protected at all. It has even become quite common for critics to be allocated places in such boxes. But the proscenium box towers in splendour above the abyss of the orchestra pit, surrounded by a crown of gilded bronze and plush. When appreciative lorgnettes from the stalls are directed at Madame von X and Mr Z the purple plush is ready to descend to shelter them from prying eyes, much as it protects Bacchus and Ariadne on the stage.

Only in the proscenium boxes is the stage able to present itself as the landscape which it really is. For only from here can the spectator who is dazzled by the light from the stage step back and create a distance between himself and the stage. It is this that converts it into a changing but eternal landscape in the first place. In the stalls he would be reduced to closing his eyes, which would turn him in on himself. In the box, however, he and his companion retire to the rear of the box and converse about quite different matters, or about how bad the play is. When they return to their balustrade the landscape will have changed: their light has become twilight. Only now does the couple recognize that it is the same.

If you are a man, never take a box with another man. Two men in a box are either boring or no men at all: they cut no sort of a figure. As for the woman with whom you share the intimacy of a secluded box, she has taken her coat as if into her own room and hastily let it fall on the little divan, as if time were pressing, for you have arrived late. She now shows herself with you so as to conceal herself. For this evening she is your mistress, even if you have never possessed her except in this dark, constricted frame which unites you as in a picture.

That the boxes really have no future is apparent from the fate of the mirrors. These are dying out. Only the theatre director still has one, for practical reasons, and here the new practicality is the instrument of an old doom. For the mirrors were the emblems of the boxes' sovereignty. They resembled the peepholes which capture the street outside and bring it into the house. They hung the stage landscapes up on the walls and caught them as they vanished. The craftsman who brought them in through the concealed door was called Dapertutto[3] and when you want to disappear from your box, in which you would otherwise burn to death in the next catastrophe, then, bored by the events on the stage to which you are too close and which therefore hold up a mirror to your soul, you must cover the image of the theatrical landscape in the mirror with your own reflection until the landscape closes over you. For what happens next the box attendant bears all the responsibility.

UPPER CIRCLE, FIRST ROW, MIDDLE

Ever since philistine collusion and the need to cut a figure have taken precedence over the genuine appreciation of opera, which itself possessed not a little of both these qualities, the expert has been on the run. Unless he is elevated to that Olympus which Schiller assigned to the poor poet after the dividing up of the world, he has found asylum in such seats as the middle of the upper circle.[4] Lacking in character to the point of anonymity, it

3. Dapertutto is the evil genius in Act II of Offenbach's *Contes d'Hoffmann*, who tries to cheat Hoffmann of his reflection.

4. In his poem 'Die Teilung der Erde' (1795) the poet finds that everyone has taken a part of the world for himself, leaving nothing for the poet whose mind dwelt among higher things. As a reward, or consolation, Zeus allows him to enter heaven whenever he wishes.

amply compensates for this with the benefits it offers the ear. Except for the few buildings with perfect acoustics, the seats in the boxes distort the sound, depending on their position with regard to the orchestra. In the stalls, especially in the front rows, the sound is frequently muffled and two-dimensional, as if it could not come to terms with being in the *juste milieu*. And in the gallery it sounds as if one were not quite present and could only catch it in snatches, like a tolerated gatecrasher. The possible combination of volume, fullness and resonance is concentrated in the circles. There instead of dissipating itself, the sound spectrum is gathered up and rounded out; there alone do you find yourself in the heart of the opera: the performance and not the printed score.

The best position for anyone who wants to listen from the inside, as it were, and not simply to the mere effect, is the upper circle during a rehearsal. Pale streaks of daylight fall on to the vast, almost empty space. A permanent morning greyness can help to break the spell of illusion just as effectively as the interruptions caused by people shouting and giving orders and rushing to and fro. If something of the initial magic is lost, it is richly made up for by the second magic, the feeling of being privy to the secret which normally just envelops you, and of sharing fellowship with conductors, directors and technicians. The work only opens out when it has been deconstructed. Once it has been broken open, you can penetrate into the interior through the gaps and joints. For this the upper circle is the right place. The spectator sits far enough away from those issuing orders so as not to be distracted and can concentrate wholly on the performance which presents itself in its true proportions.

Socially these seats are undefined; they bring neither prestige nor odium. They confer an inestimable privilege which opera otherwise frowns on: that of seeing without being seen. The fact that the spectator is invisible fits with a casual approach to the performance. No one disturbs you and you disturb no one. If in your zeal you lean forward to avoid missing anything, no other sybarite will protest, and even if you whisper to your neighbour about the music as it flies past, there is a good chance that you will escape without rebuke. Such casualness is the counterpart to what is thought seemly in the boxes. Whoever sits in the upper circle strives to forget that the boxes used to exist.

A price has to be paid for this advantage. You can see everything, but you see it badly. At best you get a good view of the audience and can look individual spectators in the eye. But the stage appears all too small down there below and it is seen from the worst possible angle from the point of view of opera. It is as if you were placed above it all. The more keenly and attentively you listen, the more the producer's skill and flights of fancy pass unnoticed. However, the expert will ask himself, Is that really so terrible? Was not the very purpose of the musical theatre to compensate those who would rather listen than see? Does this not mean the reinstatement of the opera as a performance which you experience without distinguishing the elements of the action any too clearly – something which once existed but which is now inescapably past and which reduced opera producers to despair. In the front rows of the upper circle you can learn that the opera does stand in need of the stage on which you gaze down, but that it thrives best if you see as little as possible of the particular theatrical efforts that have been made. Sitting there, you learn the wisdom of that Epicurean maxim about the theatre of the world which might well be the motto of opera production as such: *bene vixit qui bene latuit.*[5]

THE FOYER

If the theatre is a cabinet clock on which the hand of fate measures the progress of the world, evening after evening, then the foyer is the face with the second hand which duplicates in miniature the image of the world at large, as if an infinite system of mirrors were to be set up in which the world would gradually disappear. In the foyer the spectators are the players, presented to an imaginary public. The auditorium has banished them from

---

5. 'He has lived well, who has lived in happy seclusion.' Ovid, *Tristia* 3, 4, 25.

the stage. But here, eccentrically, at the edge of the theatre, they have made an entrance on a stage of their own. In the intervals they act out their own drama. It is a pantomime, an interlude whose relationship to the stage play proper is all the plainer the further removed it is from it in reality. People stroll around here visibly in the realm of ideas as genies and demons, where previously they had presided invisibly over the figures on the stage. Yet no one understands the words that are exchanged, least of all those who utter them in order to recover from the silence imposed by the stage.

They circulate ceaselessly. No one has ordered them to do so and yet they obey. Anyone who breaks ranks in order to reach his goal directly does so as a conscious rebel, and even worse, with a bad conscience. Like stars they travel in an elliptical path. They embody, without expression or intent, a pure mathematics which lays down the laws for the physics of the stage. If you speak, you at once forget what you have said. You have heard nothing of what is said in front of you or behind you. You are merely cocooned in the hum of voices in which, without your assistance, the harmony of the spheres can safely be heard. The true dramatist would be the one who was able to record this sound.

In the foyers there are buffets in the corners to the left and right. But the lady you are escorting will decline to partake. If she does so because she imagines that it is indelicate or provincial to eat in the theatre, she is mistaken. Is it not wonderful to hear the rustle of chocolate in the darkened stalls, to say nothing of the collations in the boxes. But in the intelligible world of the foyer you are but shadows. You have left your body behind in the auditorium. This explains why you constantly feel drawn back to your seats. If you were to eat here, the blood would flow back into your veins; your body would eagerly follow you, you would spring into life as mortal creatures. The sacred cycle would be disrupted and you would remain standing in front of the buffet and with your entire weight you would plummet into the abyss.

In summer, when among the green gardens, the long, colourful twilight and the warm rain the lights of every theatre make it look like an illumination, this is when the foyer comes into its own. It happens then sometimes that double doors are opened from the foyer on to the balcony. Through them the theatre-goers pass into the open air, and, finding their audience for the first time, their tongues are loosened. Those who previously had surreptitiously smoked a cigarette in the foyer, now breathe a sigh of relief and with the breath of fresh air the dramatic spectacle of their brief passage on to the balcony is revealed to them as natural. Below, on the square in front of the theatre, a fortune teller's telescope is directed at them. When, at the sound of the third bell the last people have disappeared from the balcony, the moon soothingly makes its entrance above the stone stage.

DOME AS FINALE

The opera is more than the decadent form it appears from the study of tragedy. There is no more convincing proof of this than the presence of the dome in modern theatre design. Even though theatres, whether ancient or modern, have been crowned by domes ever since the Renaissance, they only fulfil their strict function in the opera. It is not just that they shut out the sky and replace the sun, moon and stars with a simulacrum of themselves in the form of a chandelier. More importantly, they create the only acoustic space in which opera should properly be heard. The dome conceals the dialectic which is liberated by opera. It is a partition wall and a reflector all in one. Music, which as chorale once aspired to reach God's ears, now bounces back from the ceiling. But although unyielding, the dome's soft rotundity gathers up the sound which would simply be dissipated in the open air. Having gathered it in, it sends it back transformed. The dome shape of operas themselves is a topic worth pondering. True operas are composed with this reflection from the dome in mind, while false ones owe to it what life they have. Thus the fascination of Puccini's melodies lies in the way in which passion surges up in irregular waves and then radiates down again evenly to those from whose darkness it sprang. By rising above the theatre like a crowning piece, the dome completes the form which began enigmatically with the cumbersome stage of tragedy and now fades away gently, floating down from on high. For the sorrow of all those images rising up from words of lament to the edge of the space they would like to burst asunder is not shattered by this barrier, but finds its way home. Having reached the pinnacle of the dome, it is transformed into solace. The sound of the imprisoned human being which rose up as song and is not shattered, but returns as an echo to meet its origins, reverberates with the hope that a living creature that is able to sing cannot be lost. Thus the dome, which is what separates our closed theatres most clearly from the open amphitheatres of antiquity, contains the promise that whatever happens here will not be forgotten, but will be preserved, so that one day it will return as an echo, subtly transformed, and will welcome us in the sphere of this finite cosmos. *Non confundar*;[6] that is the resounding assurance which the dome gives to the cloudy, fallible impurity of song. For one day, so it would appear, the vault of the dome will draw the entire theatre into itself. The theatre will then become a sphere which has ceased to know the direction of historical time, something which our theatre had yearned to master. In the imagined spherical theatre the past becomes present and not just as our best costume play. Thanks to the transitoriness with which it transparently makes its entrance on the stage and then its exit, the present is made eternal. Here lies the justification of theatrical illusion. It is impossible to suppress the desire to create that illusion, opposed though it be to all the self-assurance of an autonomous aesthetics. The most ephemeral things will suddenly be seen to be preserved within this spherical theatre. In the domed theatre the scenery will consist of dark forests; the hydraulic murmuring beneath is like the sound of hidden springs and of the underground railway which Wedekind used to connect town and theatre in the surrealist utopia of *Mine-Haha*. But the song whose melody traces the outlines of the dome which earlier had moulded it is not vouchsafed to the

---

6. 'May I not be confounded'. From the Te Deum.

77

mute in vain. Singers will join in and the sequence of song, its reception and its echo will dissolve in the fulfilled moment of the floating space whose tranquillity hovers trembling in itself.

(1931–33)

PART II

Evocations

Mahler

CENTENARY ADDRESS, VIENNA 1960

No one who comes to Vienna from Germany to speak on the occasion of Mahler's centenary can escape the feeling that he is bringing coals to Newcastle. Mahler's innovations – and these were his essential contribution – are not comprehensible without reference to the norm from which he deviated, the norm which is itself a deviation. I am speaking of his Austrian idiom, which is also the determining musical tradition of Europe.[1] He gave ten years of his life to the Vienna Opera, years which have gone down in history as the Age of Mahler and which have made a lasting contribution both to music and to the history of interpretation. The standards they set for the entire world of music have continued to this day to exert a pervasive influence on composition. Aware from early on that the so-called tradition was losing its hold, he insisted on clarity and accountability down to the very last note, and combined this with a generous and enthusiastic vision of a composition as a whole.

From the Austrian tradition he inherited that instinct for dwelling on what is musically meaningful, as opposed to any purely mechanical sequence of events. But at the same time he

---

1. Looking at Mahler from a German perspective, Adorno thinks of Austrian as a deviation from German, even though the Austrian musical tradition is not a deviation but the core.

was acutely conscious of the threat to musical form posed by any easy-going, conciliatory attitude of laisser-faire. He resisted this much as his contemporary, Karl Kraus, assailed the corruption of language in the culture section of the papers. Hence even as an interpreter Mahler has an important place in that intellectual movement of the age which served notice on the dominant conformism. This has the paradoxical effect that the impermanent performances that he rehearsed and conducted have become immortal, even to those who were not present. A person who has lost a loved one often looks for traces of his way of speaking, moving and gesturing in the people who knew him or at least belonged to the same circle, so that what seems to be the nuance of an intonation may provide the consolation that the dead man is not wholly dead. In the same way, one would like to reconstruct what it was like to have been directed by him from the accounts of those who knew him. I sometimes play with the idea that the features of his face, suffering and tender, powerful and earnest, were shared out among the conductors and composers who succeeded him.

To hear Mahler properly it is essential to be attuned to the consensus that prevails wherever music speaks Austrian. In this respect the extremes meet, since Bruckner was on friendly terms with Mahler, while Webern was probably his most authentic interpreter. The Austrian spoken by his mother is inscribed in passages in early works like the trio of the First Symphony, which is sweet without being sugary, thanks to the richly differentiated levels of harmony. Austrian too is the long *Ländler* melody in the andante of the Second Symphony, which was probably the first piece to attract Mahler lovers to his music. It is enough on its own to refute the accusations of a poverty of melodic inventiveness, if anyone were still brave enough to level that charge. He was capable of such extended melodic passages whenever he required them, even in his maturest phase – in the first trio of the first 'Night' music of the Seventh Symphony and in the incomparable F sharp major theme of the adagio sketch for the Tenth. That he was sparing in his use of melody is due not to his lack of inventiveness, but to a symphonic conception in which the whole surpasses even the most beautiful parts. Austrian, lastly, is his counterpoint, the imaginative creation of melodies to be added to those already set, a process of condensation arrived at not by compression, but by allowing free rein to the profusion of his ideas. Even in the muted works of his last phase we find a recurrence of the Austrian tone. In the 'Dance of Death' in the Ninth, a tune reminiscent of a *Ländler* is played on the fiddle.

There is little point in defending him against the flood of long-since standardized objections, by presuming to assign him to his appropriate niche in history. What needs to be explained is why the living experience of works which have been collectively repressed is now overdue. The justification lies in the repressed music itself; it lies in what is true in Mahler and will outlive the scandal.

The aim cannot be simply to transform him into a great composer, to salvage his reputation merely by asserting that the great achievements which were unquestionably his were really wonderful. For this would be to acquiesce in the norms of the *juste milieu* and would cheat Mahler of his best claim to fame. What is inauthentic about him is not just the allusions to the popular musical idiom of Austria and Bohemia which have been criticized for their *déraciné* irony or their mawkish sentimentality. His own musical language is consistently fractured. It challenges the conventional musical belief that music is a pure, unmediated art, a belief which people cling to despite the fact that relations between people have undeniably become more complex and that the world they inhabit is increasingly bureaucratized. When Schoenberg remarked in his important study of Mahler that in the Ninth Symphony the composer's voice could not be heard directly, he put his finger on something that applies more or less to all his works and goes a long way towards explaining the unease and the sense of ambivalence he arouses.

Scarcely a theme, let alone a whole movement, can be taken at face value. A masterpiece like the Fourth Symphony has a hypothetical air about it from the first note to the last. Although the composer claims to love nature, he puts musical immediacy and naturalness in doubt and this doubt goes to the very core of his musical ideas. Unmistakable and individual though his manner is, he has absolutely nothing in common with the idea of originality as this has been formulated ever since the early Romantics, if not earlier.

His themes, which are always conceived as something other and more than what they directly are, are frequently borrowed or else open to the accusation of banality. Indifference to the norms of a fastidious musical culture, or rather rebellion against them, dominates both the form of the individual detail and the strategy of the entire work. Whereas the traditional formulae remain more or less in force, apart from the very last works, they are disavowed by the concrete shape they are given. It is not merely that the proportions of the parts within the movements are incompatible with the traditional meaning of the overall scheme. The very fibre of the music contradicts the meaning of the formal categories. This applies particularly to the sonata, even though Mahler never completely abandons it before the late period. This means that the listener who is accustomed to listening for the prescribed formal patterns sometimes receives an impression of chaos. The established concept of musical culture is thus faced with a mortal threat. At the climax of the first movement of the First Symphony there is a fanfare which seems to shatter the walls of the securely constructed form. Against all art, its aim is to transform art into an arena for the invasion of an absolute. Mahler's music shakes the foundations of a self-assured aesthetic order in which an infinity is enclosed within a finite totality. It knows moments of breakthrough, of collapse, of episodes which make themselves autonomous, and finally, of disintegration into centrifugal complexes. In its attitude to form it is recklessly advanced, despite a harmonic, melodic and colouristic stock-in-trade which seems downright conservative when set beside Strauss or Reger. As the representative of the existing cultural establishment, Debussy had walked out in protest from the Paris première of the Second Symphony. He was appalled by what seemed to him a monstrosity of inflated dimensions when measured by the criteria of clarity and distinctness. Later on people became deaf to Mahler's rebellion against the constraints placed on music by private bourgeois conventionality. He was labelled an exponent of the monumentality of the Wilhelminian age and the Ringstrasse.[2] This represented a streamlined[3] version of the old, spiteful cliché that Mahler's intentions were not matched by his achievements. The Beckmesser-like ridicule of the man who doesn't follow the rules, but learns his tunes from the finches and the tits, was now dressed up as the defence of a newly espoused modernity.

But what the apostles of authenticity really hold against Mahler, namely his thoroughgoing discontinuity, the musical non-identity with whatever stands behind it, emerges now as a necessary development. *Weltschmerz*, the disharmony between the aesthetic subject and reality, had been the posture of the musical spirit ever since Schubert. But this had not led composers to modify the formal language of music. That was Mahler's achievement. The soul thrown back on itself no longer feels at home in its traditional idiom. It feels distraught; its language is no longer able to accommodate the direct violence of its suffering. In this respect, although Mahler came from the margins of society and never disowned the experience derived from his background, he is not far removed from Hofmannsthal's high-born Lord Chandos who finds the words crumbling in his mouth because they no longer say what they ought. But unlike Chandos, Mahler did not conclude that the only solution was to fall silent.

Instead, by attributing to the traditional words and syntax of music intentions which they no longer possessed, he signalled his recognition of the rupture. The inauthenticity of the language of music becomes the expression of its substance. Mahler's tonal chords, plain and unadorned, are the explosive expressions of the pain felt by the individual subject imprisoned in an alienated society. They are the cryptograms of modernism, guardians of

---

2. The Viennese Ringstrasse replaced the old city walls which were demolished in 1860. A number of imposing public buildings constructed in various historical styles were built between then and the end of the century. They included the opera house, the principal museums and the parliament building.

3. Adorno used the English word.

the absolute dissonance which after him became the very language of music. Unstylized outbreaks of horror, such as the one in the first trio of the Funeral March in the Fifth Symphony, in which the inhuman voice of command seems to cut across the screams of the victims, were no longer really compatible with the language of tonality, least of all within the compass of the march. The scandal is that he achieved it nevertheless and succeeded in expressing the truly unprecedented with a traditional vocabulary.

Today, when music has discovered a language appropriate to such experiences, we are tempted to wonder whether that very appropriateness does not weaken and make harmonious the unspeakable experiences that flash through Mahler's music and only become reality at a later stage. But it is his banalities, the true fossils of tradition, which really establish its incompatibility with the individual subject. They are indispensable to a consciousness that abandons itself unreservedly to the historical negativity that is approaching. They are also allegories of the 'Lower Depths',[4] of the insulted and the socially injured. With supreme genius Mahler, the passionate reader of Dostoevsky, incorporates them into the language of art. The commonplaces he evokes never remain commonplace. They become eloquent and hence integral parts of the composition. In this way Mahler strives to compensate to some degree for the ancient wrong necessarily committed by the artistic language of music when, in order to realize itself, it excluded everything which did not fit in with its social preconditions, those of educated privilege.

Following the Eighth Symphony the experience of metaphysical negativity entered Mahler's consciousness. This meant the impossibility of using music to confirm the meaningfulness of the ways of the world, something which had previously been the hallowed custom that allowed for no exception, not even the tragic metaphysic of Richard Wagner. The now famous letter to

---

4. A reference to Maxim Gorki's play of that name, which was set among the outcasts of *fin-de-siècle* Russian society, as well as to Dostoevsky's *The Insulted and the Injured*, a novel set in St Petersburg, which depicts the miseries of the modern city.

Bruno Walter makes this plain. It is an early testimony to the fact that the foundations of all music had been severely shaken. This is the source of everything that sounds chaotic to the ear that loves order. Because his music can no longer profess any guaranteed meaning and because, unlike Beethoven's, it must dispense with the hope that meaning will be vouchsafed by the overriding logic of a dynamic structure, he is forced to surrender himself nakedly to individual impulse. Anyone who has allowed the lower depths to enter into composition composes from the bottom up. The only totality known to this symphonic art is one which arises from the temporal stratification of its individual segments.

In Viennese Classicism the concept of totality was the undisputed master. Its musical ideal could therefore be called dramatic. If that is so, then Mahler's may be described as epic; it is a cousin to the large-scale novel. Reminiscent of the novel are the rise and fall of passion; the unexpected, seemingly coincidental, but in reality necessary events; the detours, which are actually the main road. From beneath the trembling veil of the old, conciliatory symmetries, we witness the emergence of that musical prose which then became the language of music as such. To understand Mahler means to cast off, as far as is possible, the listening crutches afforded by the traditional patterns. Given the fact that, not infrequently, the movements are very long, this is no petty requirement. Since the music has been composed from the bottom up, it must be heard from the bottom up. The listener must abandon himself to the flow of the work, from one chapter to the next, as with a story when you do not know how it is going to end. You then become aware of a second and superior logic. It follows from the definition of the individual figures, rather than an abstract, preordained design. As Mahler developed, this logic became increasingly marked. The ability to organize a totality became fused with the ability to shape this totality from the goals of the individual components. Starting from the chance nature of existence, he transformed it into a coherent whole, without having to borrow from sources no longer authenticated. This is what defines Mahler as a great composer. None of the more recent composers has equalled him in his ability to make objective an untrammelled subjectivity. But the forces that led him to such adventurous composing were themselves anything but private and voluntary. He had no illusions about the inexorable decline of forms that behave as if their mere existence could establish a meaning which is no longer present in society. He perceived the direction this decline was taking and complied with it. Hence his power.

Mahler's music is critical of aesthetic illusion and of the culture in which it thrives and from whose superannuated elements it is composed. Wherever he falls below the level of culture, by the same token he stands above it. Having salvaged an amalgam of happiness and misery from his childhood, he refused to sub-scribe to any adult resignation or self-abnegation, the official social contract of music. By nature he was a *fauviste*, a savage, but not one who is intent on the resurrection of barbarism because he is oppressed by civilization. Instead his music envisages a human race that rises above the preordained order and its own failures, which works of art normally replicate simply by virtue of their existence. The works of art which he created dream of the abolition of art by that achieved fulfilment which his symphonies conjure up so indefatigably and in so many variations. Hence the contradictory nature of his work. The elements defined by the cliché of the gulf between intention and achievement do not point to an aesthetic inadequacy, but to the inadequacy of the aesthetic itself. I do not deny that you cannot have the one without the other. Works of art that are superior to the current culture are not able to satisfy its requirements entirely. But the most ambitious works succeed by transforming their weaknesses into strengths. Ever since the last of the *Lieder eines fahrenden Gesellen* Mahler was able to convert his neurosis, or rather the genuine fears of the downtrodden Jew into a vigour of ex-pression whose seriousness surpassed all aesthetic mimesis and all the fictions of the *stile rappresentativo*.

In the same way his lack of immediacy and virtuosity as a composer all became part of the creative ferment of his art. The austere, unpolished beginnings developed into the clarity, the unadorned terseness which a generation ago Erwin Stein rightly termed Mahler's matter-of-factness [*Sachlichkeit*]. In the words of the Chorus Mysticus [from the end of Goethe's *Faust*, Part II], which he was not too overawed to set, it really is the case that in his music, 'All that is enacted / Here is perfected'. Even his monumentality, which offers such an easy target for the ridicule of those who have the advantage of having been born fifty years after him, expresses his refusal to accept an intimacy which had degenerated into a mere ornament and which had become the particular refuge of the most sophisticated composers like Brahms and Debussy. This monumentality may be problematic in a society built on individualism, and Mahler has to pay the price for that.

But on the other hand he was sometimes able to achieve one of the ambitions of all modern music since Bach and one which was especially central to the Austrian symphonic tradition. This was the desire to fill the empty flows of time with meaning, to transform it into a permanence full of joy. That fulfilment which was present in those passages of Schubert which have been described, not without irony, as his 'heavenly lengths', or which could be glimpsed in Bruckner, where it was frustrated by his failure to close the gap between the epic design and the traditional formulae of music – that fulfilment has found its true home in Mahler's unaccommodated and fractured symphonies. If all important conceptions of art are built on an inherent paradox, then the paradox of Mahler's music is that he succeeded on the terrain of the large-scale symphony at a time when such works had already become impossible.

In the early works, that is the first four, closely related symphonies, which are generally known as the 'Wunderhorn' symphonies, the basic elements are already to be found. These include his sense of the 'way of the world'[5] and the breakthrough to something better, the closeness to dialect and the discontinuities full of inner torment. But at this stage they are just crudely

---

5. The 'way of the world' (*Weltlauf*) is a Hegelian term which is based on a contrast between the everyday world, with its multitude of more or less selfish purposes and actions, and 'ideal life'.

juxtaposed to each other. They over-assert themselves to the point, on occasion, of an intentional musical programme. This is the source of their freshness, the inextinguishable aroma of their individual characteristics. Never again would Mahler venture as far as in the first movement of the Third Symphony, which is doubtless the cause of its neglect today. With the trombones savagely erupting from the defined tonal space in the slow passages; the sequence of marches which are not heard from a fixed reference point, but from a series of shifting vantage points and which sweep the ear along in the Dionysian revelry; and in the closing section of the development, a sound that was already as completely undomesticated as anything in the orchestration of the new music – in all this we perceive Mahler's *Urphänomen*, the fountainhead of his music. Mahler renounces the traditional idea of the symphonic goal and waits, without intervening, for the din to exhaust itself. Only the drum rhythm links it with the recapitulation of the introductory section; the barren passage of time shows through, much like the canvas in early modern paintings.

The fear of his own audacity, which must have overtaken him thereafter, had become productive. In the Fourth Symphony, the epilogue to the Third, all the different strands are brought under control. But the norm against which they are measured, a perspective reduced to that of childhood, remains dislocated. The consequence is not just a work which satisfies traditional standards better than any others and which tempts the obtuse to compare it with Mozart; it is also as puzzling as the damaged paradise of Kafka's Nature Theatre of Oklahoma.[6] None of Mahler's symphonies is more deeply impregnated with sorrow than this seraphic work and it is this that makes it an act of homage to Mozart. Mahler was a late developer who was by no means utterly at home in the details of his craft. It was only with this symphony that he acquired full control of the compositional means available to him. The three great instrumental symphonies which followed are reflexions on the image world of those

6. See the last chapter in Franz Kafka's *America*.

that went before. Of course, with the new professionalism, the world of the latter is now distanced and preserved in a fully organized musical context; recapitulation in the dialectical meaning of the word. It may well be that the much-vaunted tragic character of the Sixth Symphony is itself the expression of that immanent coherence to which Mahler's work increasingly tended. This coherence allows for no escape, so that the life that pulsates in the great finale of the Sixth is not destined for destruction by the hammerblows of fate, but to an internal collapse: the *élan vital* stands revealed as the sickness unto death. The movement combines the powerful dimensions of an expansive epic ideal of music, the generous elevations of the large-scale novel, with the compelling density of thematic work: the symphonic idea is simultaneously realized and suspended.

Of equal stature to the Sixth is the first movement of the Seventh. Here Mahler's vocabulary is enlarged and sheds that hint of anachronism which hitherto had been inseparable from his boldness. The timbral range of the orchestra embraces everything from the most luminous super major to the darkest shadows. No less rich is his harmony. His use of fourths may have inspired the Chamber Symphony which Schoenberg completed a year later. Even more astonishing are the chordal contrasts of the second theme which give the music an almost three dimensional shape. Then, in the Eighth Symphony, the hand of the master attempts retrospectively to complete what had been anticipated as early as the Second. In the hymn 'Veni Creator Spiritus' there are passages where the impossibility of making a start turns into violence, as if wilfully asserting that the start had been a success.

But there is no stronger argument in Mahler's favour than his impatience with the affirmative nature of the masterpiece. And it was the very idea of affirmation that he found suspect. The idea of a breakthrough, which never left him, became sublimated into the memory of a past life as of a utopia that had never existed. It was in *Das Lied von der Erde* that the desire for subjective expression first broke through the impulse for symphonic objectification. It provided the keyword of 'universal loneliness' and thereby became Mahler's most popular work. To this day it has remained the ultimate composition to conquer all hearts, despite its autonomous nature, despite its total organization. What is puzzling, though, is a quality that goes beyond even mastery itself and which is almost impossible to account for in technical terms. The simplest turns of phrase, formulae, are sometimes so saturated with content in *Das Lied von der Erde* that they put one in mind of the everyday speech of an older man whose words go beyond their overt meaning and contain the experience of a lifetime. Written by a man not yet fifty, this work, despite its fragmented form, is one of the greatest achievements of a late musical style since the last Quartets. It is surpassed, if at all, only by the first movement of the Ninth Symphony. It lingers in the same Chinese Dolomite landscape of streams and pines, but frames the compressed fullness of the vocal part within a wide-ranging symphonic objectivity which represents a final leave-taking from the sonata form. Two themes, major and minor, alternate in dialogue. They tell a story that stretches far into the past. Their voices intertwine and drown each other out, mingling with each other until, driven by a third motive, the work becomes ensnared in a passionate present, only to collapse at a sudden blow of which the listener had had a presentiment from the rhythm of the very first bar. Only shards remain and the sweetness of a captivating but futile solace. The last work which Mahler completed, and whose third movement contains polyphonic passages that strain to escape from the thorough-bass scheme, is the first work of the new music.

Mahler drew the consequences from a development whose implications have only now become fully apparent. It is the perception that the Western idea of unified, internally coherent, as it were systematic music, whose unity is meant to be identical with its meaning, is no longer viable. It has become incompatible with a situation in which people are no longer in command of any authentic experience of such a meaning in their lives. It is incompatible with a world which has ceased to provide them with the categories of unity in happiness, leaving them only with those of standardized compulsion. Mahler is matter-of-fact even in the supreme metaphysical sense, in that he jettisoned the aesthetic illusion of a meaningful totality which no longer existed, if indeed it ever did. Mahler, whose uncompromising spirituality separated him from the hedonism of his age, from Debussy and Strauss and whose mind selflessly strove to conceive of something that goes beyond mere existence – Mahler discovered the impossibility of such a task simply by refusing to be deflected from his path. A metaphysician like no other composer since Beethoven, he made the impossibility of metaphysics his central belief, even while battering his head against the brick wall this represented. His world, like that of his compatriot Franz Kafka, is a world infinitely full of hope, although not for us. He passionately wagers everything on the absurd possibility that it will one day be fulfilled. This conviction does not hover over his music abstractly, but permeates its texture right down to the last technical refinements. Technique in Mahler is concretely deter- mined by and directed towards this idea. Mahler's technique centres on the principle of composing logically, in a manner free of caprice and indifferent to effects[7] and at the same time to transcend logicality. What he longs for is the epiphany of construction and freedom. This would be a lost cause if it were not corroborated by the construction itself. Conversely, the construction would be no more than an arbitrary exercise of power by the would-be sovereign self, if it were not filled with substance that is reconciled with it, rather than subject to it. Of course, in this account of the goal of which Mahler was unconscious, but which is implicit in his music, we may recognize the spiritual return of the quintessential Austrian, purified of all its stifling cosiness – that is to say, something passive and yielding which trusts itself to the surge of inspiration without attempting to tamper with it.

---

7. In *Aesthetic Theory* Adorno refers to periods in which art and mathematics were closely related. In such a period art emphasizes internal logical consistency. It follows from this that 'Logicality makes it impossible to grasp works of art in terms of their impact [*Wirkung*]. Logical consistency ensures that works are determined logically, irrespective of how they are received.' See T. W. Adorno, *Aesthetic Theory*, translated by C. Lenhardt, Routledge & Kegan Paul 1984, pp. 198ff.

The history of music since Mahler, even in its most recent phase, has maintained this trend towards integration and even taken it to extremes. The principle of motivic elaboration, which goes back to Bach, Beethoven and Brahms, has been extended to the point where every element of the music is determined by a latent element common to them all. Hence it has virtually excluded the idea of a variety which is to be synthesized. An individual musical fact is viewed from the outset as a functional part of a totality, and hence sheds its own substantiality. Unity, however, is undermined as soon as it ceases to unify a plurality. Without a dialectical counterpart it threatens to degenerate into an empty tautology. The recent tendency to incorporate alea-toric elements into the overall construction implies a critical reflection on this situation.

Mahler would be the staunchest pillar of this criticism. He has elicited from the process of composition a dimension which had been repressed, as he had been, and which has now been revealed as the precondition for all music. It is the dimension of functional characterization, where distinctions tend to be obliter-ated in the undifferentiated unity of the integral language of the present. In Mahler's music all the individual domains are formulated as definitely and unambiguously as possible. They proclaim: I am a continuation, something that comes after, a coda. Thanks to the clarity of this characterization, which makes everything what it is by virtue of its function, its formal meaning within the totality, the individual domain genuinely becomes something more than itself. It opens itself up to a totality which crystallizes out in consequence, without being brought to bear on the functional elements from outside. This is why these elements never remain constant, but are caught up in a continuous process of change, even though they are all unmistakably themselves.

It has rightly been observed that the first thing that impresses the listener to Mahler's music is that it always develops in an unexpected way. But by the same token, his novelistic, unsche-matic approach is far removed from the merely episodic or arbitrary. The method he uses is the variation technique. When compared to the total work, the functional elements are too independent, too evidently living beings in process, to be split up in accordance with the rules governing traditional motivic work or to sink their identity in a seamless web. In variation technique each functional element is fixed in a recognizable shape; the structure of themes and shapes is preserved.

However, particular features are modified; classical music comes to incorporate the principle derived from the oral tradition and the folksong, according to which subterfuges, minute variations, are introduced into the repetition of the original melody that transforms the identical into the non-identical. Mahler is the composer of deviation, right down to the technicalities. Variation, however, the unexpected, is the opposite of the kind of effect used by the school of Berlioz, Liszt and Strauss to achieve the *imprévu*. Nowhere do Mahler's variations introduce difference for its own sake. For all their irregularity their sequence in time is subject to a certain organic teleology which can be studied down to the very last interval. Where there is change, there has to be change because tensions and potentials which proclaimed themselves at the figure's appearance are worked through. Why a thing starts off one way and then becomes something else is always precisely motivated. In the first movement of the Fourth Symphony, for example, it can be observed how from the outset a theme waits from the beginning to enlarge one of its component intervals, but that this interval is only introduced after lengthy preparation. It is in the tensions between the variations that the breathing rate of Mahler's symphonies is established and the transition from the particular to the totality is achieved.

But it is in the functional figures, as they emerge, persist and disappear, that the substance of Mahler's music is contained. They are quite simply expression, which becomes both the function and the constituent of the form. If Mahler's art begins with the idea of breakthrough, this is objectified and fulfilled in these figures. Frequently failure itself, the celebration of the compulsion they are subject to, becomes a substitute for what has been promised. But in Mahler it is achieved; that is what is so fascinating. And if, on the other hand, Mahler's experience in a society whose spell cannot be broken means that the image of breakthrough and fulfilment is itself distorted, he nevertheless succeeds in discovering the figure appropriate to such experience – namely, that of a fully composed-out disintegration and collapse. It is already to be found in outline in parts of the first movement of the Second Symphony; then in the first two movements of the Fifth, and finally and utterly in those passages of the andante in the Ninth which follow the catastrophe.

In the final phase it may be that the idea of a music which evokes transcendental meaning is reduced to a truly Proustian search for things past, for the pavilion of friends and the blossoming beauty of slender young girls. But if so, the composition adapts itself to this with figures of disintegration and by renouncing the ambition of integration. It finds its true solace in the strength to look absolute desolation in the face and to love the world even though there is no hope. Such figures are to be discovered in the leave-taking movements of *Das Lied von der Erde* and the Ninth Symphony, which dissolve into particles which make no pretence of unity.

Mahler's non-violent violence which is formulated in such figures is the power of a true humanity. Greatness in composition does not consist for him, as it did for Luther, in commanding the notes to go where they belonged. Instead he follows them where they lead, from a sense of identification with those who are cruelly knocked about and forced into line by aesthetic norms and indeed by civilization itself. In short, he identifies with the victims. Ultimately it is because of this self-denying identification with the Other that Mahler has attracted criticism for his subjectivism. The expression of suffering, his own and of those who have to bear the burdens, no longer knuckles under at the behest of the sovereign subject which insists that things must be so and not otherwise. This is the source of the offence he gives. In his youth he composed a setting to the poem 'Zu Straßburg auf der Schanz'.[8] Throughout his life his music sided with those who

---

8. This poem from *Des Knaben Wunderhorn* describes the fate of a Swiss soldier who is overcome with homesickness when he hears an Alpine horn. He tries to desert, but is caught and shot.

fall out of the community and are destroyed – with the poor drummer boy, the doomed outpost, the soldier who has to keep beating the drum even after his death. Death itself was for him simply the continuation of the blind earthly disasters in which he was enmeshed.

But the great symphonies, the marches which reverberate through his entire *œuvre*, set limits to the sovereign individual who owes his life and glory to those who dwell in the shadows. In Mahler's music the incipient impotence of the individual becomes conscious of itself. Aware of the imbalance between himself and the superior might of society, he awakens to a sense of his own utter unimportance. Mahler responds to this by abandoning the sovereign power to posit form, but without writing a single bar which the subject, who is thrown back on himself, would have been unable to fill or to answer for. He does not adjust to the incipient external domination of the age, but nor does he deny its power. Instead his ego is strong enough to help the weak and the speechless to express themselves and to salvage their image in art. The objectivity of his songs and symphonies distinguishes him sharply from all art which makes a pleasant and comfortable home for itself in the private individual. As a metaphor of the unattainability of a harmonious, reconciled totality this objectivity is essentially negative.[9] His symphonies and marches do not express a discipline which triumphantly subdues all particulars and individuals; instead, they assemble them in a procession of the liberated, which in the midst of unfreedom necessarily sounds like a procession of ghosts. To use the term for an awakening, which occurs in one of his songs, all his music is a reveille.

(1960)

AFTERTHOUGHTS

The Centenary Exhibition in Vienna provokes the criticism that with their programme 'Mahler and his Age' the organizers

---

9. For Adorno 'negative' is a laudable quality, opposed as it is to 'affirmative' – that is, conformist art – and to 'positive' – that is, positivistic science.

formulated their aims too broadly and that Mahler's specific qualities have been dissipated in the generalities of the age, if indeed it is possible to grasp anything of them at all through the display of visual exhibits. But the very irrelevance of the exhibition to the man it is celebrating enhances our knowledge of him considerably. The period of his maturity coincides more or less exactly with that of Art Nouveau. Names like Roller and above all Moll, his wife's stepfather, are both associated with this sphere.[10] But what distances Mahler from his age, and that includes its leading literary figures, is the almost complete absence of the elements of Art Nouveau in his work. Such elements predominate in Richard Strauss; they are present in the young Schoenberg and can even be found in Reger. But of Mahler the most that could be said is that the exotic aspect of his last works reveal an affinity with Art Nouveau. But that aside he must have sounded retrograde when compared to the standards of what was then thought modern. Neither the slogans nor the formal idiom of Art Nouveau made any impact on his *œuvre*. The images which inspire it are late Romantic rather than neo-Romantic; they belong to those which people were in rebellion against. But his anachronistic element, this sense of not having quite kept up with developments, became in him a source of strength which went beyond the capacities of the age. It provided him with a sort of resistance to the process of subjectivization which enabled him to retain a quite spontaneous hold on the model of the great objective symphonic work. Even though this had now become an impossible project it none the less managed to infiltrate his works and imbue them with something of that past collective authority, as soon as his works were technically in command of themselves. On occasion the most progressive kind of art seeks refuge in the residues of what has been left unfinished or unworked out. This bypasses the sphere of what is

---

10. Alfred Roller (1865–1935) was a set designer. He worked with Mahler on redesigning the Vienna Opera in the spirit of Wagner's ideal of a *Gesamtkunstwerk* (1903–7). Carl Moll (1861–1945) was one of the co-founders and key figures of the Viennese Secession.

regarded as up to date[11] by taking up and rethinking what has been left to one side. That lack of concern with himself, with the composing subject, which is evident in his music and which must have struck his contemporaries as a lack of discrimination, was potentially the saving grace of self-obliviousness. It legitimated his symphonies as the language of the age after the style of the isolated human being, which he never achieved, had become obsolete and a matter of indifference.

'Die Lichter, die aus deinen Wunden strahlen' ['The lights which radiate from your wounds']: this line by Stefan George reads like a motto to Mahler, his older contemporary. But the fact that in his case the scars of failure are transformed into the bearers of expression and therewith to the fermentation of a second success, is no merely private peculiarity. His music inquires how the sonata form can be reconstituted from the inside so that it is no longer violently imposed on the living specificities within it, but is at one with them. This is the squaring of the circle, comparable to that philosophical labour of Sisyphus of reconciling rationalism and empiricism. All supreme art has some paradox of this sort. It is not inadequate talent, but the insolubility of an objectively posed problem that jeopardizes a work. And the threat is all the greater, the more profoundly the work is conceived and the more boldly it exposes itself to its own impossibility. Or rather, in authentic artists a subjective flaw becomes the site of an objective historical failure. Not the worst criterion of art is to ask whether its failure is adventitious, or whether its chance nature gives expression to a necessity. In Mahler's case this becomes the signature of his work.

The peculiar preponderance of march music in Mahler calls for a better explanation than the notion that he was fixated on childhood impressions. The behavioural patterns objectified in the march stand in intimate relationship to the novelistic structure of the Mahlerian symphony. The march is a collective

---

11. Adorno used the English phrase.

form of walking. It assembles the unconnected occurrences of daily experience in a single figure. At the same time it suggests a unidirectional, irreversible movement towards a specific goal. To retract, turn about or repeat are alien to it, even though such elements constantly enter the march from the dance. The time consciousness of the march seems to be the musical equivalent of narrative time. 'Time marches on.'[12] This is just as much a metaphor of an unconcentrated, linear but menacing concept of time as it is of the impulsive movement which corresponds to such a concept, if indeed it does not originate in it in the first place. Mahler's marches intend all this. His ingenuity led him to excavate them from his childhood as the fundamental models of an experience of time which in a lively consciousness stripped of its illusions is all the more potent, the less it obtrudes in the workings of the work of art.

The criticism that could be made of the principal theme of the Sixth Symphony is that it smacks of the official. It sounds a little like the epithet 'tragic', which even at that time had degenerated into a cultural reminiscence, and not only in music. But emphatic though the theme is, and even though a genuinely symphonic gesture has assumed theatrical overtones, it is more than mere trappings. Because the theme appears forced on its entry at the very beginning, it is compelled to justify itself by universal mediation – that is, by elaboration. The Sixth is so completely integrated that nothing is allowed to remain an isolated detail; but everything becomes what it is by virtue of its place in the totality. In order to understand such works the listener should not cling to themes, but instead should propose them to himself, and await events. As soon as it starts to develop the movement casts off its 'official' tone. At the point where the accompanying march rhythm is dropped the full, rounded orchestral sound of the opening is split open as if it were going to bleed. The principal motif leaps from the violins to the immoderate trombones; the violins play a counterpoint against it, and the

12. In English in the original.

entire high-pitched woodwind section plays a semiquaver, without a bass to carry the harmony. Only after this disruptive interlude does the march return with the crotchets of the opening, followed by a shrill oboe melody. After only a few bars of motivic intervention every hint of the conventional gives way to Mahler's heart-rending tone.

There is something sinister about the scherzo of the Sixth, not least because, thanks to the put-on crescendi and the chromatic *fauxbourdon* passages in the middle voices, the orchestra seems to swell like a body threatening to burst and cause untold damage. The three-dimensionality of the orchestra, its spatial volume as it were, becomes the vehicle of expression. It perhaps assumes this function because Mahler's laborious development of a full, corporeal orchestral sound only established itself in the instrumental works of his middle period, whereas the first three symphonies at least sound curiously two-dimensional, as if lacking in spatial depth, simply because of his efforts to achieve maximum clarity in his orchestration. This spatial depth appeared for the first time in Mahler's polyphonic orchestral thinking where it at once became an element of the musical meaning, the expression.

The trio in the same movement operates, as is well known, with the frequent alternation of 3/8 and 4/8 time. But since it too is polyphonic in structure the irregularity of the metre leads to such overlapping of the entries of the different parts that what has a strong beat in one voice has a weaker beat in another. This results in a highly idiosyncratic process of rhythmic interference, an unstable sense of the main emphases when it is heard as a whole. The metric irregularity is not confined to externals, the succession of beats, but extends into the core, into the simultaneous composition of the music. Under the impact of what Bartok and Stravinsky have accustomed us to think of as rhythmic, these rhythmic innovations of Mahler's have been forgotten and have been largely neglected by later composers. Down to the present there is no aspect of music in which less has changed than in rhythm – the dimension which has been the most talked about of all. Of this too Mahler is a reminder.

From the andante moderato of the Sixth we can hear how Mahler's sense of form has sapped the vigour of the traditional patterns, without ever breaking with them openly. It begins as if it were one of the *Kindertotenlieder*, with a cantabile melody in the upper part which is followed by an alternative theme. Initially the two complexes alternate regularly. But the sense of elevation to which the development, or if you wish, the final section of the movement leads endows this passage with such verve that it seems to burst its confines and then gradually ebb away. For this its intensity requires a lengthier period in order that it should not seem out of proportion and so that the development should not break off suddenly.

But after the broad, flowing movement no space would be left for a recapitulation of the chief thematic complex. It would make an academic, tacked-on impression, like a mere formal doubling of that descending movement which covers the resolution span of the elaborated section. For this reason it is diverted at the end so that it unobtrusively and without interruption takes over the function of the coda of the entire movement. For the sake of balance Mahler omits the recapitulation which would normally reinstate the balance.

This exemplifies the subtlety and delicacy with which Mahler's sense of the irreversibility of time announces itself in his mature symphonic work. His principle of the variation technique, the deviation, is applied to subverting the large-scale forms. In consequence the entire movement ends up in a different place from the one intended by the composer, or rather by the overall structural design. According to a theory in contemporary painting this is in general the kernel of truth contained in the most hackneyed concept of originality. Originality is a historical concept, not a fixed one. As long ago as the eighteenth century Goethe had praised the painter Hackert in his autobiography, observing that 'he had gradually risen to the production of some originals'. However, the idea that the path of music is one of diversion is so much more compelling than the logic of its own forms because diversion provides an aesthetic formulation of the actual experience that every life runs at cross-purposes to its own premisses. It is diversion itself which is the inescapable reality.

Mahler's music can be said to be 'concretely determined towards its idea'. Lest it be thought that this is too cryptic or that a vacuous Gundolfian formula[13] is being used to rehearse the distinction between absolute and programme music, it is important to specify what is meant, since no feature is more deeply ingrained in the physiognomy of Mahler's work. In the finale of the Sixth, immediately before the last repeat of the introductory section, which already belongs to the coda, the brass once again intones one of the principal motifs of the movement and treats it sequentially, four bars before the final strike-up. These bars contain the feeling of 'despite everything!', of success in the face of a doom which the latter can do nothing to diminish. It is a feeling which is expressed with extreme directness; it is as unmistakably present as the spoken word could be, but devoid of every unmusical literariness or anything extraneous to form. What is said, is said wholly in the language of music, by virtue of its similarity to music and not through any imitation of images and concepts. No other composer has ever been able to do this to the same degree as Mahler. Hence the utopian cast of his music, as if he had come within an ace of uncovering the ultimate mystery. He promises that music which utters the things inexpressible in words, but which keeps losing its grip on them because it has no words at its disposal, can nevertheless express them literally.

A long prehistory provides proof that it is not arbitrary to ascribe this achievement to Mahler. Even those aspects of his symphonies which have been described, following Erwin Ratz, as their 'negative space', can be dated back to Classicism in a quite

---

13. Friedrich Gundolf (1880–1931) was a well-known literary critic associated with the circle around the poet Stefan George.

unliterary way. A vivid example can be seen in the trio from Beethoven's Fifth. The grim humour in it is not anything whose existence can be disputed. It becomes unambiguous, objectively memorable, in the relationship of the concrete music to the idiom as such. After the double bar line [at the end of the first section of the trio] the principal motif enters, without being able to achieve the strong beat as it had done earlier. After its quavers, but before the next attack two crotchet rests gape. The idiom and the preceding first statement of the trio lead us to expect the continuation of the motion as something self-evident, and this expectation is disappointed. The motif's gestural language, fortissimo in the basses, suggests strength. But this strength fails. The block of granite is hurled but falls short. Or perhaps the clumsy giant hand does not venture even to throw it, or else it is not even a granite block in the first place. Without the need to resort to conceptual language, this makes quite evident the futility of strength and indeed its stupidity, as long as it fails to reflect on itself. All that becomes apparent in a flash. You can't put your finger on it, for it vanishes as swiftly as the event in the allegro, even though it is no less firmly defined. We might well say that Mahler's music as a whole, and the negative spaces above all, take up Beethoven's example and extend it to every imaginable type of expression and indeed that they colonize the symphony in its entirety. The extent to which Mahler must have been impressed by that trio can be seen from the scherzo in the Second Symphony.

Among the idiosyncratic features of Mahler's use of rhythm we find isolated notes, or under certain circumstances, accompanying motifs in which the flow of the music comes to a halt or rather is suspended in mid-air. We find this as early as the *Urlicht* in the Second Symphony where, immediately before the A major sidestep to the words, '*Da kam ein Engelein*', a minim E is included which is strictly speaking out of place [in an unambiguous B flat minor passage]. The finale, '*Wir genießen die himmlischen Freuden*' in the Fourth Symphony is particularly rich in such retarding features. The overall effect is as if everything had been displaced by two crotchets, as if the whole passage had failed to catch up with itself. This is a major source of ambiguity. There is a related effect in the '*Von der Schönheit*' movement from *Das Lied von der Erde* and the first movement of the Ninth Symphony. Unlike some expressively overextended notes in Wagner or sustained accentuated notes of Beethoven's, these do not represent any build-up of power which then motivate a subsequent discharge. Nor are they simply a pause in which the movement temporarily comes to rest, but something different again: they are the seal of permanence, of the music's inability to fight free of itself. The epic sense of form of Mahler's symphonies has penetrated right down into the motivic cell and there resists non-violently the essentially dramatic onward thrust of the symphony. The difficulties of interpreting such bars correctly, that is to say, in such a way that they acquire their meaning from the way the symphony unfolds, and not from external formal categories, such as tension, are extraordinary. One is tempted to think that the success of performances of Mahler depends on the success of these moments.

Because of their vast scope Mahler was induced to construct entire symphonies on the principle of correspondence. In the Fifth, for example, the Funeral March in the second movement is elaborated parallel to a theme of the adagietto in the finale, and between these two analogously structured parts the great scherzo acts as a caesura. In a similar way the march rhythm, the harmonic sequence with the cowbells and individual motivic elements relate the outer movements of the Sixth much more closely than would be the case merely by the use of the major/minor motif. In motivic and thematic terms a major component of the first theme, as well as of the introduction and coda of the finale, is the retrograde motion of the core motif of the first movement: instead of A–C–B–A, we find A–B–C–A. Finally, the two movements share clearly chorale-like wind stanzas in minims, whose motifs do indeed differ radically from each other, but which are brought together by their use of the chorale. Even the Ninth still works with the symmetry of large-scale architecture. The first and last movements are slow; the two are analogous in the disembodiment of their concluding sections. The discovery of techniques similar to those found in film – such as the time-lapse seen in the rondo of the Fifth – or of slow motion – which can be seen in the quotations of the episodic theme from the burlesque in the adagio of the Ninth – has redounded to the benefit of Mahlerian composition because of their need for large-scale structuring. But productive though such discoveries turn out to be later on, they pale into insignificance before the exigencies of the here and now of composition. The grand architecture has not yet become fused with the fibre of the music, but instead it sketchily frames the details. The parallels give pleasure to those who discover them rather than exercising too much power in terms of a living musical response. There are few things that make the distinction between music and the visual arts as clear as this. The very measures which in Mahler seem to be almost an afterthought are the ones which decide the stature of painters or architects. For too long the theories which have been derived from Mahler's constructs have retained the aura of bricolage. It is only in more recent times that they seem to want to become an integral part of the music itself. This is perhaps the weightiest evidence in favour of the contemporary convergence of painting and music. But Mahler was the first in whose work this convergence was proclaimed, not indeed through any mimesis [*Klangmalerei*], but through the conductor's magisterial gaze, directed at the screen of his compositions.

The more conversant you become with Mahler's work, the clearer the source of his retrograde form becomes, and with that the secret of one of the central formal impulses in his *œuvre*. The retrogrades are designed to retrieve something of the vigour of which the open march-form had deprived them. This can already be seen in the Third Symphony in the tendency to elaborate the themes of the exposition in reverse order. This is no doubt conditioned by an aversion towards the mechanical repetition of even the abstract formal structure, or perhaps in order to establish direct contact between the end of the exposition and the beginning of the elaboration. A further instance can be seen in the finale of the Sixth where in the recapitulation the sequence of the first and second thematic complexes is reversed and the complex as such is fused with the returning introduction. This tendency towards retrogrades is extended to the point of self-consciousness in the adagio finale of the Ninth, where the final recapitulation makes its entry in an enormous outburst with the second half of the theme and only responds with the first after a moment of extreme tension. The idea of retrograde movement as one of large-scale structure rather than of the treatment of detail is one which Berg may well have borrowed from Mahler, as well as from Schoenberg's *Mondfleck*. His method resembles Mahler's also in that he is less concerned with exact pitch retrogrades – although that does play a considerable role in his music too – than with the effect of retrogression as such. What it may lack in coherence in a constructivist sense, it makes up for by the drastic form it assumes. Behind Mahler's conception of the procedure lies something quite different from the desire to create a stasis in which time is retracted. The quasi-retrograde passages are a form of retrospection, of the transition of the musical present to the realm of memory. A formal intentionality which then makes inroads into the stock of technical devices, as formerly into individual harmonic or timbral significances arose originally in Mahler's case too from an expressive need. This coincided from the outset with an aversion towards musical architectonics, a dislike of mere recurrence, as if nothing had happened in the interim, whereas the whole order of music lies in developing the rigorous implications of what has gone before. But whether in the transposition of this experience to the level of the musical material anything decisive has been lost is a question which remains unresolved to this day.

If it is true that every formal aspect, every figure, every question in Mahler's works is precisely what it is and what it should be in the context of the whole, without any trace of the merely conventional, then this compels the composer to revitalize the

topoi of the received formal language of symphonic writing and
activate them by reawakening the sense of their true purpose and
of what they had forgotten as mere topoi. A sense of what this
means can be gleaned from certain instrumental mannerisms of
Mahler's late phase. The drum roll was a topos designed to use
orchestral timbre to create tension, on the dominant, for
example. With the passage of time this has become so hackneyed
that the tension failed to appear, or else appeared only as
mock-tension. Mahler needs the device but is forced to rethink it,
intensify it beyond its own capacities, renew it so that it might
become once again what it may have been on its first appearance
in Viennese Classicism. The way he achieved this is as simple as it
is ingenious. What he does on occasion in the Ninth Symphony is
to transfer the drum roll from the kettledrums to the bass drum.
This resembles the traditional roll closely enough to leave a
similar imprint in the memory. But at the same time, the bass
drum has an indefinite pitch, which is closer to mere noise, to
something undomesticated and alien to the realm of musical
culture. Hence it retains much more of the dread than it did on
the kettledrums, where it simply evaporated. What had been
convention now becomes an event. This is in general the fate of
the conventions in Mahler's music.

It is where Mahler most faithfully keeps to the sonata model for
the sake of the traditional idea of integration that his specific
formal intentions, his hostility to the schematic, really make
themselves felt. The meaning of the prevailing configurations
undergoes a significant change. The first movement of the Sixth
contains an orthodox transition. But it is designed as a chorale –
that is to say, statically and not, as might be expected, something
that drives the music forward. Moreover, its colour is altered by
dissonant clashes. This has immediate consequences both for the
structure and the further development. The chorale cannot lead
anywhere. The brutal and dazzling secondary theme which
follows is not mediated by it. Precisely because the transition does
not culminate in it, even though it stands in the usual place,
it comes as a shock. This is intensified because instead of

modulating into it, the end of the chorale, the D minor dominant,[14] is followed by the F major tonic, an interrupted progression. The striking feature of the second theme, sensation as character, is not inherent in itself, but springs partly from the formal organization. The latter continues to be affected by it. The surprise effect is unrepeatable. In the recapitulation the second theme appears only in fragments. This is not uncommon in those Mahlerian movements where the themes are unbroken melodies which become over-prominent and appear too much as partial wholes in their own right. The surprise element of the second subject is promptly withdrawn from it and is only taken up again in the coda. The movement is sonata-like, as if in defiance, but its form is dictated by the musical content.

One sometimes has the feeling that it would be possible simply to formulate the substance of Mahler's music in words: in it the absolute is conceived, felt and longed for, and yet it does not exist. He no longer accepts the ontological proof of the existence of God which all previous music repeated parrot-fashion. All could be well, but in fact all is lost. His nervous, gestural language is a reaction to this situation. But how impoverished, abstract and false such a jejune formula appears when confronted with the actuality of his work. What it overlooks in its efforts to pin Mahler down is what is unfolded and dedicated within the totality of an experience which does not disclose its secret in selective assertions. Only in this way does its truth-content establish contact with the feeling which leaves such assertions as far behind as the actual meaning of life leaves phrases which purport to sum it up.

I am well aware that the expression on death-masks is deceptive. While we imagine that the mask reveals the final facial expression of a life, we know that it merely reflects muscular spasms. But Mahler's death-mask, which I first saw at the Centenary Exhibition, is enough to make one doubt such scientific explanations. Other death-masks, too, appear to smile.

---

14. This should read 'the A minor dominant'. [Note by Eric Graebner.]

But in Mahler's face, which seems both imperious and full of a tender suffering, there is a hint of cunning triumph, as if it wished to say: I have fooled you after all. Fooled us how? If we were to speculate we might conclude that the unfathomable sorrow of his last works had undercut all hope in order to avoid succumbing to illusion, rather as if hope were not unlike the superstitious idea of tempting fate, so that by hoping for something you prevent it from coming true. Could we not think of the path of disillusionment described by the development of Mahler's music as by no other as an example of the cunning not of reason but of hope? Is it not the case that in the final analysis Mahler has extended the Jewish prohibition on making graven images so as to include hope. The fact that the last two works which he completed have no closure, but remain open, translated the uncertain outcome between destruction and its alternative into music.

(1961)

Zemlinsky

The term 'eclectic' is surrounded by the same pejorative connotations as 'mannerism'. Artists who are said to be mannered stand accused of having concentrated exclusively on one single feature which has been rigidly isolated and developed at the expense of the living totality. The eclectic, on the other hand, is criticized for having internalized every possible fashion, particularly stylistic fashions, and combined them without ever achieving a tone that is peculiarly his own. The two concepts mark the extreme points on a scale which is defined by the idea of balance and compromise. They both have their origins in neo-Classicism. In this conception works of art should neither reduce themselves to the level of the particular, nor should they dissolve into generalities. They should preserve a happy medium. The underlying model here is that of the personality.

According to the common view the personality is never fixated on any one special thing, but expands in a natural, organic fashion into a comprehensive totality. On the other hand, it is also suggested that it is capable of forming such a totality entirely on the basis of its own resources, like a windowless monad. But it never really works out like that. The artist's productivity never forms the perfect fit with his individual subjectivity that is required by the concept of genius. Even his most individual qualities are secretly the products of a collectivity and, by the same token, his idiosyncrasies exhibit the marks of the collective, of the historical context. At all events, neither category befits a state of mind which has ceased to conform to the harmonious norms of neo-Classicism and in which the continuity of the individual personality and the general context is no longer a given. It is not for nothing that the word 'synthesis' – which is equally opposed to both mannerism and eclecticism – sounds so feeble. The mediation between divergent trends can only be achieved nowadays by working through the extremes, not by any conciliatory compromise. To appeal to synthesis as an antidote to eclecticism is to imagine that the totality now inaccessible from within could yet be achieved, as always, by the man of genius. In short, mannerism and eclecticism are not the indices of individual failures, but stigmata inflicted by history. To continue to use them as pejorative terms simply demonstrates how far aesthetic thought lags behind the concrete specifics of art and how impotently it clings to the traditional ideologies. Webern, one of the most important of composers, was long regarded as a mannerist à la Schoenberg. What with hindsight proved to be the great musical tradition, that is to say, the emancipation of dissonance, and even Debussy's fastidious abstinences, once seemed to be a mannerism raised to the level of exclusivity. What is mannerism and what is style can only be established conclusively after the fact.[1]

On the other hand, we might also term eclectic the almost equally powerful tendency to organize and thoroughly unify every dimension of music. For until a few decades ago each dimension was developed independently in particular schools, and these schools were gradually being absorbed by the progressive developments in composition. It is quite common for composers to be credited with having achieved a synthesis even though they would have been labelled eclectics if they had been less successful. Objective criteria for distinguishing between the two are lacking, as is any penetrating consideration of what should be approved and what rejected. Despite all this, the term eclecticism does point to a genuine experience, but one which

---

1. The terms used in this passage go back to the magisterial discussion in Goethe's essay, 'The Simple Imitation of Nature, Manner and Style' of 1789.

does not coincide directly with quality. What *Kapellmeistermusik* means, seems clear enough; it is music which has good musical manners and is conversant with every imaginable fashion, but is unable to make any really new discovery. But even though critics of Wagner never wearied during his lifetime of pointing out those elements in his music which merited this epithet, his music possessed a power which the spokesmen of a traditional originality, Schumann at their head, tried in vain to deny. And in Mahler above all the eclectic elements are just as much in evidence as the most eloquent originality, as is the fact that this originality did not make the former harmonious as thoroughly as was laid down in the conventional wisdom he despised.

The wariness towards eclecticism, particularly in Germany, has ancient roots. We may discern in it something of that anti-Roman sentiment to be found in German Protestant phil-hellenism – that hatred of Cicero and the philosophy of his age and the one that followed, which was nurtured by the Refor-mation and crassly echoed even by Hegel. Youthfulness, elemen-tal vigour and naive spontaneity – these are the values that were pitted by a reflective culture against the values of civilization. The associations evoked by this procedure are sinister. Such hostility is unknown to cultures which are as secure in their beliefs as this one could only aspire to be.

Nevertheless, such hostility towards civilization was not with-out justification. The wholly civilized mind does away with all opposing principles, with the very thing that made it mind in the first place. It is superficial because it contents itself triumphantly with what it has created. Art which had removed every trace of what is not art, would scarcely continue to be art. Particularly in the modern age, when every work, independently of its author, simply by virtue of its complexion, aims to be wholly itself and not painted from any model, eclecticism contradicts and gives the lie to its own claim to objectivity. But because this claim to be able to realize a pure aesthetic work in the here and now cannot be fulfilled, anymore than the old models can still be deemed valid, the verdict on eclecticism always contains a false note. This doubtless stems from the feeling of irritation that neither can succeed, that the work is compelled to support a burden that will cause it to collapse.

Let it collapse then is the unconscious reaction of all who hate the eclectic. Since in reality everything stands under the spell of equality, of absolute interchangeability, everything in art must appear to be absolutely individual. That archaic taboo on mimesis, the dislike of resemblances with which man has been inoculated for millennia, becomes fused with the prohibition on betraying the secret that works of art are interchangeable. A composer who does not avoid resemblances like the plague does more than violate the cult of property, which is particularly strongly rooted in ephemeral music. He also confesses that he has too great a liking for music – that is to say, the music of other composers. He doesn't take the collective norms seriously enough; he is actually no better than a child who copies from others, certainly not the stable ego who can be taken seriously and treated as a personality. It is such bewildering considerations as these which give one pause when the accusation of eclecticism makes its premature appearance. The distinction to be made instead is between the secondary talent and the artist who has something to express, even if it is only the crisis of art.

Alexander Zemlinsky, who originates from the same spiritual ambience as Mahler, made more of the compromises characteristic of the eclectic than any other composer of rank of his generation. The sensitivity essential to artistic production was identical in his case with impressionability. He positively invited the criticism of eclecticism. The subjects and forms that he chose uninhibitedly echoed those of his most celebrated contemporaries. The *Lyric Symphony* after poems by Tagore, Opus 14, for orchestra, soprano and baritone, automatically reminds us of *Das Lied von der Erde*. The one-act opera *Eine Florentinische Tragödie*, based on a story by Wilde, at once recalls *Salome*. The presence of eclectic features in the texture of his works cannot be denied: they reflect the conductor's love for the masterpieces of his age, a love from which his sensibility is unable to draw back when he comes to compose. But of course, great works can scarcely be

imagined without such love. An originality which is on a par with
the achievement of the age, but does not spring from an intimate
knowledge of what is essential to it, does not count. Just because
music had been split up into particular intentions, each of which
had its own validity, the task facing Zemlinsky's generation was
one of unification.

Only now can we see that this task was incapable of fulfilment.
But he faced up to it to the point of self-immolation with a
musical intelligence devoid of all prejudice and preconception.
In doing so a certain casualness is undeniable, as is an intermittent paralysis which prevents him from always making what he
borrowed fully his own. But his eclecticism shows genius in its
truly seismographic sensitivity to the stimuli by which he allowed
himself to be overwhelmed. Weakness which never pretends to
be creative acquires the strength of a second nature. The
unreserved sacrifice of the pathos of personality becomes a
critique of personality and hence something intensely personal.
Soft-heartedness, sensitivity, nervousness, the imaginative
power to combine heterogeneous elements – all these result in
something quite unmistakable. And even though the subaltern,
but practised ear can effortlessly detect the models of his works
and his musical idiom, to say that it is difficult to define what is
specific to Zemlinsky himself is not to detract from his achievement. In the Schoenberg school, whose intransigence seems to be
poles apart from the everyday, conciliatory nature of the popular
conductor of the German opera in Prague, he was held in
extraordinarily high esteem. Alban Berg dedicated one of his
most mature and perfect works to him, the *Lyric Suite* for string
quartet, and gave it its title with a conscious reference to the *Lyric
Symphony*, which is quoted in one passage.

Still under the spell of traditional aesthetic idealism people still
tend to neglect the intricate threads connecting the writers of an
age, and not only personally. It is to these links that we may well
owe rather more of the collective authority of an individual
achievement than may first be supposed. Looked at from this
point of view Zemlinsky was one of the most remarkable figures
of his generation. Born in Vienna in 1871 or 1872 – sources

differ even on some of the basic facts – he was only three years older than Schoenberg. He studied in Vienna under Fuchs, and after a number of posts ending up as first conductor of the Vienna Volksoper, he was invited to go Prague in 1911. Here he worked for many years with the very greatest success. Around 1930 he moved to Berlin. He emigrated after the onset of the Third Reich and went to New York, where he died.

Brahms is not included in a list of his teachers. It was not possible to obtain a copy of a biographical sketch by Heinrich Jalowetz which appeared in 1922 in the now forgotten Prague musical journal *Auftakt*. Yet Brahms must have taken a great interest in him and have used his influence, as the saying goes, to promote his career. As early as 1926, in *Das neue Musiklexikon*, the German version of the Eaglefield-Hull's *Dictionary of Modern Music and Musicians*, edited by Alfred Einstein, he is correctly described as 'a significant representative of that synthesis of Wagnerian and Brahmsian elements which can be discerned in so many works of the Viennese school'. As conductor of the Philharmonia, the Vienna amateur orchestra, Zemlinsky met Schoenberg, who played the cello in it. He gave Schoenberg lessons in composition. It is difficult to establish the extent of Zemlinsky's influence and whether it amounted just to giving friendly advice or whether it involved more far-reaching collaboration. But the relationship must have been very close. Nor was it disrupted when Schoenberg accepted implications that went far beyond what Zemlinsky had intended. Schoenberg's first wife, Mathilde, was Zemlinsky's sister. Moreover as a performer Zemlinsky was closely involved in subsequent developments and gave excellent first performances of such crucial works as *Erwartung* and the fragments of Berg's *Wozzeck*. In his own later *œuvre* he revealed the influence of Schoenberg, in much the same way as Haydn had been influenced by Mozart. Schoenberg wrote the vocal score of Zemlinsky's first opera, the award-winning *Sarema*.

Zemlinsky must have made contact with Gustav Mahler very early on, since Mahler had conducted the première of his opera *Es war einmal*. Mahler also agreed to put on the *Traumjörg* or

Traumgörge. However, after Mahler handed in his resignation, Weingartner dropped the planned production. Mahler's correspondence makes it clear just how much he, Schoenberg and Zemlinsky saw of each other. The musical cross-references extend even further. Zemlinsky was the teacher of Erich Wolfgang Korngold, the infant prodigy, and is said to have orchestrated his *Schneemann*. He was on friendly terms with Franz Schreker. There are close similarities in the libretti of Zemlinsky's *Zwerg* and Schreker's *Die Gezeichneten*. This was obviously more than a coincidence. Lastly, Zemlinsky was probably the first composer to take a strong interest in a westerly direction. He particularly liked Debussy's *Pelléas* and Dukas's *Ariane et Barbe Bleue*. He conducted the latter work in a glittering performance at the Prague Music Festival in 1926, where he also performed Berg's *Wozzeck* fragments. Maeterlinck, the poet who had written the plays on which both operas are based, played an important role in Zemlinsky's work. Some of his most beautiful pieces, the Six Songs, Opus 13, are settings of poems by Maeterlinck. However, since they were published in the First World War, he was forced by the prevailing chauvinist climate to omit the poet's name in the piano edition. It was not introduced until the orchestral versions were published in 1922 and 1926.

Such details give some sense of the extent to which even a movement which was so extreme and so remote from the official musical life of Vienna was closely intertwined with it even in its formative years. It shows too how unprovincial it was from the outset. If in Schoenberg's works the most divergent impulses of the age met, culminating in the idea of constructivist composition, it was Zemlinsky who defined the cultural space which made it possible to compare those different impulses in the first place: apart from Wagner and Brahms, this meant, above all, Mahler, Debussy and Schoenberg. This is not to be understood as the claim that Zemlinsky possessed the composer's external understanding of the most important trends of his day. The respect in which Zemlinsky was held by his Viennese friends was based on the fact that these conflicting currents had come together in his works in a way that created the most productive tension imaginable. We can perhaps venture the cautious formulation that Zemlinsky and Schoenberg more or less simultaneously succeeded in combining Wagnerian chromaticism with the Brahmsian legacy of a movement that proceeds harmonically, step by step, avoiding the crutch of the sequence. Together they were the first to incorporate polytonal chords into movements while still taking the concept of the key extremely seriously.

Zemlinsky published as his Opus 7 a number of songs under the title of *Irmelin Rose*. They bear a dedication to Maria Schindler, who subsequently became the wife of Gustav Mahler. This work should probably be dated before 1900. Some of the texts for these songs are by Richard Dehmel and Jens Peter Jacobsen, authors whose works were also set to music by Schoenberg. But even more striking is the fact that for all their similarity to the Act II duet of *Tristan*, their peculiarly intense tone, especially in the Dehmel song 'Anbetung' is strongly reminiscent of Schoenberg's early songs. The first song, however, 'Da waren zwei Kinder', a setting of a poem by Christian Morgenstern, is a tentative model of that late tonality in which all twelve semitones have become of equal value, as it were, even though there is no chromatic sliding from one to the other – a foretaste of that harmonic consciousness that culminated in the idea of twelve-note composition. Moreover the song, which in the briefest possible space develops from a bright, airy gracefulness to the most sombre mood, is a genuine masterpiece that points far beyond the Art Nouveau ambience in which it originates.

Zemlinsky's early music differs from Art Nouveau in one respect, which then became constitutive for the new music: the deliberate simplicity of his utterance. For all the harmonic subtlety he mainly dispenses with any decorative, luxurious piano accompaniment. The musical events are presented quite nakedly, without any prinking, almost as in a conventional harmonic 'chorale'. This stands in sharp contrast to, say, Richard Strauss, but also to Hugo Wolf. The voice does not declaim; it is not interpreted in an attention-grabbing way by the play of motifs on the piano. Instead the actual music is compressed into the vocal line – again in the Brahmsian tradition, but even more emphatically. The piano exhausts the harmonies implicit in the vocal line, but barely adds anything of moment. There are no Straussian surprises or expressive effects.

Beneath the cloak of a musical idiom which a crude jargon still likes to classify as late Romantic, we sense in the young Zemlinsky a groping towards reduction, towards objectification. Needless to say, this is not combined, as it is in the very first works of Schoenberg, with powerful polyphonic tendencies. Zemlinsky, who was a true child of the nineteenth century, remained faithful to homophony throughout his life and never attempted to conceal it by superimposing a contrapuntal web. His talents doubtless drew the line at counterpoint. But his homophonic disposition did possess the virtue of a highly transparent and elegant style which never lapsed into the banal or amorphous. In his mature works as a composer he came closer than anyone to the ideal of distilled comedy: subtle and not overloaded with meaning, an ideal which Hofmannsthal had vainly looked for in Strauss.

If Zemlinsky succeeded in this it was because he had complete mastery of the means at his disposal, while possessing enough self-knowledge to remain within his limitations. His last two operas, *Kleider machen Leute* (written in 1911, revised in 1921), and the *Kreidekreis*, are true examples of a discriminating simplicity. There can be no doubt that in this he was impressed by one feature of Debussy's, namely the highly pared-down use of monody which provided opera with a new impetus. He reacted less to the dazzling variety, the dissolving forms, the whole impressionist palette, than to the art of omission, withholding, of compositional 'understatement'.[2] With Busoni he was one of the first to reject pathos. His implied aesthetics forms a bridge to the later work of Les Six. He was particularly influenced by the *Pelléas* score which showed him how to hint and intimate, instead of composing something out fully, as his own tradition had taught. At the same time a store of Viennese nimbleness of mind

---

2. Adorno used the English word.

and dynamism saved him from the monotony of the much more ambitious *drame lyrique*. The pleasures of archaic pastiche held no charm for him.

But for all his historical merits the reason for reappraising Zemlinsky is more than a matter of historical interest. Since the European catastrophe the whole concept of the cultural heritage has become dubious and nothing is able any longer to legitimate itself by reference to its contribution to the tradition. Cultural products can only justify themselves nowadays by their immediate relevance and by their ability to speak to us directly. In such circumstances Zemlinsky would have nothing to say to us if his achievement were purely historical. We would merely be left with the pointless memories of a man who, just a few years after his death, had fallen into such total oblivion that even the discovery of the simplest data and getting hold of the scores of his works are fraught with the greatest difficulties. But the force-field of his work has managed to salvage his relevance for us precisely because the so-called main trend has passed him by.

Zemlinsky's music, like that of few others, contains impulses which brought the new into being. They were then left by the wayside, but their sacrifice says something about the price that had to be paid for progress. That price was the creation of clearly defined, vivid, individual characteristics. They were perforce sacrificed to the ideal of total unification, integral composition. Only when the individual is displayed in total clarity does the music radiate something of that force which not only achieves total transparency, but which also legitimates it. Without the substantiality of the individual impulse totality can only celebrate Pyrrhic victories. Zemlinsky draws attention to the best of what must not be forgotten. Alban Berg was particularly attached to those Maeterlinck songs of Opus 13. Perhaps they really do form the centre of his *œuvre*. An inward Middle Ages 'with eyes blindfolded', the folksong tone which has become darkened, enigmatic in its own eyes, establishes the link with Mahler. This is especially so in the first song, the ballad of the three sisters, and in the last, 'Sie kam zum Schloß gegangen', which reflect the young Mahler's *Gesellen* songs as in a glass darkly. Moreover, in many passages, especially in the first, Brahmsian movement, this is to be found combined with an expanded tonality, alongside Debussyian chord shifts and chains of seconds.

What is crucial, however, is Zemlinsky's ability to formulate the most concentrated melismas, in which the lyrical sweetness runs together like honey into combs. Something of that has been captured by Berg in Marie's lullaby and Alwa's rondo passages in *Lulu*. It was because of this that Berg felt an affinity with Zemlinsky and knew by heart some incomparable passages of his music, many of them marked by their warm, wide intervals. An example is the last stanza of the 'Virgin's Song', with the major ninth leading to the word 'love' – which despite the tonal material has an expressive force that was otherwise reserved for a full-blooded expressionism, a force which is self-evident and yet also unconventional, harmonized against the grain, as it were, by reformulating the cadence. Or again, there is the tender, mournful passage about the gold ring in the fifth song, '*Zeig die offene Tür, sag, das Licht ging aus*'. And lastly, the question '*Wohin gehst du?*' in the final poem of the sequence. In the most recent developments in composition, Boulez' *Marteau*, for example, the question of the individual characteristics has once again come to the surface. With that in mind we may see such passages in Zemlinsky as amongst the last in which individual characterization was successful without any need for recourse to the traditional stock of Romantic formulae. To convey a sense of the mellowness and vividness of these abbreviated melodies, one would have to look to Verdi's *Otello*, which is profuse in such inventions. The principle underlying them has never been properly absorbed into the tradition.

Zemlinsky's outstanding quality is his melodic cadence, cadence in the literal sense – that is to say, an expressive falling of the voice, a melancholic falling away at the outset. The line mimics the composer's temperament. This is not to suggest that isolated, so-called purple patches are inserted at random. They are rather the concentrates of a large-scale form. So as to organize this in his strophically constructed songs, Zemlinsky adopted Mahler's variation technique. The ends of the stanzas

121

hardly ever repeat themselves in a fixed, invariable way. For the most part they remain identifiable, but the continuation tends to reveal something unexpected and often more intense. The variations are drawn into the harmonic construction and ingeniously follow its intensification or attenuation.

On the whole, closer scrutiny compels us to modify our initial impression of Zemlinsky's eclecticism. We discover how effectively an alien style becomes a meaningful nuance of the rest of the composition and how closely it fits in with it. This is the position with the quartal harmonies of 'Und kehrt er erst heim', which derive from the early Schoenberg. The quartal chords never clash with the circumscribed tonality, but blend in an unceasing series of resolutions with the harmonic flow which they interrupt. The Maeterlinck songs require no apology when set beside the far more radical song-cycles of Schoenberg and Webern. But it would be a grave mistake to compare him with Strauss, purely on the basis of the components. 6/4 chords and unexpected harmonic intrusions are not enough to provide a definition of music. Zemlinsky stands at the opposite pole from Strauss, since in his work such moments are never conceived as effects, but are developed functionally from the harmonic progression. For all his love of nuance he never tolerates mere stimuli and never composes *ad auditores*, but always obeys the logic of the matter in hand. This corresponds to a stylistic asceticism and also a certain habit of reticence. In his works for the stage, too, which are primarily lyrical in nature, he scorns all shrill, overemphatic gestures; in this respect he was a true disciple of the French. Above all, the content has an untheatrical, wholly unfeigned warmth. It is the direct proclamation of feeling, not its imitation. To that extent and despite his use of largely traditional methods, Zemlinsky may be classified along with the post-Straussian generation. The very pride his music takes in refusing to project itself – that is to say, its very modernity – may paradoxically prove to be the greatest obstacle standing in the way of his fame today.

His instrumental music is of high quality. Take, for example, the Third Quartet, of 1924. It moves within the realm of an enlarged but unmistakable tonality, although the last three movements close on a mildly dissonant note. The brief movements are written in the most relaxed manner. Despite his highly skilled exploitation of the quartet sound and the assured individuation of each voice, he avoids deliberate polyphony; instead, the ideas alternate with extraordinary rapidity and their variety is diachronic rather than simultaneous. The harmony is elegant and luxurious; metrically, preference is given to irregularity.

What is striking is the courage Zemlinsky displays in his readiness to interrupt the movement, never pursuing a rhythmic impulse beyond the point where it naturally comes to rest: the antithesis of anything mechanical. This waxing and waning of impulse is characteristic. It is idle to speculate whether it testifies to the feebleness of old age or the ability to translate unruffled a gesture of essence into one of musical form. That gesture was never alien to the Viennese tradition of Schubert and Bruckner. The first movement might very easily have been inspired by the idea Wagner developed late in life of writing 'symphonic dialogues'. He works more exclusively than is usual in sonata movements with two antithetical main groups, one of which has the expression mark 'leisurely, heartfelt', while the other is to be played much more quickly – 'with a sharp rhythm' – and concludes quietly with a one-bar motive. The development, in running semiquavers, is carried almost entirely by the second theme; only in the passage leading to the repetition does the concluding motif appear in an expanded form. Conversely, the second theme is absent from the extremely abbreviated recapitulation so that the development could be regarded as an anticipated part of the reprise which more or less inverts the exposition.

In short, the sonata form is dominant, though treated quite unconventionally, sketched in rather than filled out, as if by a composer who inwardly had already taken his leave of it and only turns back to make use of it for one last time. No less unconventional is the variation movement, if only by virtue of the cursorily sketched-in eight-bar theme. The equally brief variations succeed each other in quick succession. The third movement bears the title 'Romance' and contains prominent *Lied*-like melodies, with a simple accompaniment, but on a variety of instruments. The final movement, Burlesque, comes close to the rondo form; everything is full of art, yet unpretentious. With self-critical intent the impression is created of something slipping from one's grasp, something which does not care to assert itself too powerfully: a coherently formulated incoherence.

Or take the Sinfonietta, Opus 23 in D, which was not published until 1935. Its title gives no indication of the intention which may well have become increasingly conscious. The piece is set for a small orchestra, strings and double woodwinds. But also for four horns, three trumpets and three trombones. He aims throughout at striking, self-contained phrases and an almost song-like melodic line. The first movement is a presto which has distant echoes of the Mahler of, say, the scherzo of the Fifth Symphony. The main group of themes is quartal, the second subject cantabile, the development is somewhat more explicit, the repetition reduced to a mere reminiscence. The fear of overemphasis and the reluctance to dwell on anything surpasses even the Third Quartet, if that is possible. The second movement is entitled 'Ballad', rendered in a narrative style, as if it feared the complexities of a symphonic andante. The rondo with its surprisingly mellifluous main voices is almost a medley.

Altogether the Sinfonietta remains within the bounds of a type of composition in which a knowing modernity flirts with the long-submerged fundamental forms of Viennese Classicism, evokes them with a complete lack of commitment and makes use of them as if for its own relief. At the same time, Zemlinsky's Sinfonietta has nothing in common with the neo-Classicism of the Stravinsky school. It neither borrows the static tectonics of the past, nor does it parody them. Zemlinsky rather juggles the traditional forms with such supreme facility that their specific meanings do not even clash with his lyrical differentiation of the individual events. His taste culminates in an attitude to form which would prefer to solve the prohibitive difficulties which the symphonic form presents today not by direct confrontation, but by means of omission and circumvention. He is not fixated earnestly on the past, but neither is he prepared to take the risk of attempting a new reconstruction of the symphonic spirit. This attitude harmonizes well with the witty and elegant tone; the finale of Beethoven's Eighth might well have provided the model for the rondo. Needless to say, his experience ensures that his orchestration has a sure touch and the effect of the whole is entirely convincing.

But the centre of gravity of Zemlinsky's work lies neither in the songs, nor in his orchestral music. As an opera conductor he saw himself primarily as a composer of operas. Most of what he wrote was intended for the stage. The early operas are as completely forgotten as his youthful symphonies. Two of the mature operas, *Eine Florentinische Tragödie* and *Der Zwerg*, are hardly performable any more, despite their undoubted musical qualities. The *Florentinische Tragödie* has one of those crass neo-Romantic libretti which, like Max von Schilling's *Mona Lisa*, deserve only to be consigned to the flames. The *Zwerg* is based on that immortal tale of Oscar Wilde's which does not have enough substance to yield a full-scale dramatic work. It provides enough material for a single situation and whatever goes beyond that necessarily degenerates into dramatic padding.

Kleider machen Leute, on the other hand, is one of Zemlinsky's best scores and it is highly effective as theatre. Its obstinate neglect is barely comprehensible in view of the unceasing complaints about the absence of decent musical comedies and the futile attempts to resuscitate *The Taming of the Shrew*.[3] The text is tactful, albeit artisanal, crafted along the lines of Keller's story on which it is based and it salvages some of his humanity. But for tenderness and bashful grace the opera has no equal. At the same time, in the crucial scenes his inventiveness is very striking. It is cheerful and devoid of the forced musical humour so often encountered. If anything, the reluctant swindler is consoled. In *Die Meistersingers* Wagner's instinct perceived the musical comedy as the genre of individual characterization, of engraved detail.

---

3. A comic opera composed by Hermann Goetz in 1872.

And so it remained in the line passing via *Der Rosenkavalier* to Schoenberg's *Von heute auf morgen*.

Zemlinsky's disposition enabled him to fit naturally into this tradition. With extreme discretion he sidesteps the exalted ambitions of the music drama and its dynamically conclusive developments. For the most part he confines himself to motivic models for the individual sections and develops them with variation technique, without any cheap sequences, until the entry of the next model. The work contains charming songs, like the 'Schneiderlein, was machst du denn?', a burlesque interlude and a subdued, but touching love scene. The tendency to simplify the stage music in dramatic terms, a process later introduced by Kurt Weill, is already hinted at in the texture of his work, without making any concessions to commercial entertainment. With a dignity which derives from a fast vanishing tradition *Kleider machen Leute* was able to achieve popularity while maintaining certain formal standards. It is a late triumph, comparable to Ravel's *L'enfant et les sortilèges*, but Zemlinsky's work is freer of jingling. The entire movement of the new Viennese school towards essentiality, which in many respects is also a tendency towards simplification, is present in Zemlinsky, but in the opposite direction. He moves towards communication and not away from it. He is a Westerner in that his reductions move closer towards the functional forms, instead of negating them.

The most eloquent testimony to this is his setting of Klabund's *Kreidekreis*.[4] This work was performed in an excellent production in Berlin in the first years of the Hitler dictatorship. Of course, it was then swiftly dropped from the repertoire as undesirable and has probably never been put on again since. The subtle and sensitive tendency to simplification already present in the Keller opera is taken even further here. We may well believe that Zemlinsky, who was familiar with *The Threepenny Opera*, may finally have fallen under its influence and tried to soften the

---

4. Klabund (the pseudonym of Alfred Henschke 1890–1928) wrote his version of *The Chalk Circle* as an adaptation of a Chinese play in 1925. It served as a model for Brecht as well as Zemlinsky.

brutality of the Weill songs by blending it with exotic charm. The aura of the Wiener Werkstätte really does surround the entire work.[5] But if we look at the trajectory of Zemlinsky's work as a whole, we become aware of the injustice of such assertions. The method of basing everything on the briefest possible individual characteristics which Zemlinsky adopted to the exclusion of any symphonic or dramatic expansiveness, is already clearly anticipated in *Kleider machen Leute*. No more than a minute leap was required to enable him to achieve comparable results to those of Brecht and Weill. It might almost be said that Zemlinsky forestalled them in inventing the type of *The Threepenny Opera* for himself.

The word 'almost' points to his failure in the manner which is familiar to us in science, where scientists are said to have almost made crucial breakthroughs, but are then inexplicably denied the credit for them. Here, rather than in the notion of inspiration, is the place to seek the irrational element in composition. This element is that of a bad society and is comparable to the situation of a man who is doomed because his discoveries lag behind those of a competitor. In a great composer a clarinet must sound as if it had been precisely imagined beforehand, even if that is not the case in reality. Or, to give a slightly different example, he must fully articulate the form to which he is unconsciously aspiring, and he must do this without hesitation and without looking to the right or left. It is the sort of thing that makes one despair of the concept of greatness, if one has not done so long since.

In certain circumstances a man may be cheated of his deserts by nothing more than a lack of ruthlessness. It is possible to be too refined for one's own genius and in the last analysis the greatest talents require a fund of barbarism, however deeply buried. This was denied to Zemlinsky and to that extent he lacked the element

---

5. The Wiener Werkstätte (Viennese Workshops) were established in 1903 as an offshoot of *Jugendstil* or Art Nouveau. Under the influence of Klimt and other artists of the Viennese Secession they attempted to reform the style of domestic life by applying the decorative techniques of the movement to household objects. It is this combination of the decorative and the artisanal that Adorno has in mind.

of luck that according to popular belief goes along with genius. He provokes the verdict that he is too quiet and refined. But such a criticism endorses the idea that force is an integral part of greatness, and this view casts its shadow even over an extreme of delicacy. In artists like Zemlinsky the significant factor is precisely the absence of force; he surrenders himself to the so-called trends of the age and becomes their spokesman. Anyone who has managed to emancipate himself from a residual belief in success will come to regard talents of this type in a different light, even when their sensitivity – the exact counterpart of Webern's implacable hardness – sometimes induces them to make common cause with the criteria of popular success. But there is all the more reason to revise such judgements when we reflect that the survival of works of art of the past does not follow automatically from their once palpable modernity. Even though it is essential for critics of contemporary works to inquire whether they have drawn the logical conclusions implicit in their situation without making any compromises, it remains true that such criteria cannot be projected into the past and applied to the state of musical consciousness that obtained then. For the logic of that consciousness was not yet evident, since it may have contained possibilities which were discarded or forgotten at the time and only came into their own at a much later date. Once works of art have lost the tension of their immediate here and now in their relationship with their observer or audience, they reveal quite different dimensions from those visible in the material at the time. To borrow an expression from the plastic arts, we could call these dimensions those of *peinture*. On occasion they often prove more durable in the retrograde art of a past era than in the erstwhile avant-garde. It is in this sense that we might even today give the rather more moderate Ravel greater chances of survival in posterity than the Groupe des Six. Much of their radicalism now stands exposed as a disdainful take-it-or-leave-it attitude, incomparably less well worked out than Ravel's impressionism, which they consigned to the scrapheap.

It would be rash to predict a similar future for Zemlinsky with any confidence. In his case everything stands on a knife's edge.

But at all events the overwhelming proportion of what passes for opera nowadays is vastly inferior to him both formally and technically. Indeed a level of uncreativity has been reached compared with which his feeblest and most fragile work would surely merit a revival, but for the insistence on being up to date[6] and the abstract cliché, 'This no longer has anything to say to us'. This and the simple appeal to the sheer passage of time have enabled people to deceive themselves about the decline of the ability to react to art and make aesthetic discriminations. If for once we state frankly just how little good music, past and present, there really is in the world – in complete contrast to the situation in painting – and if we deny ourselves any illusions about how much of the official stock of cultural goods is subjected to objective judgement, while the media of mechanical reproduction pour out endless floods of music, then we shall feel better able to ask for a hearing for Zemlinsky who was a true master. We can do so in the full knowledge of the objections that will be raised even before he has been given a proper hearing. They only conceal the wish to confirm yet again a historical judgement which proves that the power of chance and the injustice of the world also hold sway in the realm of art.

(1959)

---

6. Adorno used the English phrase.

Schreker

Music has not been left unscathed by that loss of a sense of historical continuity after the Second World War which has been so widely remarked on in Germany. Many composers who exercised a considerable influence before the Hitler dictatorship have now been consigned to oblivion. The most famous of these was Franz Schreker. Admittedly, the theatrical success that he sought, like the hero of his first opera, forsook him during his own lifetime. An aura surrounded him in the early 1920s when every stage of any significance mounted productions of *Der Schatzgräber* or *Die Gezeichneten*. Then, probably after the première of *Irrenlohe*, public taste turned against him, just as the faces of idolized stars are suddenly turned into objects of ridicule by the unconscious revenge of their enslaved worshippers. In the period of his greatest successes, after 1918, he was regarded as one of the protagonists of the new music. In the book that bears that title[1] Paul Bekker eulogized him as its greatest dramatic representative. Even then, of course, he was as far behind Schoenberg and the early Stravinsky, both in style and compositional material, as Secessionism, with which he had much in common, lagged behind Cubism and Expressionism.[2] But the history of music does not run absolutely parallel to the other arts.

---

1. Paul Bekker, *Neue Musik*, Berlin 1919.
2. Secessionism includes the Munich Secession (1892), the Viennese Secession of Gustav Klimt and others (1897) and the Berlin Secession led by Max Liebermann (1898).

'Non-contemporary' works still survive in a way that would never be tolerated by the most progressive forms of painting. Initially, the Klimtian aspects of Schreker's artistic landscape were not found objectionable. His scores did not lack features which brought him closer to those of younger composers.

They may perhaps have been an integral part of the climate, rather than something which could be pinned down technically. The Frankfurt première of *Die Gezeichneten* was surrounded by an atmosphere of scandal. It was rumoured that the conductor, Ludwig Rottenberg, had insisted on an unusual number of rehearsals. One had visions of some huge, surging monstrosity, something altogether excessive and perhaps even alarming, triggered off by the term naturalism and the name of the composer, as well as shocking erotic scenes. Even if not all of this promise was fulfilled, at least as far as one fourteen-year-old listener was concerned, and even if the work as a whole proved to be much easier to grasp than his desire for something exorbitant had led him to expect, the rumours that surround a work of art are sometimes closer to the truth than a precise analysis. The conjunction of lavish profusion, uninhibited daring and a confusing, disorganized image of modernism beckoned seductively from Schreker's works.

Schoenberg himself always treated him with the greatest respect and quoted a passage from *Der ferne Klang* in the *Treatise on Harmony* as one of the first instances – one among many – of unresolved chords with six or more notes. However, the younger generation reacted vehemently against him. This reaction was even shared by Schreker's own students at the Berlin Academy of Music where he was still artistic director. They rejected him much as avant-garde painters rejected the successful figures of their own age and their own circles as the purveyors of kitsch. He met such protests with the slightly obtuse naivety of a professional artist who possessed what the late nineteenth century called an artist's head. He was surrounded by a studio atmosphere. His most successful scene was set in an artist's studio. Lavish décor, the wealth of the ornate orchestra of the New German School, musical scores simply covered with the fleeting notes of glissandi and arpeggios, all these combined with the sensuous sweetness of Debussy and Ravel. On occasion, as a man of the theatre, he lashes out with Puccinian octaves. He loosened up and dematerialized the viscous flow of the post-Wagnerian school and at the same time surpassed it in timbral intensity. He brought a shimmering Mediterranean note into the monolithic orchestra. But even these achievements were already obsolete when he introduced them. It was as easy to reproach his great canvasses for their lack of stringency and spiritual power, as to snipe at the tastelessness of his texts. His music was only too well suited to such stage directions as this one from *Der ferne Klang*: 'She raises her arms, as if to leap into the lake. At this moment the moon rises and transfigures the landscape. The lake glitters in its light, glow-worms dance, a nightingale sings and deer go to the lake to drink. Sultry breezes envelop the girl. The magic of the forest by night. Nature breathes love and promise. Grete stands silently, lost in wonder at the view.' This drags a cautious Wagnerian note on the Good Friday music into a dubious realm halfway between oleograph and Art Nouveau.

In general, like Wagner's other successors, what Schreker borrowed from Wagner was the element of the phantasmagoria which he then made into the centrepiece of his own work. Just as damning as such literary abominations were the objections which specialists raised to the musical side of his work. These included the impoverished grasp of harmonic movement; the clumsy chord-shifting from one pedal-point to the next, as if from one cushion to another; the absence of thematic clarity, which had a disastrous effect on the later works especially; and the frequently amorphous rhythms. All of this stands in striking contrast to the skills to which his pupils have testified. It was said that he wrote an extraordinarily good and strict movement in the style of Palestrina during a class and, in general, even where his harmonies appear slapdash, he was always able to explain them in terms of their functions in traditional harmonic theory. The lavishness of his orchestration has been attacked, but never disputed. To the figure of the artist in his studio we may add that curious blend of fancy-dress ball and professorial manner. For all his love of the mellifluous the provocative image he presents is decidedly deficient in ordinary common sense, and we should note his ability to come to terms with a world to which at bottom he was by no means hostile. Both these features are enough to give one pause.

On the other hand the taboos he flouted are not just those which the idea of the coherent work of art imposes on a self-indulgent intoxication. There is something not quite domesticated that struggles for self-expression in Schreker. This is why judgements on his technique are often too hasty. If, as was common, critics sought to oppose Schreker's garish colours by calling for allegedly pure and cleanly distinguished lines and complexes, they were not only responding to their legitimate dislike of a euphemistic charm and of what was felt to be a mere whitewash, a scrawl. Schreker also provoked the hostility of stuffy ascetics to the discontinuous, shimmering and seductive – qualities that they defend themselves against by assuming a patronizing attitude. The Schrekerian syrinx is the exact counterpart to the recorder. It is unlikely that all those who discerned the devil in Schreker's orchestra could have orchestrated better than he. The ambiguity in the obsolete elements in Schreker – the undeniably tawdry and dubious features – as well as the fear of throwing off all restraint that is the goal of his best music, justifies reopening the file on Schreker – if this image from the criminal world can be used in the sphere of art. But it does not seem entirely inappropriate in view of the slightly scabrous nature of the aura surrounding him.

In the jargon of those years it used to be said of Schreker that his music was founded on the experience of sound. There is some truth in this. Ideas about 'sound' [*Klang*], to use the term employed in his first opera, run through his entire *œuvre* like a red thread: the music box [*Spielwerk*], the diffuse designs of *Die Gezeichneten*, the treasure-seeker's [*Schatzgräber*] lute and, lastly, Amandus's organ in *Der singende Teufel*. The sound not only forms the subject and the symbolic theme of the work, but also musically, as the unity of harmony and instrumental timbre, it was more important in his eyes than every other dimension of composition. In his later period he attempted to retrieve what he had neglected hitherto, but the result was unrelieved sterility. It is often difficult to distinguish specific talents at work in art from a simple incapacity to do those things which have been voluntarily forgone.

But what Schreker actually understands by sound must remain open. People who use the term imagine for the most part that nothing more need be said. Perhaps their example should be followed. For the phenomenon resembles the 'sound' [*Klang*]. It attempts to retranslate into music the onomatopoeic word which itself imitates something musical. What is conjured up is the idea of something which resounds but comes, as it were, from nowhere and returns to the same place. It is suddenly there, as if strings had been plucked. Like an auditory Fata Morgana it hangs in the air, colourful, transparent and denatured. It proves too elusive to grasp and then disappears. In the shape of a phantasmagoria it aims to snatch music from time and conjure it up in space. It arouses nostalgia, like the nostalgia that attaches itself to the traces of smells which involuntarily recall happiness in childhood. Schreker's ideal of sound is music that puts down roots in mid-air. It denies both cause and effect, indeed every actual determinant of composition. The factors which usually define the musical structure – developing variation, the logic of composition in its broadest sense – are virtually excluded. Thus despite the moderate nature of his material, this lends him a radical streak which justifies classifying him along with the avant-garde rather more than the façade of his music would lead us to suppose.

Bekker, who has studied Schreker in greater depth than anyone else, once noted the impulse which induced him to formulate his creative ideas [*Einfälle*] indecisively. This may have been based on an intentional programme. He scorns themes which have been identified as characteristic and have been preserved both traditionally and even in Schoenberg, or perhaps he has no ear for them. It is as if they are to be lost to any precise memory and the listener is supposed only to recognize involuntarily what are no more than vague intimations. To that extent

Schreker may be seen, remarkably enough, to participate in the critique of the traditional conception of melodic line, which in advanced music had taken quite a different direction, namely that of condensation and restructuring. If there is anything at all topical about Schreker, then it lies in such elements as this. They teach us that changes in material and consciousness do not necessarily move in a straight line along the same track as the new music. The pressure to dissolve all existing practices may perhaps have expressed itself before the First World War in a variety of categories, and not just in those of the great historical trend. But today, when that trend threatens to become universal and mechanical, we have to revaluate many things which previously appeared to be of minor importance.

Schreker's ideal of sound did not remain an empty cipher, a matter merely of attitude. He created his own technique by which to give it reality. In this his academic bent stood him in good stead. The isolated 'sound' [*Klang*] is associated in the first instance with the harp, and in fact the imaginary *chef d'œuvre* of the hero of Schreker's programmatic artist-opera is named after that instrument. The harp was a major symbolic prop in Art Nouveau. Thus there is not only a programmatic poem by Dehmel, but the sublime harp [*hehre Harfe*] also features in Stefan George's *Der siebente Ring*, while the number of harps used to decorate books at the turn of the century is legion. For freethinkers they symbolized magic. They feature prominently in Schreker's arsenal and are without doubt a major factor in the reputation for idiosyncrasy which his name evokes to this day. The same may be said of the triangle which Krenek, his disciple, denounced as 'a load of rubbish' in an aside in his first opera, *Der Sprung über den Schatten.*

But the fleeting vision of the non-identifiable, the curious supersensory sensuousness of which his music dreams, prevents him from opting unambiguously for any settled orchestral timbre. Schreker, who was anything but a theorist, once admitted this with surprising candour: he found the undue prominence of any single instrument, such as a celeste, which always attracts attention, quite unbearable. He really only acknowledged one possible instrument as an accompaniment for an opera: the orchestra itself. The shimmering intangible quality requires nothing less than the integration of differences, of the significances which have only just been emancipated as a ferment of sound. This trend is taken further in the orchestral art of the new music, particularly that of Alban Berg. In the orchestration of his *Lulu* the Schrekerian chiaroscuro is intensified to the point where it achieves fulfilment as one strand in a fully articulated composition. But the sound of Berg's orchestra in his late works would be unimaginable without Schreker's. There is a passage in *Wozzeck*, where the Captain says, 'I too have once felt love', which indulges in all the delights of the Schrekerian sound. It would be idle to speculate how much of it is parody and how much elective affinity. Moreover, there are a number of scenes in Berg's operas, those with Alwa, for example, which are stratified in a way which is not markedly different from that of the best of Schreker's. An instance would be the scenes in Carlotta's studio, with their refrain-like formations.

The analogy with the 'mixed drink'[3] which is sometimes applied rather blusteringly to jazz, fits Schreker's elixir exactly. They shimmer; the individual detail lights up for an instant and then subsides into the mass where it can no longer be distinguished, and barely even felt – the dripping of the harp, solo violins in a high register, a clarinet doubled by the celeste or horns dispossessed of their own weightiness. The association with jazz may give us a clue to the otherwise scarcely comprehensible fact that a famous composer should have been able to disappear in so short a time, not just from public consciousness, but that he should have been buried by oblivion as if beneath a heavy stone. The fermentations of the Schreker sound have been entirely absorbed by light music, whether because its matadors learnt a thing or two from Schreker, or because his manner of simply sampling sounds is one which was itself moving in the direction of popular music and the latter spontaneously produced effects of the kind which had very different intentions in

---

3. In English in the original.

him. But in the meantime the sharp dichotomy between high-brow and lowbrow music has been erected by the administrators of musical culture into a fetish which neither side may question. In consequence the guardians of highbrow music are shy of sounds that have found a home in lowbrow music and might discredit the lucrative sanctity of the highbrow variety, while the fanatical supporters of lowbrow music wax indignant at the mere suggestion that their music could have claims as art. Yet Schreker cherished lofty ambitions for his confections. The intoxication they induce conjures up the vision of some lukewarm, chaotic effusion, like something from the age of courtesans. It is music without firm definition of any sort. It resists it as if it were reification itself. It is art which resents its own purely musical materials, as if they were amusical, alien to art as such.

It is this unruliness and nothing else that links Schreker with the avant-garde of modernism. It was aided by his harmony, which, after his use of colour, was his most abiding contribution, especially when taken together with the weakened, irresolute basic progressions on which Specht has already commented. As his music advances above them, it seems to hover on the same spot. Something of this too has transferred itself to Berg. On occasion it appears to fall unresistingly into an abyss. A characteristic feature is the so-called Schrekerian false note. Consonance and dissonance are interwoven. Melodious sounds are enriched by searing pain. Frequently groups of dominant-related major keys are stacked one above the other, intensified to a kind of 'super major'. Their aim is to re-establish something of the glow that has long since faded from the simple major triad. This device was first used by the Impressionists, as well as by Mahler in the first movement of the Seventh. Schreker cultivated it as far as it would go and indeed he intensified all the possibilities of Impressionist luminosity with heedless extravagance.

Sonority of this kind is the goal of his music, but equally of the yearning, the boundless desire for happiness that inspired it. In a pre-artistic way he ignores the gulf separating the culinary – that is to say, music as a literally physical stimulus – from the well and truly formed and shaped. He remains indifferent to the disciplines of construction. But equally, he will not allow himself to be fobbed off with anything less. *Der ferne Klang* is the immediate, unconfined promise of sensual pleasure. Because he is unwilling to renounce it, the feeling of the unattainable is inscribed in his music and functions as a stimulus. Schreker's music reproduces this contradiction, even where its voice is at its most human, in the gesture of hopeless tenderness: tenderness for the heroine of *Der ferne Klang* as she enters the theatre bar, a hunted, destroyed woman of the streets; the tenderness of the treasure-hunter towards his outlawed beloved.

Complete with kitsch and a halo, Schreker's utopia is that of the king's children, albeit stripped of the aura of petty-bourgeois idealism which they possess in Humperdinck's opera. It celebrates those who go out into the world, abandoning their ordinary walks of life and preferring to perish than to give up following their impulses to the point where they become amorphous. The English story of the man who searches for the end of the rainbow exactly fits Schreker's vagrants and seducers. His vision fixes on a single element of musical Impressionism, the one to which Debussy's most Schrekerian piece owes its name: *L'Ile Joyeuse*, Pleasure Island. Two phantasmagoric acts, Act II of *Der ferne Klang* and Act III of *Die Gezeichneten*, are set in Cythera. Like the Schrekerian sound, the vision of the island is separated from empirical reality by a heaving abyss, and yet it is essentially sensuous.

But Schreker's music does not simply dwell on the idea of such a utopia: it invites the listener to join him there. With unconscious surrealism the aesthetic distance is reduced, the listener's body is immersed in pleasure. This, more than any aesthetic superiority, is doubtless responsible for the denunciation of Schreker's work. The consciousness of unattainability, however, of the power of prohibitions, encumbers Schreker, who strove for the opposite, with that reputation for impotence which the malicious are so quick to emphasize. Nevertheless, for all its ambiguity, there is a subliminal seething, sulphurous quality in the Schrekerian sound and, in its supreme moments, a sweetness of the kind which thrives where tears are as little repressed as exultation.

Those to whom Schreker is an unknown quantity would be best advised to begin with the Chamber Symphony and the overture to *Die Gezeichneten*. Both were composed at around the time of the First World War, when Schreker was already wholly master of the means he required, but before the idea had become hackneyed and his hand too facile. The Chamber Symphony is clearly an occasional work, written for the staff of the Imperial Academy in Vienna who gave it its première in 1917. At that time chamber symphonies were not yet fashionable and the only available model was Schoenberg's Opus 9. Admittedly, Schreker's work has scarcely anything in common with Schoenberg's apart from the fact that both have one movement. That aside there is perhaps only the tendency to slip imperceptibly into the repetition of sections while omitting their initial phrases. In extreme contrast to Schoenberg the texture is homophonic throughout and unmistakably Viennese at times. The orchestra is not at all used soloistically, but produces a comprehensive body of sound, particularly so thanks to Schreker's use of the harmonium which he must have studied much as Stravinsky studied percussion.

The iridescent Schrekerian sound is conjured up in the first bar of the introduction. This then reappears at every formal turning point. In a compressed form the piece contains the main parts of a four-movement symphony: an allegro exposition, an adagio, with the Schrekerian false note in the third bar, and a relatively extended scherzo. As in Schoenberg the finale is replaced by a free recapitulation of the exposition and the adagio. Like his model, Schreker brackets the four symphonic movements into a main sonata movement. Yet the individual parts, particularly the exposition and the first subject, are rather static and episodic instead of being developed progressively, as in a symphony. Sections of varying sound complexion are strung together instead of thematic elements being varied dialectically and propelled forwards. Even in the Chamber Symphony defined themes are avoided in preference to sounds that waft ethereally away. Moreover the individual formal sections flow into each other without any tangible articulation, instead of providing sharp contrasts. In order to profit from the music at all it is necessary to go along with his intentions here, instead of objecting from the outset that things are not going the way a good musician expects. Few pieces of music are as vulnerable as this one to standards which are self-confidently imposed from outside.

The overture to Schreker's opera *Die Gezeichneten* probably represents the quintessence of his work in general. The subject of the opera, which is unquestionably his best, is a neo-Romantic Renaissance drama based on Wilde's fairy tale of the dwarf and the princess which Schreker also used for a ballet in his youth and which has continued to attract composers to this day. The overture is more concerned with the atmosphere surrounding the main characters than with the trajectory of the plot. This overture, incidentally, also exists in an expanded concert version, in sonata form, but this seems somewhat external to the music. The stunted dwarf obsessed with his lust for beauty; the mortally sick artist by whom he is destroyed; his gloriously vital antagonist – for all these the music invents tonal expressions. Richly figured and distinguishing the main emphases with its use of rhythm it is developed in its way with obvious care and great consistency. It is built up from a slow introduction and an allegro whose main components derive from the festive music of Act III. But the climax of the allegro is followed by the Italianate theme of Tamare, the ladies' man. This is not actually an elaboration, but a fade out in a composed-out ritardando leading to the motifs associated with the heroine, Carlotta. By the end the whole thing, which is devoid of schematic construction throughout, slips back imperceptibly into the clangour of the introduction.

The beginning is exemplary, the Schrekerian phantasmagoria *par excellence*, an opalescent resonance as of countless orchestral timbres all blended in together, forming the groundplan of the hero's three principal themes which appear in sequence in the tenor register – a polytonal pedal effect composed of the triads D–F-sharp–A and B-flat–D-flat–F. The result is paradoxical: the clangour moves into the foreground, the three themes become peculiarly insignificant, as if they were only counterpointing their own accompaniments. Despite the rapidity with which stimuli are blunted in the history of music, we can still feel the impact of the beginning of the overture of *Die Gezeichneten*, so original was it when it was first heard. Following the allegro exposition, whose colouring is exaggerated to the point of burlesque, the oscillating harmonies of the introduction are balanced by the diatonic, brilliantly set and at the same time, with its pronounced rubato, strangely elusive counter-subject which trembles between major and minor in the iridescent mirror of his orchestral sound.

In reality, the curve of Schreker's production already began to turn downwards after *Die Gezeichneten*. His most successful work, *Der Schatzgräber*, is not able to sustain the high quality of the earlier opera. In the difference between the two works we can discern the defect to which his great talent finally succumbed. After *Die Gezeichneten, Der Schatzgräber* starts off as if the composer were in full possession of his own style. But ever since modern art came into being, its authentic exponents – among them Kandinsky, who is explicit on this point – have been aware that for an artist to make such an assumption is the beginning of the end. In *Der Schatzgräber* Schreker opts for an easier route, perhaps from a desire for greater popularity. Vagueness becomes a formula; the details are no longer so well elaborated and in the over-long orchestral interlude in Act III, the erotic centrepiece of the work, the emotional surge becomes a splurge, the representation of inarticulacy itself becomes inarticulate, in glaring contrast to Debussy. Presumably, Schreker wanted to exploit his talent while at the height of his powers. He revels in his idiom, but although still no more than forty, was unable to muster the strength necessary for self-reflection.

He whose conception of opera issued a challenge to the spiritualization of music, just as Wedekind's formula of the carnal spirit had challenged the idealist drama, was also prevented by that conception from going beyond it. The sensuous realization he aspired to – Cézanne's idea of *réaliser* – itself stood in need of the spirit, and Schreker was by nature incapable of this. He was able to compensate for the technical shortcomings of his method of composition by an increased facility, but he was not able to rethink it, imprisoned as he was within the limits of his own cast of mind. Nor, precisely for this reason, was he able to enlarge these limits. He lacked the musical intelligence, the ability to resist musical stupidity. Such intelligence is the pre-requisite for the production of ambitious works. Only where there is a controlling energy can a composition fulfil its potential. The naivety which gave Schreker his sustained *élan* also proved his undoing. Spirit, not as the artist's consciousness, but as an internal aspect of the music, took its revenge on him: without it the magic failed to work. What he conjured up now failed to materialize. He must have suspected this. If it were not so repugnant to speak of the tragedies of artists – it is only works of art that can be tragic – the inflated term might well be applied to Schreker. There would be something unutterably wretched about the failure of such an outstanding talent, were its downfall not equivalent to the stake which he, like a dulled but magnifi-cently reckless gambler, did not hesitate to pledge.

In order to be properly in tune with Schreker's music, it is probably necessary to have encountered it as an adolescent, just as the novels of Péladen have to be devoured at that age.[4] No art fits better into the increasingly narrow world of childhood, or finds quicker access there, than art which is not suitable for the young. Schreker's music is music for puberty; it had its roots in an adolescent frame of mind and remained attuned to it with all the defiance of incorrigible immaturity. This is how a highly gifted fifteen year old spends hours improvising at the piano, pressing down chords with the right hand and arpeggios with the left. The composer must have ceased developing in order to write all that up, but he must also have been unwavering in his desire to do so. To distil a consistent style from such material does indeed call for

---

4. Joséphin Péladan (1859–1918) was a popular novelist whose *La décadence latine* in 21 volumes presented a broad panorama of life in Paris and the provinces. It depicted the snares and pitfalls facing the 'Latin race' in the spheres of political, private and also religious life.

genius. Something survives in it of the radiance which only those years possess and which maturity irrevocably destroys; something too of the productivity which we often despise because at that age everyone possesses it, only to lose it in later years. But it is seldom that it finds expression. The utopia conveyed in these operas is too unsublimated for it to survive. They are altogether too literal in their advocacy of the rebellion of art against nature. In revenge they are thrust back into the crude materiality which Schreker so detested in music, thinking it far too obvious.

The essence of modern art is that utopia enters into the power of negation, into the prohibition on its own name; that the variety of life is salvaged in obscurity, happiness in asceticism, reconciliation in dissonance. All this only brushed him fleetingly. For all its virtuosity – Schreker was probably Strauss's superior in orchestral imagination – his music failed, as the psychologists would say, to construct an ego. It stands outside the demands of culture. But because it springs from a compulsion which is more potent than shame and testifies to the truth of things that culture proscribes, it gives expression to doubts about the value of culture as such. Schreker consciously deserts to the realm which culture has distanced itself from and consigned to the vulgar. The fact that culture has to reject this reminds us of the limitations of its power and, ultimately, of its own failure: unable to effect a reconciliation between the drives and itself, it holds them down by force. This has led to those increasingly powerful feelings of discontent which Freud described in that late essay.[5] Schreker, a minstrel in a world without minstrels, refuses to join in the repression of the drives. When Frank Wedekind ironized the fatal word 'art-painter' [*Kunstmaler*] and introduced the 'art-artist' [*Kunst-Künstler*] in one of his uncompleted works, and confronted him with his antithesis, then in music we may think of Schreker as playing the role of this opposing type. The verdict which culture and cultivation have pronounced on him, and which no court of appeal can quash, accepts his sacrifice. If Schreker remains dissatisfied with the established criteria, then

---

5. Sigmund Freud, *Civilization and its Discontents*.

this is at least partly because he throws a spotlight on the element of fraud and ideology they contain. Culture withholds a fulfilment without the promise of which it is itself quite unthinkable. Schreker was no Balzac and no Dostoevsky, but the possibility of something splendid, some great breakthrough flashes from him. And this is something from which great art is increasingly alienated, the more purely and utterly it subscribes to the internal logic it shares with civilization. It is the possibility of transcending culture, of forging a unity between the effervescence, the 'foaming forth', of absolute spirit[6] and the proscribed materialism to be found in garish penny-dreadfuls: it is the gesture with which Natasha hurls the banknotes into the flames,[7] and in Esther's letter of renunciation to Lucien Rubempré.[8] The profession of Schreker's father would have been the true title of the opera he was never able to write: the photographer of Monte Carlo.

(1959)

---

6. Adorno alludes here to the epiphany achieved at the end of Hegel's *Phenomenology of Mind* where the depth of spiritual life is reached in the Absolute Concept. To illustrate Absolute Knowledge, or Spirit knowing itself as Spirit, Hegel quotes from Schiller's 'Die Freundschaft':

> The chalice of the realm of spirits
> Foams forth to God His own infinitude.

See G. W. F. Hegel, *The Phenomenology of Mind*, translated by J. B. Baillie, George Allen & Unwin 1964, p. 808.

7. In F. Dostoevsky, *The Idiot*.
8. In Honoré de Balzac, *Splendeurs et misères des courtisanes*.

Stravinsky: A Dialectical Portrait

In memory of Walter Benjamin

After the Second World War the work of Igor Stravinsky entered an entirely new phase. Earlier on, around 1930, he had been the stylistic model for every composer who wished to demonstrate his contemporaneity – except for the immediate disciples of Schoenberg. Now, however, he emerged as a 'grand old man',[1] the only survivor of that group of composers to have a niche reserved for him in the pantheon of modern classics, an honour which inexorably results in the loss of that modern quality which it was intended to preserve. Parallel to Picasso, Stravinsky had launched neo-Classicism in the early 1920s. But unlike Picasso he practised the style for more than three decades. Not until after his opera *The Rake's Progress* did he try out his compositional method on any material but that of a restored tonality. But the neo-Classicism which generally prevailed between the wars has now all but vanished. It can scarcely be found anywhere except among the belated converts in the music academies.

This means that anyone who wished to criticize Stravinsky's claims to authenticity and validity as a model would find the ground cut from beneath him. When the tide turns against someone as powerfully as in his case, it is tempting to leap to his defence. The task of theory is always to take sides in unresolved disputes, not to slip into what has always been the disreputable role of the messenger who brings the latest news. With the victory

---

1. In English in the original.

of what had been a minority and wanton proliferation of twelve-note and serial composers, even Schoenberg, who had originated the entire movement, began to feel uneasy. The avant-garde is incompatible with victorious triumphalism. The fact that Stravinsky fell victim to a process of repression disguising itself as praise is reminiscent of the inane habit of ridiculing obsolete fashions. Employing a backward-looking and in many ways intentionally conventional material, whose very traditionalism gave it a certain similarity to language, he dreamed of a 'distantiated'[2] sort of music that might have given that similarity to language the slip. Such music could only have been created in a material wholly divested of language, such as that of contemporary music.

In his aspirations, then, Stravinsky may have come closer to the spirit of the most recent music than Schoenberg from whom it more visibly derives. But there was a discrepancy between that dream and his actual composition that was comparable perhaps to the gulf between the utopian dreams of functional industrial forms and the cast iron of the nineteenth century. Stravinsky touches a raw nerve in the younger generation because they detect a like-minded spirit, but are ashamed of the stigma of that complicity with the past which he so assiduously put on display and which raises doubts about their own modernity. Moreover, a mistrust of their in many cases all too simple need for objectivity may be projected on to Stravinsky. Since his objectivity now appears to be merely contrived, they secretly fear that the same fate might one day befall their most recent, rather more tangible version, namely the belief in sound in itself and its pure qualities.

Stravinsky remains a scandal because, as a lifelong conjurer, he made visible the inauthentic aspect of objectivity and gave it shape as a grimace. This removed his music so far from the realm of the provincial that he was able to produce his tricks and to explain them at the same time, something that only the most

---

2. Adorno uses the word *verfremdet* – alienated, distantiated – which Brecht employed to describe his innovative theatrical effects. These 'alienation-effects' are designed to foreground the artificiality and theatrical nature of the events on the stage.

preeminent magicians can allow themselves. His instincts were magnificently aware that in music the linguistic and the organic were only possible in a state of decomposition. This instinct was the controlling factor in the structures he himself created. He borrowed their idiom from tonality, which had preserved the illusion of the organic right up to the threshold of modernity but which now manifested itself as something on which history had pronounced judgement. If his works owe their authority to their objective gestural language, they have also done objectivity the honour of disavowing the gesture and unmasking its authority as a fiction. The man who has the whole of moderate modernism on his conscience was a radical in his thinking. Of this his affirmative works, with their damaged sound sequences and their montages of dead material, provide ominous testimony. This is reason enough to direct attention to him once again.

I myself feel a particular need to do this since my discussion of Stravinsky in *The Philosophy of Modern Music* is commonly deemed to have played its part in causing the demise of neo-Classicism. I see no reason to retract anything I wrote in 1947 and much of what I note there could be extended in a process of critical self-reflection. Hans Knudszus, in an essay which places me deeply in his debt, has leapt to my defence against my critics.

> At all events it is at least possible to surmise that . . . criticism of Adorno is only possible because it fails to appreciate the way in which the structure of his thought is reflected in its literary form and hence judges his ideas by reference to criteria which are wholly alien and which have been explicitly repudiated by Adorno's Hegelianism![3]

This may explain why I so seldom learn anything from my public critics. Not that I have nothing to learn, or am unwilling to do so. But the misunderstandings on which these current objections are based are so gross as to astonish even someone who is as acutely aware as I am of the extent to which intellectual

---

3. Hans Knudszus, 'Die Kunst versöhnt mit der Welt. Zu den literatursoziologischen Essays von Theodor W. Adorno', *Der Tagesspiegel*, Berlin, 25 March 1962, p. 45. [Adorno's note.]

interactions are beset by misconceptions. Now that chapter on Stravinsky has been more thoroughly misunderstood than any other. It began with the accusation that I had no feeling for order, for ontology, in music – whereas what I objected to in Stravinsky was not order but the illusion of order. At the other extreme I was rebuked for calling him a schizophrenic, whereas what I repeatedly insisted on was that the complexion of his music was derived from the lesson of obsessional neurosis and schizophrenia – that is, that he had chosen this method as a stylistic principle, or had constructed schizophrenic models, to use another term to be found in *The Philosophy of Modern Music*.

Obviously one of the greatest stumbling blocks for readers of philosophical interpretations of music is the failure to understand that their findings refer to the objective substance of the music and not the subjective state of mind of the composer. What I attributed to Stravinsky was probably only available to him because he was not under the spell of the processes inscribed in his works. It never occurred to me to treat Stravinsky himself as a pathological case or to diagnose him with the aid of some intrusive psychological theory. As an individual Stravinsky's actions have been remarkable for their nobility, courage and humanity on many occasions, notably on the death of Schoenberg and during the McCarthy period in the USA, and it would be simply despicable to hold him or his attitudes responsible for certain historical or philosophical implications of his works. It is the act of a philistine to confuse the objective form of a work of art with the psyche of the man who created it and who, like Stravinsky, did everything in his power to eradicate the traces of the psyche from his work. Only if you fail to comprehend the thing will you seek to make up for it by attacking the person.

My critics make me want to begin by giving them a helping hand. Even a straightforward text-based criticism might have found more damaging objections to my Stravinsky chapter. If it is true that his music represents an objectively false consciousness, ideology, then conscientious readers might argue that his music was more than simply identical with reified consciousness.

They might insist that his music went beyond it, by contemplating it wordlessly, silently allowing it to speak for itself. The spirit of the age is deeply inscribed in Stravinsky's art with its dominant gesture of 'This is how it is'. A higher criticism would have to consider whether this gesture does not give it a greater share in the truth than music which aims to give shape to an implicit truth which the spirit of the age denies and which history has rendered dubious in itself.

A not implausible objection to my argument would maintain that I had analysed the ideology which developed out of Stravinsky and which has since evaporated, rather than his actual *œuvre*. Subjectivity, I assert in *The Philosophy of Modern Music*, assumes the character of the victim in Stravinsky – but is that not the fate of subjectivity? The thesis on which the entire dispute hinges, namely that his music identifies not with the victims, but with the agents of destruction, is one that I have at the very least not worked out in any detail. In the absence of proof it could be objected that it was unimportant to establish what he identifies with as long as he has succeeded in objectifying the impotence of the subject as an actual state of affairs in which everyone is reduced to the status of potential victim. Was not the objective despair which I discerned in *The Rite of Spring* a more appropriate response to the state of total impotence *vis-à-vis* the murderous collective? Did it not represent a more complete indictment than the expression of musical subjectivity would have done? Is not the taboo that Stravinsky's static music imposes on life the manifestation of a negative truth? Is not the regression whose formulae are invoked in his works the faithful and unadorned image of an emergent truth?

Stravinsky, our plea for the defence would continue, had introduced into music what literature had possessed ever since Flaubert: the conviction, devoid of any trace of sentimentality and hence falsification, that a pure and consistent statement about the way things are is more persuasive than any vain lament. His cool objectivity [*Sachlichkeit*] provides proof that in art the power of the human can be transformed into an inhumanity which acts as the mirror of inhumanity, whereas it degenerates into ideology as long as it continues to quiver tremulously like the voice of humanity. Such sobriety is identical with the artistic principle governing Stravinsky's works. He recoils fastidiously from the communicating subject, his feelings and his will. This imparts to his music that manner of 'Thus it is and not otherwise', which I had attacked as an ontological illusion, as the use of stylistic devices to create the fiction of a valid essence. It is not possible to defend, as I had done, the idea of art as appearance [*Schein*] against the ideology of meaningful statement and authenticity, and then to criticize that appearance as mere illusion [*Schein*]. With my accusation that Stravinsky's music was no more than a masquerade I was in danger of finding myself in the embarrassing company of critics who don a pious expression in order to bewail gloatingly the loss of the centre.[4] My rejection of Stravinskian form, of that compulsive repetitiveness from which there is no escape, of a type of music whose structure recreates the inexorable bonds of fate with their hopeless recurrence, the snares and entanglements of myth, is not all that far removed from the unctuous rhetoric of those who pick on Thomas Mann's *Dr. Faustus*, of all novels, as the manifestation of a world without transcendence.[5] By opposing the static ideal of Stravinsky's music, its immanent timelessness, and by confronting it with a dynamic, emphatically temporal, intrinsically developing music, I arbitrarily applied to him an external norm, a norm which he rejected. In short, I violated my own most cherished principle of criticism.

The plausibility of these criticisms is not to be underestimated. But they ignore a factor of cardinal importance. There is something intrinsically amiss with Stravinsky's music; '*il y a quelque chose qui ne va pas*'. As a temporal art, music is bound to the fact of succession and is hence as irreversible as time itself. By starting it commits itself to carrying on, to becoming something

---

4. The reference is to Hans Sedlmayer's influential *Der Verlust der Mitte* [The Loss of the Centre] (1948) which bemoaned the contemporary decline in values.

5. Adorno alludes here to Hans Egon Holthusen's controversial article 'Die Welt ohne Transzendenz', which criticized Mann's novel from a right-wing, Christian standpoint.

new, to developing. What we may conceive of as musical transcendence, namely the fact that at any given moment it has become something and something other than what it was, that it points beyond itself – all that is no mere metaphysical imperative dictated by some external authority. It lies in the nature of music and will not be denied. Beckett's '*je vais continuer*', with which his novel of absolute despair[6] comes to an end, without our being able to say whether that end is still one of despair, neatly encapsulates a factor unifying modern literature and music of every kind. Ever since music has existed, it has always been a protest, however ineffectual, against myth, against a fate which was always the same, and even against death. Nor does it lose its anti-mythic status, even when, in a state of objective despair, it makes the cause of despair its own. However feeble its guarantee that there is an alternative, music never abjures its promise that one exists. Freedom is an intrinsic necessity for music. That is its dialectical nature. Perhaps under the pressure of objective despair, Stravinsky has denied music's commitment to freedom for the most cogent reason then, one that would force music to be silent.[7] What he writes is music that has been stifled.

---

6. These are the concluding words of Samuel Beckett's *The Unnameable* (1952).

7. Attention has recently been drawn to *Svesdoliki* [The King of the Stars] for male chorus and orchestra. The work, by no means a masterpiece, provides more food for thought about the origins of Stravinsky's manner than almost anything else. Composed in 1911, it interrupted his work on the *Rite*. A first impression would not lead to the conclusion that Stravinsky was the composer; a closer scrutiny reveals a surprising similarity to the third psalm-like piece for string quartet [Three Pieces for String Quartet (1914) – translator's note]. The poem is by the symbolist poet Balmont and the music fits perfectly into that context, one of ecstatic expressionism, not far removed from Skriabin in tone. There is no trace of the technique of shifting rhythmic patterns. It may be surmised that the self-denial indefatigably practised by Stravinsky ever since involved the suppression of an impulse he detected in himself and which he subsequently only allowed to surface in his choice of religious subjects. These clash oddly with the impassivity of his musical style. The myth-making ideal of the sacrificial victim which then acts as a secret law governing all his work, may itself derive from that same neo-Romanticism; a celebrated piano piece of Scriabin's bears the title *Vers la flamme*. In German symbolism too the praise of the sacrificial victim is central (cf. Theodor W. Adorno, 'George und Hofmannsthal', in *Prismen*, Frankfurt am Main 1955, pp. 277ff. [*Prisms: Studies in Contemporary German Social Thought*, translated by Samuel and Shierry Weber, London 1967.] It is conceivable that this self-denial has its origins in a sense of inadequacy which may have befallen the perspicacious composer when confronted by his own chorus mysticus; in short, that he denied himself what was denied to him. The chorus for its part is as homophonic as that piece for string quartet of three years later. The harmony, on the other hand, is texturally as dense, with its layers of superimposed thirds, as the *Rite*. In character it is 'auratic' through and through. For decades it was thought unperformable. [Adorno's note.] Adorno's friend Walter Benjamin, the literary critic, thought that traditionally works of art were endowed with the status of cult objects. They possessed an 'aura'. This aura disappeared in the modern age where art, especially painting, was deprived of its uniqueness.

But music cannot endure the idea of an avenue from which there is no escape, and the more condensed the music, the less it can endure it. This is the source of the internal inconsistency. Whereas his music advances simply by virtue of existing in time, and so like all music, satisfies the requirement of otherness, in essence it remains stationary, since it is made up of repetitions. In substance it is turned on its head. Instead of overcoming the fate of Sisyphus by virtue of its intrinsic historical structure, it comes to grief on a concept of time as the unconnected sequence of ephemeral events and on the illusion that salvation lies in using art to conjure it away. Ernst Bloch's comment that Nietzsche's Eternal Recurrence was simply a poor imitation of eternity consisting of endless repetitions applies literally to the inner core of Stravinsky's music. Either his works create the impression of progress, only to disappoint the listener, or – and this may well be a more accurate description of them – they bow to the order of time only to suggest obsessively that time has stopped, that they have abrogated time and achieved a state of pure being. Infatuated with mythic consciousness it violates a fundamental category of myth – that of contract; it fails to comply with the contract it signed with the very first bar of music.

Musical content is not indifferent to temporal form. If the two are not to break apart into irreconcilable opposites, the sequence of musical events must be concretely determined by time, by the qualities of before, afterwards and now, and the relations between them. Conversely, the temporality of the musical events gives shape to the passage of time itself. Stravinsky's repetitions negate both these processes. But with his repetitions another factor emerges which turns out to be the same thing in another form. This is the element of mimicry, of clowning – of constantly busying himself with something important that turns out to be nothing at all; strenuously working at something without any result. Schoenberg, infuriated by the automatic criticism that his own music was a historical cul-de-sac when compared to the ostensible vitality of Stravinsky, his polar opposite, retorted with the pun that no cul was sacker (i.e. *Sacre du printemps*) than his. Unconsciously he touched a raw nerve. This music, which is celebrated for its static nature, worships the cul-de-sac as its secret ideal; it refuses to move on and marches on the spot like Vladimir and Estragon when they set off at the end of *Waiting for Godot*. Critics have often emphasized the importance of parody in Stravinsky, the use of more or less apocryphal musical models which he mockingly distorts, dislocates and provides with caustic little additions. These would give pleasure to modest listeners who have reached the point where they can enjoy a laugh at the expense of the polka and the gallop.

It is an insult to Stravinsky to praise him for cheap triumphs over objects of universal ridicule. A more urgent task is to explain in purely musical terms what sounds like parody and frequently functions as one. The apparent progressions in every one of Stravinsky's movements are not real, but instead are dammed up to create the illusion of a static timelessness. However, Stravinsky is subtle and sensitive enough to recognize that succeeding passages should have more than a purely mechanical resemblance to each other. Having himself organized all music as a set of dance-like repetitions, he was as hostile to literal repetitiveness as anyone from the opposing camp. In every bar he presupposes the emancipation of music, especially where he voluntarily enters into bondage. Naive symmetries are to his mind musical stupidities which deserve only scorn. He is beset by the crisis of the time-less products of a time-based art which constantly pose the question of how to repeat something without developing it and yet avoid monotony, or else to incorporate it integrally. The sections he strings together may not be identical and yet may never be anything qualitatively different. This is why there is damage instead of development. The wounds are inflicted by time, something which identity finds offensive and which in truth does not allow identity to persist. This is the formal, unliterary significance of the parodic style in Stravinsky. The necessary damage to the form appears as mockery of it. What Stravinsky's music does to his stylistic models, it also does to itself. He permanently wrote music about music, because he wrote music against music.[8] His

8. Cf. Theodor W. Adorno, *Philosophie der neuen Musik*, 2nd edn, Frankfurt am Main 1958, pp. 168 ff. [Adorno's note.]

own bowed freely to a principle which was not just alien to itself; it was hostile. It inscribes itself in the music in the form of repression. Its identification with collective violence is technically inherent in it and no mere ideological appendage. This would be my first retort to the criticisms I have made of myself.

My second would be the claim that the emphatic nature of his music tends to assert what is represented in it ostentatiously. For music – and no one would admit this more readily than Stravinsky – cannot represent at a distance, unlike drama. It is primarily the presentation and hence the affirmation of what it represents. Late Romantic composers like Mahler and, in a very different way, Richard Strauss rebelled against this. Stravinsky would like to go even further by banishing from music every element of representation including the sudden emergence of the composer's intentions, followed by their extinction. But the more energetically he pursues this course of action, the more his music represents the element of confinement and unfreedom as positive.

The transition from Stravinsky's surrealist and, according to the bleating of public opinion, destructive works to his neo-Classical, cultic compositions was not simply, as I claimed in *The Philosophy of Modern Music*, an easy matter, but the essence of his music. The fact that music can be nothing but its own disposition is the shadow cast by its obverse, its privileged nature, namely, its freedom from anything alien. Like a primitive it confines itself rigorously to its own nature. In this respect its intellectuality [*Vergeistigung*] paradoxically discovers its own limitation: art which is not intellectual [*geistig*] from the outset is more likely to become so from the need to work on its material. In his pursuit of myth and the archaic Stravinsky was really in search of a spiritual chimera. The pharisaical reproach to be directed at his music is not that it knows no transcendence; what is pharisaical is its very claim to transcendence.

The function of transcendence in art today can only be that of protest. But Stravinsky creates, as if by wizardry, the absolute opposite of transcendence within transcendence itself; he creates a hell within heaven, damage within order. He celebrates cruelty towards himself and against all hope, as if hope were spirit cured of addiction. In this, of course, he shows himself to be in profound agreement with the entire cultural tradition of domination over nature, both external and human. But as long as intellect suppresses instinct, it is not yet true intellect. In Stravinsky's music by virtue of its intrinsic nature as performance – it is not for nothing that it would prefer to dispense with actual performers – the paralysed cripple is transformed into a *monumentum aere perennius*.[9] Nothing remains of the fact that it is no such thing but the gesture with which it sticks its tongue out at him. Virtuoso pyrotechnics replace true transcendence. It is this positivity alone that is open to criticism, not the artistry which has established his reputation among his supporters. But this artistry behaves as if it were the unvarnished truth, or even emergent meaning.

His neo-Classicism has been unjustly treated in consequence; above all by the stupidity of all those, down to and including the whole neo-Baroque movement, who imagined that the models provided by the supreme virtuoso could supply a canon of what is permissible or forbidden in music, and that the reintroduction of a universally accepted style and the elimination of what they thought of as a loquacious subjectivism was merely a question of energetic determination and will. The experiential core of musical neo-Classicism, like that of the equivalent phenomenon in contemporary painting, which had a less widespread impact than Stravinsky, was not primarily concerned with the reconstruction of obsolete forms, however tempting a composer might find this. Neo-Classicism became an accepted style because it enabled individuals sated by their individuality to colonize the libidinous space of a past age not yet fully individuated.

But Stravinsky's anti-subjectivism did not function directly as a stylistic model. Schoenberg's sarcastic rhymed dictum, 'Classical perfection, strict in each inflection', all too readily lumped him together with a reawakened academic fashion. What really happened was that the original source of neo-Classicism,

---

9. 'A memorial more lasting than bronze' (Horace, *Odes* xxx).

Winckelmann's 'noble simplicity and tranquil grandeur', received its just deserts. It was not installed as a norm, but appeared
as if in dreams, not as a whole genre, but in the form of plaster
busts on wardrobes in the houses of the older generation,
individual pieces of bric-à-brac and remaindered goods. In this
process of individualizing a whole style into a set of monstrosities,
the style was destroyed. It was damaged and rendered impotent
by dreams hastily cobbled together and arranged. The basic
stratum of neo-Classicism is not far removed from Surrealism.
Stravinsky's Baroque revenants duplicate the statues in Max
Ernst's *Femme 100 Têtes* which tumble among the living beings
and whose faces are frequently missing as if they had been erased
by the dream censorship.

To extend the interpretation of Stravinsky's neo-Classicism
beyond the now obsolete stylistic controversy, it would be
necessary to reconstruct the way in which a small child responds
to one of Handel's sonatas for violin and piano. It perceives the
power of the figured bass in its effect on individual harmonies:
this was how a sixth once sounded, so youthful and fresh and
powerful that you could sate yourself on it, as the spirits of
Homer's Nekyia could sate themselves on blood.[10] But since what
Krenek once called the 'restoration of primeval meaning' can no
longer be applied to worn-out chords, Stravinsky, who is secretly
more Romantic than any Romantic, stages them with the aid of
over-exposure, the magnifying of individual effects which he has
stored up in the chords. A very instructive example of this can be
found in the Serenade for Piano [1925]. It is easy to imagine that
the great curved female figures in some of Picasso's cartoons
were done with similar intentions: the Stravinsky of the 1920s
designed Baroque cave drawings. The shifts of perspective were
wrung from a historical form, from the accidentals, ornaments,
non-harmonious notes in general, and above all suspensions and

10. The Nekyia was a magical rite in which spirits were conjured up and
questioned about the future. See Homer, *The Odyssey*, Book 11, in which Odysseus
descends to Hades to consult the prophet Tiresias. The spirits of the dead are
attracted by the blood of sheep flowing into the sacrificial trench after Odysseus has
cut their throats.

appoggiaturas. These were always equivocal; they concealed the normality that could be heard beneath them as a subtext, but still stood on their own. This technical wizardry lends the harmony something of the contrariness not envisaged in the figured-bass system.

In the age of the figured bass these devices had a function. Their task was to bind scale degrees, which were perhaps felt to be too far apart from each other, more closely together. They acted as correctives to the geometric monotony of bare scale-degree progressions. Stravinsky's neo-Classicism robbed them of this task. What functioned as an organic whole in the seventeenth and eighteenth centuries, and ensured that one sound grew into another, was now converted into an anti-organic appendage. What emerges is a connected style without inner bonds [*Bindung*] in either a technical or metaphysical sense.[11] What had once been perceived in these non-harmonious structures, ceased to exist as soon as they were understood in a one-sided way, made into absolutes and hence misunderstood. The historical process which paved the way for dissonances is sarcastically imported by Stravinsky into those very aspects of harmony which helped to prepare it. Hence the perverse attraction sometimes exerted by his neo-Classical sounds. But since such features are detached from their accustomed context and made generally available, this perversity is extended to their content. They are turned into the traces of the violence done to the idiom, and this violence, this arbitrary manipulation, which as it were rapes the life of the music, becomes the source of pleasure. If dissonance was once the expression of subjective suffering, its painful aspect now becomes the mark of social compulsion. The agent of this compulsion is the composer who creates the fashion. He assembles the musical structures from the emblems of the *contrainte sociale*, from a necessity which is external and inappropriate to the individual and inflicted on him. Not a small part of the collective effect of these pieces by Stravinsky may be connected

---

11. *Bindung* means connection, relationship, commitment. But in addition it has metaphysical overtones suggesting deeper 'bonds', 'rootedness'.

with the fact that in their own way, they schooled their listeners, unconsciously and at the aesthetic level, in something they were soon to experience systematically on the political plane.

Like jazz, Stravinsky's imitation of the compulsion to repeat has its origins in the mechanization of the labour process. Through the adaptation to machines and the jerky reflexes they produce, Stravinsky's music tended to prescribe modes of behaviour rather than to crystallize out an intrinsically coherent compositional manner. Its outwardly displayed authority was achieved at the cost of the authority derived from the logic of musical structure. This explains much of its subsequent fate. Not only has an internal shrinkage become apparent over the decades, but also the ambivalent attitude of listeners to authority of every kind inclined towards the side of rejection following the Second World War, when authority, already somewhat frayed, was placed under a social taboo.

Stravinsky had hosts of followers and imitators, but hardly any pupils and certainly no school. To explain this it is not enough to point to the biographical fact that he obviously disliked teaching – a readily comprehensible aversion. But his essential achievement, modes of behaviour that are gathered together in a canon of refusal and discrimination, was more or less unteachable. Every bar of Stravinsky's music is the product of stylization. It is possible no doubt to be immersed in a style, but it is not possible to learn one, least of all a style based on whim; that can only be copied. Even earlier, in Wagner, with whom Stravinsky's aesthetics would least like to be connected, the will to style was the opposite of style, and he was condemned to learn how difficult it was to transmit it.

The will to style was Stravinsky's tribute to the hated nineteenth century, particularly to Art Nouveau, to which in a curious comparison of Schoenberg with Oscar Wilde he showed himself to be allergic. For Stravinsky, whose outlook was heroic in the Baudelairean sense, it must have come as a bitter realization that an *œuvre* whose manner lays claim to collective coherence and whose innermost strategy is designed to achieve it, should end by failing even more completely than if it had no style at all. The same collective weakness which once drew all musicians looking for cover towards him, has now scattered them to the winds. The only one to have remained true to him at one level was Carl Orff, who paid for this loyalty with a musical sacrifice. By subordinating the percussion effect wholly to the exigencies of drama, he renounced the vestiges of his autonomy as a composer, an autonomy which even in Stravinsky had already been destroyed by the functional character of the ballet music. Stravinsky became isolated because traditionalism as such cannot be transmitted, but only the subcutaneous labour by means of which a composition's objectivization is organically brought about, without the composer having had one eye on objectivization from the outset. As soon as music ascribes such a goal to itself, it discounts its own chances of survival and condemns itself to inauthenticity. Only that art can survive which refrains from trying to build its own immortality into itself by eliminating everything that might develop in time. Instead of dedicating himself to the stringent requirements of true and false, Stravinsky erected tablets to the desirable and the undesirable, and they crumbled in his hands. His collectivism was isolated from the moment it was born. His music desperately opened its arms and overplayed its sociability just because it was no more able than any other music to abolish single-handedly the atomization that has its roots in the social principle of the age. To that extent his gesture bears witness to the state of consciousness and reality which it obsessively denies. Stravinsky would have despised nothing so much as to move and stir his audience, and the electric shocks he dispenses are intended to forestall such an effect. But by a kind of conciliatory revenge, this is the very effect he achieves.

More urgent than the issue of the quality of Stravinsky's neo-Classical works and their ups and downs would be the question of what motivated him – not psychologically but in terms of the logic of composition – to opt for such constraints that he was forced to work under a hopeless 'handicap'.[12] It is

---

12. Adorno used the English word.

important to imagine to oneself what is involved when a world-famous composer of truly Straussian virtuosity only composes works which bring him neither widespread acclaim, nor even the negative and esoteric rewards of a *succès de scandale*, but instead cut him off from the general interest which had once been the essence of his fame. Perhaps the only comparable case would be that of the late Brecht. Of course, thanks to the prestige stored up from earlier works, he was able to have all his late pieces performed internationally. But I suspect that only *Oedipus Rex* and the *Symphony of Psalms*, and then finally *The Rake's Progress* have found a lasting acceptance by the public. In the last case Stravinsky's pastiche benefited from the absence of contemporary operas worthy of the name, as well as from a libretto that promises to be what the Anglo-Saxons call 'sophisticated'.

Stravinsky would have been the first to feel horrified at the prospect he himself opened up with the *Rite*. And this horror – which he doubtless felt more acutely than anyone – transmitted itself to the less revisionist composers of his generation. The total musical freedom which had only just been won, must have appeared as a threat. Suddenly he must have perceived the hopeless situation of all music: how was music which had emancipated itself from all established reference systems to achieve a coherence based purely on its own inner resources? To do him justice it must be observed that to this day it has remained uncertain whether total emancipation can bring about the objectivization of art and hence make art itself possible in a society which provides the artist with nothing by way of substantial, valid forms. This question has not mellowed with time, but has become more acute, the more thoroughly the material of composition became internalized and the less it was possible to have recourse to external cultural and philosophical aids and so-called 'models'.

Standing at the beginning of this development, Stravinsky's misfortune was that he was in a position to perceive the abyss that was opening up. Steeped in the musical tradition, he looked to it for support even though its inexorable downfall had been partly brought about by the very sources of his own inspiration. No one who feels more fear of reality than can be compensated for by art and who has experienced as a concrete possibility the reversal from total freedom to total unfreedom will want to sneer at the undoubted anxiety and unfreedom of Stravinsky's stance as a composer.

The affinity of that transformation to his own freely chosen unfreedom was his most striking characteristic thirty years ago. Today a second quality has emerged. This is the emergence of freedom as mere culture, as epiphenomenon. He has seen through the spurious aspects of that freedom and vainly tried to respond with the meaning of order. He was shocked by the vision of meaningless random events since this seemed to him a travesty of freedom. He had a nasty foreboding that the individual whose autonomy is presupposed by autonomous art, was socially anything but autonomous, and that his autonomy was spurious. The aesthetic image of freedom which is played off polemically against ideology, is itself ideological. All this exploded in Stravinsky, causing a short-circuit. But it called for an expenditure of nervous energy in which few could equal him. His radicality expressed itself not so much in composition as in his reaction, his ability to face up to an extreme situation. This raises him above all those who mistook the short-circuit for a style. Their attention of course was focused on the neo-Classical results. Their ultimate aim cannot have been anything much more than the ambition of becoming his successor. Stravinsky supplied exercises for shaping musical consciousness at the price of all other musical qualities, and this price then deprived him of the ability to stamp his imprint on anything else.

Not that it would be right to imply that there was any waning of his powers in such scores as the Octet or the Pergolesi adaptation. But his refusals could not fail to harm whatever throve in the confined space he had carved out for himself and they continued to exert their atrophying effects. Stravinsky's music is music which retreats from music, which feels panic when confronted by open sound which has not been imprisoned. Its rigidity is the moulded cast of that panic. His objectivism is just as powerful a testimony to alienation as the sound of pure interiority in

Webern. Both move towards each other, just as, according to an ancient philosophical *aperçu*, absolute interiority tends towards emptiness – likewise a phenomenon of the late Webern. It may be categorically asserted that Stravinsky, unlike Strauss in *Der Rosenkavalier* ten years earlier, did not turn the clock back in order to achieve popularity. What his musical ingenuity wanted was to see what emerges when the musical impulse is denied, is reduced to the bare minimum. This aim may be compared to an experiment with chance. If Webern denied himself everything which he could not fill, Stravinsky, in his hysterically intensified distrust of subjectivity, denied himself everything that could be filled. Subjectivity only expresses itself in his music in what he omits of himself, just as in Webern's case, it only expresses itself in terms of the material he omits. The vanishing point of Webern's music is silence; in Stravinsky's it is mute deafness as of someone bereft of his organs.

His sensitivity towards subjectivity was nothing new. It has accompanied the emancipation of the subject right through the history of music, just as throughout the history of Enlightenment that emancipation went hand in hand with the progress of the ideal of scientific objectivity. Through the indefatigable *reductio ad hominem* of every spiritual substance, autonomous subjective reason itself has striven to eliminate man as the trouble-maker who disrupts the purity of the object. Isaiah Berlin was right to have drawn a parallel between Stravinsky and neo-positivism. In music that sensitivity to the role of the subject, which varies from one epoch to the next, is concentrated in the notion of taste.

The difference between the subject as an immediate entity and a social adaptation which is imposed on it, but never wholly succeeds in doing so, is experienced not just as a happy surplus, an ability to assert oneself, but also as a negative factor. Its self-assertiveness jeopardizes every form, every manifestation of culture in which art, or at least one aspect of art, would wish to function as the anti-barbarian principle. Ultimately, therefore, it puts at risk the subject itself. The dynamization of aesthetic forms through the process of subjectivization does not just change those forms. It is also the enemy of form as such. The subjective definition of musical form as infinity in the period following the French Revolution, supplanted the existing understanding of music as the fitting balance of genre and subjective consciousness. But it also appeared to that understanding as something excessive and destructive. A form which is wholly taken possession of by the shaping subject, thereby perpetuates that act of violence.

When the sovereign subject distances itself as far as possible from its mere destiny as nature, it comes round full circle to resemble nature unconfined. In artistic autonomy we see the resurgence of the barbarism which it destroyed with the pitchfork, and we find it in Beethoven as well as in Fichte. The fact that wholly organized works of art come to resemble organisms also brings them closer to the brutish aspects of nature. From the outset of its struggle against absolutism the revolutionary bourgeoisie together with its rationality had insisted on this.

Taste in art is the unity of all the factors that resist this credo. Under its aegis Stravinsky rigorously eliminated every reminiscence of nature, of whatever kind, as if impelled by an absolute sense of shame. His links, through Debussy, with the Paris of the Symbolist movement made him more of a Baudelairean in this respect too than an elemental Russian force of nature. What taste consistently castigated in musical subjectivity in the era of its dominance was the impertinence of the unintegrated subject; the rubato as the thief of culture,[13] the voice of humanity as an exaggerated emphasis on the humane – in short, everything which exposed the failure of culture as seen in its exponents, the impossibility of reconciling the general and the particular in society and art hitherto.

In Stravinsky's eyes this failure is total, to judge by the subjective mediation of all music which still has the power to speak; and no less total is his hatred. In his ears every utterance, every undomesticated impulse, even up to and including Florestan's *Dir werde Lohn*[14] must have sounded no better than any

13. In Italian *rubato* literally means 'robbed'. [Note by Eric Graebner.]
14. Cf. *Fidelio*, Act II, Trio No. 7. The opening words are actually '*Euch werde Lohn*' [To you the reward].

other example of musical culture, a mere tactless ritardando from salon music. His taste runs amok; it becomes inhuman from the sheer excess of culture and lapses into a repressiveness that vies with that of the subject he excoriates. His maxim is to kill off everything that might wound him. Nothing is immune to this threat. Reactions of this kind are boundlessly subjective in tendency, certainly no less so than what they rebel against, for they are part of the texture of the same historical process of subjectivization. This is why everything is forbidden and why at the same time all prohibitions can be flouted and permitted as *haut goût* against the prevailing taste. As a mere negation of the subject taste is chained to it, and its norm is the ephemeral reflex of what objectively has ceased to be valid. Stravinsky is implicated in the curse on all modern ontology; it took its revenge on him more swiftly than on its philosophical counterpart.

His taste also rebels against taste. Insatiable sensitivity recoils from everything even remotely sweet and sugary, qualities that were once closely allied to taste, sociability and conformism. Musically he is overwhelmed by the nausea that overcomes the spoilt person in the pastry shop, while simpler palates are enchanted by the promise of refined pleasure. It is astonishing to see what can be transformed into patisserie. It can even include painful dissonances in which pleasure still survives in their stacked up thirds, as the goal of the subjective impulse that is expressed in such chords. The inspiration of Stravinsky's idiosyncratic attack on culture in the name of culture could be traced back to the strand of sensuousness in Debussy and Ravel, or in comparable figures in painting, such as the late Renoir and perhaps even the decorative elegance of Matisse.

Stravinsky was fixated on this realm of experience. While his musical structures juxtapose sound sections like Debussy, they rage against their flavour and rob them of their vitality. But however varied his different phases may appear, he always negates the principle of development as a constituent of music – and this is why a division into phases and works is far less relevant than one into stylistic categories. Through this negation he really circumvents the problem of large-scale form in a way reminiscent of the Impressionists. Even in the symphonies he only appears to tackle it. The virtuoso composer does a *volte-face* when confronted with the decisive and inescapable difficulties of composition. It is this far more than his obsession with ballet, a related phenomenon incidentally, which relegates his extensive *œuvre* to the category of a speciality, despite that talent for the unexpected which never forsook him.

A detailed comparison between the use of brief sections in Schoenberg's last orchestral pieces and the role of the different sections in Stravinsky's Symphony in Three Movements would be most instructive. If Stravinsky recoiled in horror from the nineteenth century – even the shudder was exploited artistically – this idiosyncrasy may well conceal what always accompanies it, namely a resemblance. As a secret genre composer he was Debussy's direct heir. There is room to speculate whether the distinction between genre and symphonic scale has not become obsolete; whether Stravinsky was not perhaps acting on a tip from the World Spirit when he placed the genre work on the tottering pedestal of aesthetic totality. At all events it was incompatible with the innocent interpretation of the Classical ideal and he undermined it by reproducing its façade like a death's head and discarding it in a single gesture.

The musical analogue of the transition from Impressionism to Cubism in painting exhibits manic features in Stravinsky. All life must have tasted like saccharin in his mouth, just because music cannot rid itself of the memory of life. Yet it is precisely that which Stravinsky yearned to achieve. Despite a surface integrity even the symphonic side of his *œuvre* obeys a logic of decay, when set beside the symphonic tradition. Beethoven's symphonies, unlike his chamber music, achieve their specificity through the unity of two elements which can only be reconciled with difficulty. His success was due not least to his ability to use each to counterbalance the other. On the one hand he remains true to the general ideal of Viennese Classicism with its belief in thematic development and hence the need for a process unfolding in time. On the other hand, his symphonies exhibit a characteristic accentual dialectic [*Schlagstruktur*]. By both compressing the unfolding of time and mimicking it, time is abolished and, as it were, suspended and concentrated in space.

The idea of the symphonic, which has since established itself as if in a platonic realm, can be found in the tension between these two elements. In the nineteenth century they broke apart, like the systems of German Idealism. Either the organizing force was lost and gave way to the stringing along of supposedly important or at least striking moments. Or else – and Brahms is the prototype here – the large-scale symphony sacrificed the accentual dialectic [*Schlagstruktur*] to the principle of developing variation. Hence the distinction between the symphony and chamber music was reduced to the almost accidental choice of instrumental forces. The first movement of Brahms's Fourth Symphony could equally well have been composed as a piano quintet. In contrast to this development, Stravinsky returns to the accentual dialectic which he perceived to be an essential ingredient of the symphony. But the ballet composer did not go beyond this. Whereas he hoped that his use of lapidary accentuation would restore the symphonic structure after its loosening in the hands of the Romantics, he now, as always, avoided the task of thematic elaboration in his symphonies and quasi-symphonic pieces. This is the origin of the sense of impotence and the illusory in his symphonic work. The concentration of energy, the intensity with which the music is articulated suffers from the absence of any opposing force, any resistant, temporal dimension against which it could test itself. Something non-existent is overcome. This is the price to be paid by the use of the symphonic to imitate the gestures of synthesis in an age when the intensive epiphany of musical form has been destroyed. To overstate the matter, Stravinsky's symphonic structures are forms minus any dialectic with a pure musical content. The more imperiously the form asserts itself, the more it becomes a simulacrum of itself.

His percussion effects are no less than assassination attempts, echoes of archaic war drums, blows of the sort that sacrificial victims and slaves have to endure. In his percussion the shock disrupts the continuity of living matter. His achievement here goes far beyond the mere invention of new percussion effects, though there is no lack of these. Having negated every other musical emotion, he has invested the percussion with emotion. It absorbs what is elsewhere repressed. Pregnant with energy, the percussion section now joins in that emancipation of timbre which had been the prerogative of the strings and wind instruments ever since Wagner. But only when the musical beat was emancipated and treated as material in its own right did it become involved in the actual construction which it had traditionally lagged behind. In the sound of the attack, which has become excessive in more recent music, Stravinsky found his true home. He was the first to use percussion, not as a set of spotlights on harmonic perspectives, but in response to its own sound significances.

In this respect the finales of the *Rite* and the *Soldier's Tale* have never been equalled. In the *Rite* the specific and quite precisely realized conception of the sound of the percussion is combined with the most subtle differentiation. In the *Soldier's Tale* it is combined with a feel for the individual small drums. His projection of the attack literally hits the nail on the head. Stravinsky could activate the sound of percussion from intimate knowledge of how the instruments are played. This is something he shares with Paris in general and it distinguishes him profoundly from the Viennese school. In the latter, ever since Beethoven's remark about 'the wretched violin', the tonal imagination has held undisputed sway. The productive creation of sounds that have never been heard before goes together with a certain indifference towards their execution. This indifference can have an adverse effect on the imagination itself: it fails to envisage possibilities open to it.

Stravinsky proceeds much more positivistically, or as the positivists would say, instrumentally. His idea of sound is guided today, as it was fifty years ago, by his 'know-how',[15] in the sense of Berlioz's programme of composing on the basis of his knowledge of what the instruments are capable. This approach has served him extremely well. His taboo on subjectivity has a liberating

---

15. In English in the original.

effect on the instruments which, instead of playing a subservient role, now begin to speak for themselves. The power that accrues to them is one of dissociation. Their own characters declare their independence of the overall intention and are thereby made new and fresh. Nowhere else did Stravinsky approach so closely to the idea of doing justice to the material, without ever slipping into the artisanal approach of the skilled orchestral practitioner. The voices of his instruments are like animals whose very existence seems to express their names. For all his hostility towards subjective intentions his sounds retain something of the nature of signs, of *écriture*; they exist by relinquishing their hold of playing 'techniques' while continuing to demonstrate them stolidly. However, this is done cryptically, as if every sound evoked its entire prehistory. This is the salt that is missing from all those who have modelled themselves on him, whereas the best of his work retains a subjective element that is involved in a passionate game of hide-and-seek and for that reason makes a mockery of every attempt at translation into self-confident technique.

The wind instruments which had always been the allies of percussion – namely, trumpets and drums – share in Stravinsky's achievements in percussion writing. Here too he has an attacking approach. From the idea of a music without development, the imago of a primeval oppression as something timeless, he extracts from the wind instruments the exaggeratedly hard, spiky tone colours which, down to and including his love for the piccolo, conquered all scores at a time when everyone had long since ceased to emulate the man who had made all these discoveries. His sense of the appropriate sound never falters, even where, and indeed especially where it sounds terrible, as in the *Mass* and in many parts of the *Rake*. The distortions to which the music condemns itself are masterly. He was the first musician to attempt something which became accepted only later in literature, namely a sadistic gesture which before him had only appeared in a rationalized and hence vicious form – as the clash of swords or the swell of triumph.

The liberation of this structure of feeling through play and imagination is ambivalent. It tallies with the resurgence of physical brutality and at the same time it acts as the catharsis of that brutality through the aesthetic image.[16] Dehumanization also marks the unexpected rapidity of the trumpets and trombones which lead the melody. In contrast the Wagnerian horn, as it were the stringed instrument of the wind section, recedes in importance or is given a different function. The strings, however, are stripped of their string-like quality, their ability to provide a perspective, and this applies not just to the pizzicato, but even to the double-stopped passages which are driven into sforzato and held there. They are scarcely any less denatured than Webern's use of 'col legno' and 'sul ponticello'. Their sound is split between a momentary percussion-like plucking and the accordion.

And in general Stravinsky's sound does not lack sympathy with ostracized, *déclassé* musical elements. This was well understood by Weill when he wrote *The Threepenny Opera* and *Mahagonny* for the Brechtian theatre. The term 'distancing effect' is appropriate to the sounds Stravinsky has coaxed from the instruments ever since he has composed for small orchestra. The combinations he uses are no less striking than the individual timbres. The ideas that characterize his late style, with the harp as the most brittle instrument carrying the melody, with various combinations of trombones and over-prominent violins in the *Agon*, and with a cunning use of pianoforte timbre, are admirable, despite a certain discrepancy between the excesses of timbral abstinence and the purely musical events. All too rich is the imagination Stravinsky deploys in the cause of denouncing it. The comparison between the performance of one of his pieces as conducted by him, and one conducted by someone else shows precisely what a musician he is: events juxtaposed become tautly integrated; the intensity of the entrances transforms them into a second life. The sound of the full orchestra above all simply abounds in such effects which cannot be reduced to the mere exploitation of 'instrumental technique'. That his music is sober and without a

16. On this dialectic see Max Horkheimer, 'Egoismus und Freiheitsbewegung', *Zeitschrift für Sozialforschung* 5 (1936), pp. 161 ff. [Adorno's note.]

trace of neo-German sweetness has often been observed. But it is never debased into a set of blunt, superficial sounds. For all his cruel economizing, they have spatial depth. Intentionally, the simultaneous complexes are denied an inner life, but each one is spiritualized in a way that is very hard to define; each one seems to be conceived from within. Stravinsky the instrumentalist thinks it a mortal sin to make 'all resound', and yet it does.

By the time the old man finally wearied of the dry, didactic tone of the New Tonality and was ready to play the devil once more, he had long since replaced it with something even worse. After the Septet the late works, which make greater or lesser use of serialism, introduce no qualitative innovation, with the exception of the extreme five-part Movements for Piano and Orchestra. That Stravinsky continues to write in his own unmistakable hand, as the phrase goes, is no effective reply to this criticism. Similarly, in Webern the unprepared ear would be unable to distinguish between the last free compositions and the earlier twelve-note pieces. Berg, too, was proud of the extent to which his use of twelve-note technique left his own voice unimpaired. As long as that technique remained satisfied with the definition of the succession of intervals and did not aspire to total serialism, it left a space for so-called individual style.

This may be not the least of the factors that aroused the ire of composers after 1945. They were irritated by the discrepancy between the principle governing the musical construction and the music itself. Incidentally, Webern's late works, from the Symphony on, already exhibit a slight diminution of his individual style. Placed in this context, Stravinsky's serial compositions evidently belong to the earlier phase, as might be expected. In *Agon*, the most ambitious instrumental work after his change of direction, there is even an alternation of free and serial passages just as in Berg's *Lyric Suite* of 1926. But the execution is as neo-Classical as ever.

The first of Stravinsky's serial works, the Septet, is in reality a suite in three movements, although the passacaglia theme would hardly be conceivable without the one in the second movement of Webern's Symphony, not to mention the variations in

Schoenberg's Serenade. It is not just that the three movements correspond to the old prelude, passacaglia and gigue. The internal texture as a whole is what we expect from Stravinsky. Note patterns are fixed and oblique, and are repeated with sustained shifts in emphasis. Intrinsically static sections alternate. The principle of the developing variation, which ultimately led to twelve-note technique and also legitimated it, is no more evident in Stravinsky's serial compositions than in his earlier works. He remained true to himself.

Of course, his total refusal and the compulsion to repeat also force him to repeat himself. By evading serialism's task of articulating thematic development, he contrived to convert it into a stylistic device, just as he had done with the other idioms from the inception of neo-Classicism. It can be said at least that his late works are as alien to twelve-note technique as his earlier ones had been to tonality. They exploit this alienness as a source of fermentation. Hence the large number of old effects arising from new means. Needless to say, the static shuffling of the rows reveals a potential which was already implicit firstly in Viennese techniques involving the total chromatic and then in serialism. Their total dynamism, that of the motivic, thematic, 'obligato' style, which fits every element of process into pre-established structures, ends likewise in stasis.

It is not for nothing that in Schoenberg the invention of twelve-note technique goes hand in hand with the use of non-developing dance forms. With his flair for historical trends the late Stravinsky intuited this convergence with his adversary, took matters to their logical conclusion and thereby implicitly provided a certain critique of twelve-note technique whose static nature contradicted its own origins. On the other hand, in his serial scores, Stravinsky's pseudomorphisms become a compositional liability, for all his undiminished musical virtuosity. Music which illustrates the programme of matter-of-fact objectivity better than any other, should do more than merely illustrate it; it should also objectify composition itself. This would call for a balance between what has been composed and the means required for doing so.

The pleasure one feels at Stravinsky's departure from the reactionary camp which had once elected him its champion does not suffice to make good this claim about his serial compositions. What is especially striking is how uneconomic the would-be economic threnodies are, for all the rigour of their twelve-note technique. There is nothing novel about the idea that serialism is only necessary as a way of organizing something both subtle and complex that would be dissipated without it. But both these qualities are ruled out by Stravinsky's steadfastly upheld stylistic ideal. The late works are neither so polyphonic, nor so varied and highly articulated as to stand in need of serial organization. In the rudimentary analytic instrumentation of the remarkable *Agon*, for example, you simply find one instrument cutting in on another. Neither in his treatment of the row, nor in his modest efforts at writing canons does Stravinsky surpass those who fondly imagine that the system will provide a support, without noticing that it becomes superfluous as soon as it fails to shape the musical events. But where he does excel is in the experience and *savoir-faire* stored up in his long life: it is the sound that gives the construction its strength. He would not need to call on this, but he permits heterogeneous materials to enter with the courtesy of a great lord who has no need to guard his past like a miser protecting his hoard, and who enjoys taking the risk. Boulez has summed this up with an elegance worthy of its object. Stravinsky, he said, is a master '*préférant la recherche à la sécurité, gardant contact et communication de la façon la plus éloquente*' ['who prefers investigation to safety, maintaining contact and communication in the most eloquent manner'].

The old gambler seduces us into imagining how utterly differently things might have turned out in a man who might not have shuddered at the thought of an apotheosis in the style of the seventeenth century, but undoubtedly did so at the thought of his own. When I heard one of the first performances of the *Symphony of Psalms* my feelings of respect could not prevent me from writing, '*Paris vaut bien une messe* – even a black one'. Since then 'black' literature has made such strides that it scarcely tolerates any rivals who would be equal to the challenge of the age. But the possibility open to Stravinsky was that of a 'black' music, in which the word 'black' is not used in the sense of an *Ebony Concerto* or a *période nègre*. He might have accompanied his soldier to the place he had driven him to, an absolutely darkened space in which lights only flicker in order to render the darkness visible.

The *Soldier's Tale* seems as fresh as ever because the modernity of dull aimlessness formulated at the beginning or in the soldier's violin, has only revealed itself fully today. The question of what happens to the individual subject in the age of his total impotence and regression is not just reactionary. It raises the issue of the metaphysical subsistence level – it is as if art were attempting to rehearse the real modes of behaviour that might permit a damaged life to hibernate and survive the onset of the new ice age. This might have resulted in music whose blows might have split time into segments, the image of a negative eternity rather than a mirage of the everlasting; music built out of ruins in which nothing survives of the individual subject but his truncated stumps and the tormented awareness that it will never end. It would have exposed the power of the individual who had succeeded for once in creating in music the whole world as his inner reality, and unmasked this as the power to hurt without consolation or protest. The subject matter might have been drawn from the Marquis de Sade, whose orgies are arranged like mechanical ballets. The most modern music, whose greatest practitioners come close to this conception, seem to recoil from it.

In terms of experience and the reactionary nature of his chosen musical form, Stravinsky would probably have been uniquely capable of it. He could have transformed the interiorized, subdued space of all music into the space of the Nameless One. If his music had consciously gone to this extreme, which is what consistently lurks implicitly within it, from the *Rite* up to the Movements, he would have liberated himself from his unfreedom by acknowledging its existence, and the immanent inadequacy of his compositions would have been exorcized. It may seem easy to advocate such music after Beckett, but Stravinsky himself provided something like a literary manifesto for it in the scandalous hymn in the *Soldier's Tale*, and he never forgot it. But he never put it into practice either. It is futile to ponder whether he might have succeeded, whether he might have cast off the curse of positivity. In the upshot the very name of absolute negativity is deformed. Complete identification with it, Stravinsky's entire energy, compels it to appear as if it were the truth. If the devil did not lie, he would cease to be himself. The negative truth only just came within Stravinsky's power. The myth to which his music committed itself without hope cannot endure the truth; absolute negativity is essentially illusion [*Schein*]. Stravinsky settled for that and renounced the more extreme option. His inconsistency in so doing is the consistent expression of the boundless anxiety which alone makes the extreme what it is.

With this taste celebrates its last triumph: the objectification of all anxiety as the dominant norm. Taste is able to lay its interdict on every aspect of culture. The only thing it cannot do is to find the redeeming word which would force culture to drop its veil. His imprisonment within eternal sameness is also an imprisonment within culture. This chains him to affirmation and establishes a sinister alliance between his music and the gruesome abominations it documents. But its complicity with untruth lies cheek by jowl with the truth itself. The parodist also parodies the dialectic. This latter defines the new as the inverted, self-reflecting figure of the old. In it the old is immediately confirmed, but the violence that always exerts pressure on the identical, robs it of its identity and decapitates it as it overcomes it. In the moments in Stravinsky's music when feeble-minded or idiotic characters make themselves heard, for example in the imagery of the clown that has recurred again and again ever since *Petrushka*, the reified consciousness, of which he was the exemplary composer, dramatizes itself without turning itself into something else or acquiring another identity by false pretences, and yet it becomes something greater than itself. He is indebted for this to that form of comedy in which unspoiled nature helplessly, speechlessly, opens its eyes. It alone allows his music to suspend for a moment its identification with the objects of fear, without depicting false meaning in a rosy light. Repetition is a characteristic of what has been reduced to the animal plane. By entrusting itself to it music transforms the extreme remoteness from nature into its own animal nature. Its spirit becomes animal. The passages in Stravinsky in which this transformation occurs successfully are indelible.

(1962)

PART III

Finale

Berg's Discoveries in
Compositional Technique

After 1945 ambitious young composers generally took Webern as their model. In doing so they went some way towards making amends for the malice and stupidity which had consigned his indescribably incorruptible and uncompromising work to the margins of musical consciousness because of its very consistency. What distinguished Webern, unbeknown to himself, from his teacher, Schoenberg, and his friend Berg was the energy with which he emancipated himself from the methods of the traditional musical idiom which survived in their works despite their introduction of new principles of construction. The energy he brought to this task satisfied, on the one hand, the German need to start from the beginning and to construct music from what were thought to be its primal elements; and on the other hand, that extension of serial techniques beyond twelve-note procedures which he inaugurated and the tendency towards total serialization in his late works which came to fruition in the next generation of composers.

Ten years ago [that is in 1951] it was impossible to rid oneself of the feeling that everyone was following in his footsteps. At the same time it was difficult to avoid the sense of a certain monotony, of an excessive similarity in the numerous works composed from pitch particles and discrete individual sounds. These works frequently seemed all too mechanical and lacking in tension when set beside authentic compositions by Webern, such as the Bagatelles, Opus 9 or the Five Pieces for Orchestra, Opus 10.

179

What was known at the time as pointillist [*punktuell*] music, a very one-sided and inappropriate word, incidentally, was really Webern transformed into a technological model. Needless to say, these musical tyros failed to include the very element that made his work into great music. I am referring to his extremely subtle sense of spontaneous relationships, his ability fully to articulate what had been pared down to a bare minimum. Every single note in Webern fairly crackles with meaning. In the absence of the accustomed surface continuity, it is this that gives the work what Schoenberg called internal flow: that breathless breath amidst events which seem wholly uneventful in traditional terms.

Pointillist music and the attractions of Webern have now all but disappeared among the gifted composers of the younger generation. This is not just, or even especially, because their pointillist works were too much alike. The abandoning of Webern as a model has more compelling motives than the concern for one's own individuality, something which disappears anyway as soon as you start to dwell on it. This disillusionment does not imply any devaluation of Webern. On the contrary, it is the precondition for a proper reception for his works – much as Schoenberg can only be truly appreciated if his works are listened to in their own right and not just as the products of the inventor of twelve-note technique. By its very nature music demands to be allowed to breathe out, to adopt a different approach to composition, as well as to breathe in, as in Webern's manner.

This brings about a change in our view of Berg. It is high time that his contemporary relevance was recognized. The suspicion that he is too sociable and moderate, that he is a man with his eye on the main chance, is contradicted not merely by his irreproachable personal attitude, but in equal measure by the shape of his work, in which every note avows what he learnt from Schoenberg. On the decisive issue, the ideal of the composing out of a work in every aspect and dimension, Berg showed himself to be no less rigorous than Webern or Schoenberg himself. The defensive reaction towards him could rationalize itself by pointing to those aspects of his work which did not quite fit into the stylistic picture of strict atonality and dodecaphony. In particular, the row in the last work to be completed, the Violin Concerto, contained 'triadic' successions. They made possible a peculiar simultaneous interplay of twelve-note technique and tonality which may easily give offence to ascetic ears, especially in the introduction and treatment of the Bach chorale. In opera the need to create characteristic figures inevitably surpasses that of instrumental composers and with the development of twelve-note technique the search for them was conducted with growing anxiety as dissonant sounds lost their specific characterizing quality and slipped automatically into the material. The role of tonal complexes in Berg is comparable to the discontinuous characterizations of the banal in Mahler, with whom Berg has so much in common – both in tone, in the approach, in the very fibre of his utterances, as indeed in the conception of entire structures. The March from the Three Pieces for Orchestra, Opus 6, is scarcely conceivable without the finale of the Sixth Symphony, and the same can be said of the relationship of the scherzando from the Violin Concerto to the second movement of the Fourth Symphony. This is not to deny the break in style, only to show its derivation. At worst, it suggests a certain crudeness in the initial reaction of the composers who followed Berg, a slightly petty interpretation of modernism, in their readiness to allow themselves to be misled and their occasional confusion of colour with *peinture*.

The issue at stake is not so much a matter of doing justice to Berg, of gaining a hearing for his music and not just shouting 'kitsch' whenever a dominant function is encountered. What has really changed is the actual state of composition itself. The question simply of the evolution of musical material is less urgent today than the problem of what can be achieved with the new methods, even though the productive application of these methods still has repercussions for the stock of available materials. The renewed and genuine need for extended forms makes an overview just as urgent a priority as the elimination of dross from individual details. It is evident that it is as difficult as ever to achieve this simply on the basis of the row. The fascination composers have felt for the principle of indeterminacy [*Zufallsprinzip*] may be a symptom of the new situation which can harbour doubts about the primacy of the row, whether this is due to the fact that composers no longer trust its organizing power, or that they fear the sacrifices which a total organization makes necessary.

In Berg, however, whose work is not dodecaphonic for the most part (and where it absorbs the technique, it softens its rigour) all those organizational forces which a puristic approach to the materials of music did away with, are stored up. He is relevant to the present situation in composition because, independently of twelve-note technique, he developed techniques which come closer to atonality's primary impulse, a *musique informelle*, than to the rationalized forms of atonality. This has scarcely been comprehended today, let alone become productive for other composers, even though most recent needs seem to correspond precisely to what Berg envisaged in some of his most important and hence analytically unobvious works. What he has to teach us is not the means of composition, whether diction or principle, but how the already-existing, emancipated material can be used to construct large-scale musical structures without sclerosis, without renouncing spontaneity.

The distinction between small-scale forms – in Webern – and larger ones – in Berg – is not just quantitative. In the most ambitious music extension determines the quality of every detail. In Webern detail-work means defining the detail so sharply that the brief structure requires no more than a few figures to establish contrast and transition. In Berg elaboration of detail means something akin to the Hegelian *Aufhebung*, that is to say, their abolition and subsequent preservation on a higher plane. What he retained from tonality – voice-leading, the omnipresence of the smallest steps – was a traditional means of bringing about an untraditional end, namely the destruction of the musical detail by the totality. Berg's music is panthematic, like that of the Schoenberg school in general. It contains no note that cannot be derived from others, which cannot be inferred from the motivic connections of the entire work; not, at any rate, since

Berg shook off the burden of tonal harmony which was incompatible with the panthematic approach.

However, in his work, this approach has a paradoxical result. The basic units which go to make up Berg's utterances, at least the most Bergian of them, and which are varied unceasingly, are consistently pared down as far as possible. They are basically just minimal distinctions. If music of any kind can remind us of tachism, then it must be this principle which anticipates by decades the term as applied to painting. It is the source of that disturbing aspect of modernism that people are so quick to reject in Berg. He offends against the taboo which civilization has placed on vermin. In a similar vein the painter Bernhard Schultze speaks of 'the milling masses'.

Berg's music inclines towards that experience of the amorphous and the diffuse in erotic impulses, which tends to be repressed. It is the antipode to everything spick and span, to the clean lines of Cubism which confuse form with the will to extirpate all impulses alien to the self in all the restorational schools of modern music. Form, however, is only authentic where it takes up this element which is so alien to it, sheds light on it and effects a reconciliation with it. The fact that the cliché of the psychological late Romantic is continually applied to Berg is probably nothing but a defence against what might be termed the unhygienic aspect of his work: anything which is not as clean as the bathroom must be sick. The purely musical reason for Berg's microtechnique is obviously not the shortage of original ideas, which is what the prejudiced and the malicious accuse him of, but the attempt to atomize the compositional material, a sort of quantitative analysis, in order to achieve a totality of unparalleled density, without fissure or edges, without the disruptive factor of effectively self-contained partial segments. Whenever Berg needed them, he could find the most vivid melodic ideas at his fingertips. Obvious examples are the closing section of the variation-theme of the Chamber Concerto [mm 25–30], the opening of the second movement of the *Lyric Suite*, and the scherzando themes of the Violin Concerto. The concept of an interwoven, instinctually expanding organism has deprived the individual figures of their accustomed sensuousness; but this does not mean that such sensuousness was absent from Berg's musical make-up.

The tendency to compose in minimally distinct units is not confined to the nuclei of the music. The initial atomized material is fragmented still further, in so far as that is at all possible. The entire set of compositional interconnections arises in Berg from such dividing and subdividing. Thanks to this everything pushes up against everything else in a way that suggests that *Tristan* might have been its distant forebear. But the structural inferences drawn from that work's chromaticism are surpassed so adventurously here that the outcome is something wholly new. Total continuity, the most concentrated rigour in the progression of the music, that is to say, organization to an extreme degree, and all this is not just combined with a jungle-like density, a tendency towards the chaotic – the two are actually equated. We may speak of the dual character of Berg's talents, one side of which is vegetable-like and instinctual while the other consists of architectonic clarity. But these are tendencies which should not be thought of as separate and opposed to each other. They are in fact identical in his actual mode of composition, his concrete technique.

Berg's greatest achievement and the one which compelled him to make the greatest efforts may well be that the impulse away from form remained in control and gave his music shape. It is all clearly articulated despite its densely interwoven texture, its concreteness in the most literal sense, and despite its dislike of contrasts, a kind of musical sense of tact which recoils from abruptness. Similar to one another though its various elements are, there are still important differences between them. We might speak of organized chaos in Berg, especially in his youth, when he gave his natural temperament free rein. Incidentally, one of the most remarkable experiences available to the listener nowadays is the discovery of the resemblance between the *Rite of Spring* and Berg's Three Pieces for Orchestra – two very different works in most respects, but they share a savagery which separates them from middle-of-the-road cultivated taste.

In the long run their common origin in the same years is of greater importance than stylistic and technical differences. The later Berg, say, from *Wozzeck* on, was more cautious than the younger one. It sometimes seems as if he were afraid of something in himself. The really chaotic utterances of the earlier period are formed less by discrete sections set off against one another than by the impulse that governs the whole and which carries the music on from one thing to the next, to sections of differing structure and above all of changing intensity. Dynamic organization replaces a static one based on contrasts.

However indebted Berg may have been to Schoenberg – much of his work consisted of developing at length succinct Schoenbergian models – he achieved effects not unlike Schoenberg's by antithetical methods. In Schoenberg's middle phase, and even more markedly in Webern's, the concept of thematic work is made problematic by the way in which the details become autonomous and because the structures are based on contrasts. Schoenberg's *Erwartung* is the paradigmatic instance of this, one which has not been surpassed to this day. Berg, however, so intensifies the thematic work, musical progression as permanent analysis, that ultimately the very concept of thematic work loses its meaning. Faced with his minimal units and whole sections in permanent dissolution, it is sometimes no longer possible to speak of tangible themes contrasted with one another and undergoing modification. In both composers a tendency towards an athematic style becomes visible.

More recently, large forms, like Stockhausen's *Zeitmaße* and *Gruppen* have made this their goal again. In his tendency to liquidate the thematic Berg, who was the more moderate in terms of his material, undoubtedly showed himself to be more radical than his friends. This explains the difficulties which are caused, even today, by some of his most crucial works, unlike almost all those of Schoenberg and Webern. With unfaltering courage Berg's formal instincts very soon recognized the incompatibility of his approach with the traditional forms defined by themes. He distanced himself further from this than Schoenberg and Webern, at least in instrumental music. Apart perhaps from the last of Schoenberg's *Five Pieces for Orchestra*, Opus 16, no music came closer to the ideal of musical prose than some pieces of Berg's.

This is perhaps the point of contact between Berg and the spirit which is in process of formation today. It is well known that Schoenberg justified twelve-note technique by pointing to the impossibility of creating large-scale and truly autonomous instrumental forms within the bounds of free atonality. If, in reply, it is objected that no one ever tried, then the answer is that if, truly, no one has ever made the attempt, then this relegates the claim to the level of an abstract assertion and proves that it was not a real option. This argument and with it the systematic claim of twelve-note technique to totality is refuted by some pieces by Berg which were written before twelve-note technique was discovered, or else in its early years.

In the well-known quarrel about the figure of Adrian Leverkühn and his music, a quarrel which was settled during the lifetime of the two men, Schoenberg asked Thomas Mann why he did not turn directly to him for help in devising Leverkühn's fictional works.[1] Schoenberg maintained that he could have told him about countless methods of construction other than the twelve-note technique which he practised himself and which appears in *Dr Faustus* as Leverkühn's own. Schoenberg's criticism was aimed at my own contribution to the *Faustus* novel. This criticism, which Schoenberg can hardly have made without irony, trusting as he did in the supremacy of twelve-note technique, may yet contain more truth than he supposed. Since the technique consists of a number of prescriptions, it is not devoid of an arbitrary, voluntaristic element.

---

1. Adrian Leverkühn is the fictional hero of Thomas Mann's *Dr. Faustus* which appeared in 1947. Adorno had advised Mann on the history of music and on Adrian's own compositions. The logic of German intellectual history in its turn towards National Socialism was paralleled in the novel by the development of music from late Romanticism through free atonality to twelve-note technique. Adrian's music was the product of a Faustian pact with the devil which reversed the humanism of Goethe's *Faust* and reverted to the anti-humanism of the original Dr Faustus of the sixteenth century. Schoenberg was highly incensed by the use made of his theory in this construction without any attribution. Mann was forced to print an acknowledgement in subsequent editions of the novel.

Berg, who, unlike Schoenberg, had something passive about him and resisted anything stubborn or self-righteous, wrote some really large-scale, internally coherent instrumental movements without twelve-note rows, which are every bit as logical as twelve-note works. In them he has managed to dispense with those forced and arbitrary features which are discernible in the present crisis of serial composition and which doubtless gave rise to aleatory experiments. The large-scale, free, atonal forms, the possibility of which was denied in the early days of twelve-note technique, were made reality by Berg. Many vestiges of earlier approaches, simpler sequential formations among them, arise from the need to establish interconnections where they are not guaranteed by the notes in the row. In Berg the effort to avoid the arbitrary is undertaken without any polemic and coincides with his concern with large-scale form. This latter should be plausible in terms of its own structures and not be legitimated by an appeal to any principles or procedures laid down in advance. The question of specific relevance to Berg is how it can be possible for an act of constant yielding, listening, a gesture of gliding, of not asserting himself, to culminate in something like a large-scale form.

The first piece of Berg's which ventures to tackle what we may regard as his latent specific ideal, is the finale of the String Quartet, Opus 3. Because of the refrain-like, admittedly strongly varied recurrence of its initial motif [m 47, 151], it might superficially at least be classified as a sonata rondo. It also contains a repeat section with correspondences to events in the exposition and its aftermath. At the same time, the finale is closely related to the unquestionably sonata-like first movement. It is not just that the latter is quoted; thematic components from it are taken up and varied. In his analysis Redlich perceives the entire movement as a sort of elaboration of the first movement, just as in Schoenberg's F-sharp minor Quartet the vocal movement *Litanei*, a sequence of variations, functions as a development of the two that preceded it.

To structure one movement as the development of another is an idea that may have its roots in Mahler's Fifth Symphony, whose second movement is a more tempestuous, though less far-reaching reworking of the first, a traditionally laid-out funeral march. However, by overlaying the rondo form with this developing function and also the numerous slow interpolations which modify the main tempo, the finale of Berg's Quartet develops into a structure which has barely anything in common with the traditional quartet. The use of the term 'rondo' loses all its meaning when the rondo theme fails to fulfil its purpose of creating the definite sense that something similar is recurring, something lasting, a genuine refrain. Even pointing to the presence of repeats does not count for much where the repeated elements are themselves so dissolved and transformed that they are scarcely perceived as an identity, and where no appeal is made to a feeling of architectonic symmetry. The complexity of the motivic elaboration, as well as the overlapping formal ideas, transform the work into a piece of free prose despite, and because of, the bound nature of every note. The only listener to take it in properly will be the one who follows its flow from one bar to the next, following wherever it chooses to lead him. The attentive listener must expand and contract with the music, instead of listening attentively for correspondences.

What is decisive for an appreciation is simply and solely the course of the music itself, not its articulation in terms of familiar patterns. Thus the very insistent entry of the initial motif turns out in the further development not to be the main thing – again, the similarity with some of Mahler is plain – but rather a kind of putty. Far more thematic in its effects than this main theme or indeed anything else in the movement are certain striking procedures which recur and are instantly recognizable. They may consist of the obsession with a particular note, or a complex which halts the flow as soon as it makes its entry. Such figures, as well as some of the tremolo chords or figures which dissolve into arabesques, take the place of what is normally accomplished by themes. The use of harmonic leitmotifs is especially worthy of note, as in some of his later works as well. The radically contrapuntal Schoenberg of the twelve-note period considered that harmony was simply not a relevant issue. It should just emerge from the serial structures and counterpoint as a by-product, without constituting an essential dimension in its own right.

Berg's disposition, which combined extravagance with forbearance, obviously found this verdict unacceptable. This may not be the least important factor in explaining his borrowings from tonality. Redlich was absolutely right to point out that of all Berg's works the Three Pieces for Orchestra, Opus 6, owed least to Schoenberg's ideas, despite its having been dedicated to Schoenberg. His harmonic motifs are atonal sounds, but they are unmistakably characteristic, never just results. They are repeated at nodal points in a form-creating manner, and even become thematic at times, as in the field scene in *Wozzeck*. There had already been signs of this in Schoenberg himself, from the famous forbidden inverted ninth chord[2] in *Verklärte Nacht* on, up to the harmonic motifs of passages in the *Pierrot Lunaire* such as *Die Kreuze* or *Heimweh*. Through the cultivation of such harmonic motifs Berg strove to salvage the specificity of the vertical dimension in the midst of the twelve-note structure, probably without this ever becoming a conscious intention on his part. All these formal devices organize the flow of the music without imposing themselves upon it from above or from outside.

However, the actual dynamism of that finale of the Quartet, that unconfined onward-driving force, succeeds in redefining motivic and thematic method in a highly original manner. Unlike Brahms, and certainly unlike Schoenberg, Berg does not begin by defining figures graphically in terms of rhythm, and then using them as models to be subsequently modified. Instead, one aspect of a complex, no matter which, is singled out because it is felt to contain seminal force. It is then spun out and transformed into the next one, without reference to any fixed point. The whole thing develops in a quite unschematic way. This may serve as the technical formula for that rampant proliferating growth in

---

2. This occurs in m 42 (B♭, A♭, E♭, G♭, C, E♭). See Schoenberg's account in 'Criteria for the Evaluation of Music', in L. Stein, ed., *Style and Idea* translated by L. Black, Faber 1984, pp. 131–2. [Note by Eric Graebner.]

Berg's work, for that sense of an impenetrable undergrowth which may have been the core of his nature. The implications of this for musical structure have only become visible in the most recent musical developments.

Composers now work in terms of 'areas' [*Felder*], instead of themes and thematic complexes. A path leads from each area to the next, but none is the logical inference or result of its predecessor. They all have equal status and stand on the same plane. They serve as the prototypes of what must become of the symphonic form once the sonata system, and even more import- antly, the spirit of the sonata, has been exhausted. The units within the movements are segments. They are connected by motifs which are divided up and shared between them. Their characteristic nature, which they retain as partial wholes, is established by the predominant feature of their area.

The transfer to large-scale musical prose, with the tendency towards wholly informal composition, was reached, then, in the finale of the Quartet with that revulsion from the sonata form. But the full development of a free compositional style had to wait for the last movement Berg composed before *Wozzeck*, the March from the Three Pieces for Orchestra, Opus 6, which he wrote instead of the projected symphony. Despite its rather modest proportions when set beside the Mahlerian movements which served as precedents, the March undoubtedly has symphonic weight. Its problematic nature is evident from the fact that even today no one has yet succeeded in a convincing analysis. In Willi Reich's book on Berg, which appeared in 1937, I undertook such an analysis. I wrote it under great time pressure and regard it as unsatisfactory. In particular, I no longer think of the third, self-contained entry of the March as a recapitulation. In reality the piece simply moves forward inexorably, much as marches do, without looking back. It is as if Berg had been the first to explore from within a large-scale work the fact that the irreversibility of time is in profound contradiction to the recurrence of an identical being.

I therefore looked to Redlich's biography for guidance, but found that the author had been kind enough to rely on my own analysis which I had come to find wanting. If two musicians from the Viennese school who had been intimately involved in Berg's work for decades, were defeated by this March, the cause of the difficulty had to lie in the music itself. The only help lay in a detailed analysis which would proceed motif by motif and note by note. This would have called for many months of highly concentrated study. I can only report on some of the ideas that came to me after reading the score many times and listening repeatedly to Rosbaud's recording.

At any rate I would now be happy to risk the hypothesis that it is precisely the enigmatic nature of the piece that makes it relevant today. Moreover the March reminds us of Mahler, thanks to its allusions to certain formulaic basic components of the march, its rhythm, articulation, appoggiaturas and fanfare triplets. These molecules are all that remain of the traditional march. They were first excised from their original context and then, through a montage-like procedure, long before Stravinsky, they were inserted into a new framework where they generate a whole flow of new ideas. The memory of the traditional architecture of the march – the march strophes, trios, return of the strophes – has been displaced as if in a dream and has faded; the music advances inexorably.

If we wished to apply to Berg's music a distinction made several times by Kant, we might call the march-form dynamic, in contrast to mathematical form, as if the music desired to cast off the burden of a static architecture, which always contains an element of the inauthentic, and wished instead to define its own flow simply in terms of its own medium, that of time. Where music does not unfold entirely according to the laws of development, but is composed, as with certain derivatives of dance, of segments whose meaning is not altered all that much if their sequence in time is changed, then a static architecture is not only possible, but it also assists the articulation of events. If, on the other hand, the compulsion towards development is rigorously insisted on, such symmetries and correspondences increasingly lose their function, their meaning and their *raison d'être*. They become incompatible with the immanent goals of such music.

191

Consciousness of this among composers has a long prehistory stretching back to Beethoven. Berg, however, was the first to face up to the problem, fearlessly and without resorting to temporary expedients, at the point where it becomes most critical, namely in extended instrumental movements about which a stubborn superstition persists that symmetries and repetitions are indispensable. Apart from the finale of Mahler's Sixth, with its climactic development from the disparaging, via the sinister to the final catastrophe, one could point to the first movement of his Third Symphony. Berg's March is no longer divided up into parts that correspond structurally to one another, but instead each segment is distinguished from its predecessor by a change in tempo as soon as a new main segment is reached. At the same time, the segments are not separated, but stapled together, mainly towards their conclusion. A new segment only signals its presence when the development flows in a quasi-definitive way into a new tempo. The whole is held together by the irresistible onward flow. This rises from motivic interconnections far below the surface. He has no recourse to insistent rhythm or ostinato.

The most important method, however, of creating an irresistible flow is the unrestrained, opulent overlaying of voices and constructs. It was not without pride that Berg once told me that his score was the most complicated that had ever been written. In its time the only score that could match it for complexity would have been Schoenberg's *Die glückliche Hand*. It is not just that the orchestral polyphony surpasses everything attempted hitherto, but that entire strata are piled on top of each other. In this respect, in the creation of a powerful orchestral space through the unfettered increase of simultaneous sounds, the piece represents one extreme version of modernism. Compared to the March, Webern's simple approach to the production of simultaneous sound has a traditional feel.

Berg's advance here remained without successors for a very long time. Only today, when the pure evolution of the material of music has reached a certain threshold does the composer's imagination find itself coerced, in its desire to break out of eternal sameness, to venture into that vertical infinity. Such insatiable overlaying, however, tends to create a new form. This is distantly comparable to Bach's polyphony, little though the organized chaos of overlapping lines and sounds in the March has in common with the spirit of the well-tempered clavier. The more tightly the voices rub up against each other – one is tempted to say, the more they get tangled up together – the more they come to resemble a knot in an almost literal sense. The simultaneity of countless melodic events is an immediate source of tension; the relations they form with each other point beyond themselves, towards progression and resolution. The energy stored up in the simultaneous becomes that of succession.

At the same time Berg's plenitude and Webern's reductionism are complementary, not absolute antitheses. Reductionism, as long as it is nothing but frugality and not the reduction of something, of plenitude, would be nothing more than a wretched poverty. Webern stands head and shoulders above his posthumous successors, because behind his asceticism what has been omitted remains a palpable reality, something rich and luxuriant which still shines through in his early works. Conversely, a plenitude which does not concentrate on what is essential to the depiction of the musical idea – I have in mind here many of the scores of Strauss's middle period – would become ornamental, decorative or, at best, inflated.

Berg proves himself in the March by his vigilance in ensuring that plenitude is possible as a constructed reality. Nowhere does he allow himself simply to wallow in the sound, although where splendour is warranted by the logic of the construction, he does not shrink from it puritanically. His ideal was that of a constructivist plenitude: one in which every line, every feature and sound complex is deduced from the rudiments of the March as expounded in the introduction; while at the same time all these elements complement each other so that each such line or complex fits precisely into another. While the very opulence of the score is confusing to the eye, it is in reality economic in the extreme and, paradoxically, simple. It contains no superfluous padding; nothing is written which you cannot actually hear. Again and again air is allowed to enter by means of piano passages, general pauses or whatever. Berg's extraordinary talent for extracting clarity from the impenetrable undergrowth – a talent which alone allows him to immerse himself in the chaos without drowning in it – can be seen at its most spectacular in the score of *Wozzeck*. The Three Pieces for Orchestra are its prolegomenon although they are not yet fully ready to accept the economy of what is visibly inscribed in the score.

Berg's exorbitant plenitude goes together with the need to make music over lengthy periods of time. It would not be appropriate for short forms. Webern avoided it, not from any deficiency in simultaneous imagining, but with a sound instinct for his own formal ideal. The more, and the more compulsively, simultaneous events are presented, the more they strive to expand. Confined to a few seconds, they would break off unfulfilled. For a long time strict limits were set to simultaneous plenitude in twelve-note technique. Schoenberg, who had an incorruptible ear for the relationship between form and means, once wrote of his Variations for Orchestra, Opus 31, that the principal difficulty with the twelve-note technique had been to satisfy the requirements implicit in a large orchestra, rich in timbres, of a movement in several parts. In the March Berg conceived a way of doing this, but then allowed it to atrophy for a time.

Twelve-note technique suffers, if we may be allowed to caricature it in this way, from a chronic deficiency of notes, especially where the strict ban on octave doubling is adhered to. Freedom in the selection of notes to be combined in non-serial atonality makes it possible to heap up incomparably more than when possible combinations are laid down in advance. In this sense it requires much greater courage to compose without the twelve-note palette than with it and from within the safety of the charts. The most recent experiments in music for multiple orchestras may perhaps represent a continuation of what Berg aspired to in the March, namely the complete freedom of the ear to integrate combined musical sources, even though this was occasionally guided by the drift of tonality.

This freedom is intimately connected with the quality which, when I reflect upon it after all these years, originally attracted me to Berg, as well as to Benjamin's philosophy. This was the quality of inexhaustibility, of a profusion of ideas which constantly regenerates itself and flows in superabundance. In a real world in which matter-of-factness (which was fully justified as a critique of false plenitude) has degenerated into a statement of bankruptcy, a kind of spiritual meanness, the need for compositional freedom converges with the need for this sense of the inexhaustible. The sterility of functionality is a mere surrogate for the rigour of the work of art. The happiness of the latter lies in the qualitative variety which is not terrorized from outside, by the lie of purity and the pure.

But if it is objected that the plenitude of Berg's March exceeds the bounds of the comprehensible, I would be inclined to retort simply that what is well cooked with many ingredients will find people to eat it, if it is not withheld from them, and sooner perhaps than things which make it a point of aesthetic morality to frustrate the need for unfettered satisfaction. But what one person has once heard correctly, can be heard in principle by everyone.

The Three Pieces for Orchestra are anachronistically modern. Dissociation at the level of detail, the elimination of all pre-established, large-scale interconnections, invokes the immanence of construction. Its signs are everywhere in evidence. To a large extent, the orchestration follows the principle that as far as possible registrally adjacent colours are always different, not the closest. Thus, the de facto coherence of a simultaneity is lifted apart, like the separate pitches in particularly dense and complex chords. If the composer is prepared to think this negative principle of orchestration through to its logical conclusion, he will see that it contains a canon which would make clear what a positive system of orchestration would look like. It gives rise, in a procedure which is both unified and infinitely differentiated, to an iridescent sound spectrum, above all in the second piece, with which only the *Farben*-movement from Schoenberg's Opus 16 is comparable.

This sound spectrum, highly varied and multi-coloured even

in terms of successive events, but quite free of any suggestion of pictures or moods, could be termed abstract Impressionism of the kind that could be found in painting after the Second World War, in painters like André Masson, for example, and in music above all in Boulez. It is obvious that Berg was the only member of the entire Viennese school to have been influenced by Debussy. It is more important, however, that he should have transformed Debussy's achievements into absolute musical means of representation. We should point to at least one of the highly unexpected consequences. In Debussy, in tune with neo-Romantic aesthetics, the precise technical dramatization of the vague, the imitation of the indeterminate, plays a very definite role. As a descendant of Romanticism, Berg shared this taste for the vague with the French composer. But in his music it turns into a quality which one is tempted to describe as one of musical absences, in memory of those moments of absent-mindedness which were so characteristic of Berg himself.

In the Three Pieces for Orchestra, especially in *Reigen*, there are areas which are not wholly there, where the organized sound makes itself independent of the composer, as if he were momentarily no longer in control. We may distinguish between varying degrees of presence or non-presence in the music itself. Many such areas sound as if they were the fruits of an admittedly carefully planned accident, were it not for the fact that it is aesthetically discontinuous, is not taken seriously and thereby submits to the subjective formal intention after all. Many such discoveries of Berg's could be discovered today in quite different places, without there being any question of influences. Pre-figurations of twelve-note technique have long since been pointed out, above all by Krenek.

The most striking are to be found in the *Altenberg Songs*. Even the affinity between composition and graphic art was discovered by Berg in his playful way, in that passage of *Wozzeck* where at the words 'Circular lines, figures', such shapes actually occur in the score. But he also explored the expansion of serialism beyond the organization of intervals. He had already used rhythms thematically in the Three Pieces for Orchestra and subsequently in

Wozzeck, the Chamber Concerto and in the monoritmica of *Lulu*. In the latter a large-scale form is dredged from the rhythmic variation in conjunction with a total retrograde. Likewise the treatment of the instrumentation often has an underlying 'serial' feel. For instance, in the prelude of the Three Pieces for Orchestra, a percussion introduction moves imperceptibly from pure noise to a definite, comprehensible tone, whereas the end of the piece reverses the process, back into amorphousness. The principle of the smallest possible transition, which Berg inherited from Wagner and applied universally, transferring it to every parameter, incorporates the desire for a comprehensive musical continuum.

More noteworthy, perhaps, than such anticipations, little observed though they have been, are the differences between Berg and Schoenberg in the choice of principles of construction. One of the most important, the retrograde motion inherited from the Netherlands in the late Middle Ages, had been used by Schoenberg for the first time in the *Mondfleck* section of the *Pierrot Lunaire*. Subsequently he also developed the retrograde forms of the twelve-note basic rows. Berg in contrast learned something from the *Mondfleck* which was just as visibly implicit in it as the serial structures. In this he was inspired by his interest in the autonomous organization of large-scale forms. He designed entire structures using the concept of retrogression. This was done in a rudimentary way in the prelude to the Three Pieces for Orchestra, the allegro misterioso of the *Lyric Suite* and in the monoritmica of *Lulu*, as well as the great orchestral interlude in Act II.

These structures may have been captivated by the mirage of reversing the passage of time through music. But Berg's unmechanical implementation of this idea is admirable. He understood retrogression as an aesthetic idea, not as a literal, rigid step-by-step process. Thus yielding to his instinct for rejuvenation in the allegro misterioso of the *Lyric Suite*, he abbreviated the retrograde in the main section. In the adagio of the Chamber Concerto he repeated the main components of the numerous principal themes in reverse order and in retrograde. But here too he maintained his freedom of action and changed the course of events where it seemed necessary. The first thing to learn from Berg is that none of the perspectives of integrated construction which opened up to him were understood naturalistically, in the sense of tangible, demonstrable relationships in which everything went according to the rules. Again and again the principles of construction are cut across or overridden by the artistic intention. He always inquires into the claims of every such logical procedure at the point where it calls for sacrifices. What this costs Berg in terms of stylistic purity and the so-called correctness in construction is made good again by his indefatigable efforts to eliminate the external, imposed aspect of objectivity and to reconcile the musical construction with the impulse of the heart.

In the period following *Wozzeck* Berg wrote one further piece which belongs with those other large-scale forms, the finale of the First Quartet and the March from the Three Pieces for Orchestra. This is the rondo from the Chamber Concerto. Its complexity and difficulty of performance is hardly inferior to the march. It owes something to the *Mondfleck* – Berg has drawn attention to this in the famous letter commentary – since a straightforward form, the variations of the first movement and a retrograde form, the adagio, are counterpointed with each other. In the same way Schoenberg made the retrograded double canon of the *Mondfleck* accompany a non-retrograded piano fugue. But here too Berg showed greater independence. The two movements are not joined together literally as Milhaud was to attempt subsequently in two string quartets, but only combined in a general way. What could not be combined polyphonically in a meaningful way was simply dropped. It may be objected that it is inconsistent to adopt a highly rigorous form and then only follow its rules when it suits you. This is legitimate criticism, but it oversimplifies the situation. A composer who appears to make things easy for himself by making arbitrary decisions, makes matters more difficult by confronting the alienated necessity of abstract prescriptions with a living, subjective art.

The finale of the Chamber Concerto is one of those enigmatic constructs we owe to Berg. The power of the conclusion, without precedent in its way, confirms the overall conception. But it remains an exception in Berg's mature *œuvre*. It certainly can no longer be described as *musique informelle*. No one will question Berg's mastery after *Wozzeck*, a mastery from which the Chamber Concerto also benefited. No one will overlook the fact that from a definite point in time the composer began to incorporate in his works the experience he had gained from the actual performance of his scores, and how much his music profited from this both in the economy of means and in transparency. If the term 'maturity' ever had meaning, then it must apply to Berg's works following *Wozzeck*.

But the thought of the large-scale informal works awakens doubts, not about the later Berg, but about the idea of maturity itself. When scholars excavated early versions of literary masterpieces like *Faust, Wilhelm Meister* and *Green Henry*[3] they did so from rather more than mere historical and philological curiosity. They were probably motivated by the premonition that there is a price to be paid for what we call maturity which frequently outweighs what is gained by it. At any rate there are undoubtedly artists, painters like Klee or Kandinsky, whose basic image is not easily reconciled with the primacy accorded to maturity. Much the same may be said of Alban Berg with his eternal youthfulness. Maturity, the assured control of the tools at the artist's command, the balanced awareness of the relation between these and his artistic aims – all this also suppresses something. It suppresses what goes beyond those aims and refuses to bow to the rules of culture, to its tacit call for works that are self-contained and complete in themselves. Instead it hankers after utopian possibilities which are renounced as soon as art has learnt wisdom and henceforth confines itself simply to what it can do. Mature works are not just aesthetically superior. Often they are also the works which, by wholly incorporating the prevailing aesthetic norms, make their peace with the world and its values.

From this point of view we may with all due sensitivity, reject

---

3. *Faust* and *Wilhelm Meister* are by Goethe. *Green Henry* is the major work of the Swiss novelist and short story writer Gottfried Keller (1819–90).

such a stance in favour of the larger conceptions of Berg's youth, whose imperfections from the standpoint of mastery are easily perceived. For they preserve the traces of what has never existed and it is this that the yearnings of music aspire to. To respond to them would be to inherit the true legacy of Alban Berg.

(1961)

Vienna

For Elisabeth-Charlotte von Martiny

Some years ago Ernst Krenek published an article in *Forum* in which he drew attention to a number of young Viennese composers of the Serial school. Although these composers in no way lagged behind their like-minded contemporaries in Germany, France and Italy, they had received scarcely any notice outside their own country. I too was unfamiliar with the names and works of this group which was so highly thought of by a competent judge. This confirmed me in a long-held belief, which was reinforced in my visits to Vienna after 1956, that a strange paradox was at work here. Music that had been regarded during the inter-war period as Austrian, or at best German, was distinguished from the mainly post-Impressionist or neo-Classicist products of Western nations and the more folkloristic music of the East by its lonely intransigence and the absence of what was doubtless felt outside the German-speaking world to be musical good manners. Yet in the intervening years this same music has come to be accepted as a sort of universal modernist style.

Nevertheless in the city in which this movement came into being all recollection of it has faded. Those who still maintain the Schoenberg tradition there are as isolated now as they ever were in the heroic days of their resistance to the musical roast-chicken culture. The three Viennese composers who basically constituted the Second Viennese School, Schoenberg, Berg and Webern, are dead. Schoenberg died, at an advanced age, in emigration. Berg died in straitened circumstances which were the direct result of the way in which he was maligned by the National Socialist rulers. Webern fell victim to the sort of monstrous stroke of fate in the early days of the occupation after the war that Karl Kraus might have imagined. Still living in Vienna are Helene Berg, Schoenberg's pupils, Joseph Polnauer and Erwin Ratz, Webern's pupil, Wildgans, and Berg's pupil, Apostel. But a genuine Schoenberg circle no longer exists. In the first instance this is undoubtedly the fault of the Hitler regime. In other countries, however, even in America, where formerly no one wanted to know about radical Viennese modernism, the great Viennese composers and their techniques have gained an authority never granted to them at home. All this gives rise to reflections that may throw some light on the direction and significance of modern music as such and may help to break the stranglehold of the blinkered technological approach which emanates from modern music down to its very latest serial ramifications.

The compact world of Viennese society has made a natural monopoly of musicality that once and for all absolves people from any effort. In this world modern music has always had a hard time: its great scandals had all the flavour of initiation rites. Nevertheless, even today, within a limited circle, there is probably a greater understanding of the problems of modern music in Vienna – and a more genuine sympathy – than anywhere else. Krenek is undoubtedly right when he argues in his essay that the receptivity of the Viennese is not inferior to that of the Parisians who were so captivated by Pierre Boulez's *Domaine Musical*.

But there is still room to inquire why Vienna should have been singled out as the birthplace of that modern movement. For in both literature and painting Vienna probably lagged behind Paris and even Berlin. The city's social structure, half feudal, half dependent on trade and luxury goods, was as unfavourable to abrasive intellectual innovations as was the climate of Viennese psychology. The latter was better suited to Impressionism and Art Nouveau than to an exacting rigour that resisted the identification of the work of art with the individual and his characteristics. Hence the great musical revolution in Vienna did

202

not occur as a straightforward recoil from subjectivism, as was common in the West, but was in fact mediated by the subjective: in 1910 Schoenberg was closer to Kokoschka than to Picasso.

Despite this, in a milieu that was as sensitive aesthetically as Vienna before the First World War, opposition to the Viennese qualities of flattery and seduction was necessarily a feature of the most rigorous elements of modern music. Viennese culture permeated the whole of life like ether and although it was secretly in conflict with everything culture really stands for, it had consolidated itself as the status quo, as the tacit affirmation of the existing state of affairs. For this very reason it was inevitable that the greatest talents would rise up against it and prove to culture that it was insufficiently cultured.

In this respect Schoenberg, Karl Kraus and Adolf Loos were of one mind. They were the enemies of the ornamental, the comfortable enjoyment of an art that committed you to nothing, that relied all too complacently on its own stability while lapsing inexorably into the merely sybaritic. Their polemics were directed at hacks in every realm, not just in journalism, against everyone who offered his own individuality, which was the same as every other, for sale in the marketplace. That complacent conciliatoriness of the Viennese softened the brutal demands of material production and hence created a space in which the intellect could move and thrive. But it also infected it. This is why true intellect had to rebel and defend itself against the circumstances that had given birth to it. For otherwise, by colluding with society, it would have ultimately betrayed itself and sold out to the unsavoury materialism of industry and the needs of the cultural consumers.

It was not just that the nonconformist intellectual was prevented by his principles from concluding a pact with the intellectual *juste milieu*. Rebellion surfaced in the primary artistic responses. The fact that another Austrian, Franz Kafka, the admittedly rather younger citizen of Prague, could note in his diary 'For the last time, psychology', points to something of the nature of the innovations of the oppositional Viennese artists. Even where they document dreams, as does Schoenberg in

Erwartung, this is done with a sharpness which precisely registers his hostility to that attitude for which Kraus coined the term '*Seelenschlieferl*'.[1] Moreover, in Freud's own psychoanalysis, which Kraus detested, there is an element of materialist resistance to an empty cult of the soul. Beneath the sceptical gaze of the psychoanalyst, as indeed of the musical Expressionist, that cult loses its aura and assumes a sober, objective aspect, like the later works of art of the great Viennese innovators. The exponents of the radical movement originating in Vienna, individualists through and through, were broadly intolerant in the largest sense of the word. Kraus, whose relations with Schoenberg at least became more relaxed in later years, turned against Expressionism as a school and coined the expression *Neutöner* [New Musician] as a term of abuse.[2] Schoenberg rightly loathed the epithet, but thought very highly of such unconventional writers as Georg Trakl and Else Lasker-Schüler. They agreed in their rejection of an ideological conception of culture in the face of a bad, historically already-condemned reality, against whose untruth their truth measured itself. Their truth in its turn would not have been conceivable without that well-known Viennese spirituality. This could be seen in travestied form in the way in which the youngest daughter of the most insignificant tobacconist would be familiar with the names of the celebrities of the Burgtheater and the Royal Opera.

In Vienna a consistent traditionalism protested, and not just in music, against the tradition itself and revolutionized it with the demand that it take itself seriously. Schoenberg's entire output could be discussed, without doing it violence, in terms of the idea that he honoured obligations which according to the standards of Viennese Classicism a composition assumes from its very first

---

1. *Seelenschlieferl* was Kraus's term of abuse for psychoanalysts. It suggests that psychoanalysts are people who worm their way into your mind for their own advantage. They are 'soul-creeps'.

2. *Neutöner* is derived from '*Tonkunst*', an old word intended as an alternative, more Germanic word for 'music'. Words derived from it nowadays have a pedantic or archaic flavour. Adrian Leverkühn, Thomas Mann's composer hero in *Dr. Faustus* is described as *Tonkünstler*, literally tone-artist. Kraus's neologism may also contain a pun on 'Newton'.

bar. That Kraus was chained to the city he denounced has been repeated so often by those whom he castigated that it has ceased to be true. A similar point could be made about Loos, although in his case the links between his aesthetic views and the ascetic elements of earlier Viennese Baroque have barely been investigated. Of course neither Kraus nor Loos founded a school. In Kraus's case the mere idea would be inconceivable.

The situation in music was different and the impulse of radical modernity was more powerful there than in the desperate attempts of the Expressionists to break the fetters of conceptual language. If this was so, we may explain it by pointing out that the material of music is non-conceptual and that the idea of technique is a more integral reality in music than literature. But the specific musical traditions of the city also played a role, dubious though it is to attempt to explain *post factum* why something came into being in one place rather than another.

The direction of Schoenberg's production throughout his life was towards integral composition, initially under blind compulsion and subsequently in the full awareness of what he was doing. This impulse had been decisively prefigured in Vienna in the tradition running from Beethoven to Brahms. At the end of the line Schoenberg proves to be the executor of their objective will. It is a striking fact, however, that both those composers had moved to Vienna from Germany. The rationality of integral composition, in which nothing is left to chance and everything unfolds according to fixed laws, has something of the flavour of bourgeois autonomy of the kind that throve in Germany, but hardly in semi-feudal Austria. An anecdote about the Emperor Franz Joseph throws some light on the matter. It is reported that when the inexorable Mahler refused to allow an archduke who had arrived late to take up his seat in his box, the Emperor did indeed acknowledge that his Director of the Opera was within his rights. But he also asked Montenuovo, the Master of the Royal Household, whether an opera really was such a serious business.

For Beethoven and Brahms music was so serious because of the power of the idea of autonomy. This continued to hold good for Mahler and then for the Schoenberg school. But it could hardly be said of a native Viennese. In the aversion of Mahler and Schoenberg to hierarchic mediations of whatever kind we may discern traces of a secularized Jewish theology. Perhaps it was that subliminal rebellion against the aristocratic Viennese tradition going back to the Josephinian Enlightenment that finally broke through here.[3] This anecdote which links the aged Emperor to the history of modern music in such a curious manner also helps us understand why the integral mode of composition should have succeeded in finding a home in easy-going Vienna. Franz Joseph's liberal gesture which enabled his Director of the Opera to assume an attitude that might provoke a smile in the habitués of the Hotel Sacher, also permitted a genius to manage the Vienna Opera for ten years in such a way as to make those same people proud of it. But such liberalism is distinguished from bourgeois rationality in that it is content to ask whether a thing is good, while neglecting to inquire what it is good for and whether it can prove itself in the marketplace.

In the hierarchy of offices Mahler was Director of the Opera and master in his own house. He simply would not allow an archduke to interrupt the performance, and that was that. The protection of such a system – protection in a double and by no means despicable sense – permitted artists in whom bourgeois rationality had truly become intensified to the point of autonomy to realize this autonomy in practice, unimpeded by the disadvantages of bourgeois alienation – namely, the commodity character of art. Thus Beethoven was protected from the need to choose between poverty and competition by the consortium of his aristocratic friends. Something of this survived, even if it were no more than a certain tolerance and freedom from outward controls, and under cover of this the conditions were created in which the achievements of Schoenberg and his pupils could come into being.

---

3. Joseph II became Emperor in 1765, but he ruled initially as regent along with his mother, Maria Theresa. The Josephinian Enlightenment dates from the period of his sole rule in 1780 until his death in 1790.

Not that they received any official encouragement. On the contrary, Schoenberg was despised and when he was finally given leave, as the phrase went, to give a course at the Academy, the invitation sounded more like an insult. Incidentally, this did not prevent him from retaining monarchist sympathies throughout his life. But only within the archaic laisser faire of a social system in which the laws of exchange were not yet omnipotent – its parody is the still current Viennese maxim 'that everything can be fixed' [by a word in the right ear] – did he find something of the comfort in the midst of poverty, and above all the support that comes from an established and unquestioned society. It was from this that he was able to draw the strength to assert his own freedom.

It would seem that a powerful and substantial tradition is required before advances beyond it can be made. Where it is absent, there is no option but to acquiesce in the demands for social utility which are peremptorily issued to the individual without any escape clause for putative fools and idiots. In Vienna as in Paris the avant-garde could only thrive in reservations for dissenters, which is what the old-time coffee houses literally were. If such refuges are liquidated on the grounds of their notorious irrationality, such realized rationality liquidates mind itself. Up to now, for freedom of thought to develop an authoritarian structure has been necessary. However, it does not demand total control, but both produces and nurtures resistance.

Nowadays the tendency is to eliminate tensions between such authorities and the individual. The latter is left with no alternative space within an order in which, shivering, he feels at home. He is cast adrift in a world alien to him, as it is euphemistically formulated by contemporary philosophy,[4] and he survives by selling himself to it lock, stock and barrel. He may persist in misrecognizing himself as free and equal, but through his identification with unspecified compulsion, he sacrifices his free potential.

---

4. Adorno alludes here to Martin Heidegger's concept of *Geworfenheit* which refers precisely to this condition of being hurled into existence.

Like Beethoven and Brahms, Schoenberg, although born in
Vienna, had something of the newcomer about him, like many
residents of the capital of the Danube monarchy – and not only
because his father came from Slovakia and his mother from
Prague. He himself was surrounded by an aura of the alien, the
stranger who does not quite belong or fit into Western civilization. The hatred he encounters to this day, both inside Austria
and outside it, is undoubtedly connected with this. When I saw
him for the first time, I was amazed by his gypsy-like appearance.
Cupy Jószi, the first violin in the gypsy orchestra who used at that
time to play in the Renaissance Bar near St Stephen's Cathedral,
could have been his brother. Schoenberg's foreignness reminds
one of the role played by Spaniards in Cubism. Schoenberg
himself felt that tradition was the precondition for going beyond
tradition. He expressed it for example in a letter in which he said
that his family was no more musical than any other in Austria. If
that is so, the breakthrough presupposes that one does not quite
belong in the tradition.

The constellation of a substance already present and an
element of undomesticated strangeness presided over Schoenberg's life. But this also describes something characteristic of
Vienna as a whole. It is no doubt true that in the wake of the
Josephinian Enlightenment, Viennese traditionalism carried a
ferment of scepticism within itself. In an individualistic petty
bourgeoisie, whose material aspirations had for generations
been locked in conflict with its precarious living conditions, this
scepticism was intensified to the point of permanent dissatisfaction – to the point which Germans call grousing [*Raunzen*] and
which has since become an integral part of the Viennese
tradition. It was present in Schoenberg's self-opinionated attitude as it was in Webern's general manner. Webern indeed had
something of a genius for grousing. In the greatest talents a
smouldering sense of dissatisfaction with culture became intensified to the point where it gave them the strength to transcend
culture.

A contributory factor was that the musical tradition in the city
of Beethoven was by no means as firmly established as it

appeared to the outside world, even in its own eyes. The archaic, not yet fully bourgeois element in the social make-up of Vienna exerts as great an influence in its music as the powerful contact with the East. The negative side of this is that fatal natural monopoly which defines the waltz as an article for export and provides the tourist industry with the advertising image of cheerful natives hopping around in the street. What actually is debatable is whether people in this city of music really knew their music as thoroughly and as well as elsewhere. Othmar Schoeck, the Swiss composer who was also Hugo Wolf's only true pupil, rightly criticized his teacher for a certain technical ineptitude that he never really overcame. And indeed it really is very difficult in music to learn in later life what you failed to learn at the conservatoire between the ages of fifteen and twenty-five. Of Mahler it is reported that because of the talent he had shown in the youthful compositions that he later destroyed, he was let off attending classes in counterpoint – an astonishing fact to anyone who can picture Mahler's dogged efforts in later years to master counterpoint, something which came anything but easily to him.

Such laxity, however, to which we are tempted to add Bruckner's obvious awkwardnesses, also helped to ensure that Austrian composers remained free of that academicism which stifled so much composition in the French and German styles. This has left room in Austria for phenomena which became historically important precisely because they diverged so uninhibitedly from the established mainstream of good academic music. This tendency culminates in Schoenberg and it is not for nothing that he rebuked Strauss, the German, for being such a model product of the conservatoire. Schoenberg did not even study at the Academy, but as an autodidact, he acquired what he needed in his private lessons with Zemlinsky which it seems were not exactly formal. That he escaped the mill of ordinary school instruction probably facilitated his achievements, as did the inevitable Viennese immersion in music. It is a paradox that he should have been the first to have brought to a pitch of technical perfection a musical culture which made no effort because it had a virtual monopoly, and that he should have been the man to make good the cultural deficit. It was he who remarked of the Third Quartet, evidently with its particularly elaborate twelve-note structure in mind, that it was furnished with all the comforts of the modern age. If the Viennese tradition of integral composition provided him with his measure of rigour, ultimately the idea of compositional freedom which he equated with rigour turns out to be the supreme example of Viennese casualness.

So deeply rooted is the new music in Viennese life and so close to its object is the spirit of the city, that their relationship can sometimes only be summed up in slang. *'Bandeln'* – pottering – can barely be translated into High German at all. What is meant are activities with which to pass the time, to squander it, without any evident rational purpose, but also activities which are, absurdly, practical. As when someone spends hours cleaning his electric shaver. Its premiss is a busy idleness. But it also calls for the obsessive love for small things familiar from the prose of Adalbert Stifter.[5]

The obsessive preoccupation with the futile and useless is a pre-school for art; it is the anticipation of a playful interest in technique. Socially such an interest thrives best where solid middle-class attitudes know how to appreciate the value of things, but where bourgeois values have not prevailed to the point where time is money. The person who potters around is attuned to a mode of production that has not yet been fully industrialized. An example is the leather industry which is marked by the natural properties of a material object and where the process of mechanization is kept within limits. At the same time the potterer's love of concrete detail fits into a way of life that is structured to a certain extent, but has not yet been dissolved by reflective rationality. Where this way of life survives, despite its

---

5. Adalbert Stifter (1805–66) was an Austrian novelist and short story writer. In a debate with the German dramatist Friedrich Hebbel who maintained in a Hegelian manner that drama should deal with the great turning points of history, Stifter argues that such moments were by definition exceptional and that literature should focus instead on the underlying routines of nature and social behaviour, which might seem petty but were decisive in reality.

having been rendered obsolete both technically and econ-
omically, isolated individual activities may easily assume an
excessive significance in it.

It is hard to imagine the Viennese climate of modern music
without its naive addiction to seemingly trivial everyday things.
In the same way it is no less difficult to think of it without that
polite concern for the culture of sensuous things which cannot
bear the idea that something evil might happen to objects that
have been shaped by human hand. Schoenberg's interest in
stainless steel cutlery, practical drinking vessels and similar
objects may indeed have relied on Kandinsky and the Bauhaus
for its theoretical justification, but its origins are rooted in that
Viennese climate. Berg, who found himself in such demand in
rural Hietzing that he had no time to compose and so had to take
flight to the mountains, tended to potter in a big way. The spirit
of pottering then found its way into his music. In the same way
Webern's canon writing makes a deadly serious business of what
major composers before him had regarded as brain-teasers to be
solved, partly at least in a spirit of fun.

The insatiable, loving devotion with which the Viennese school
refined the details in their scores, as if they were polishing,
cleaning or sanding furniture, is the finest legacy of the tradition
of pottering. In the long run this is also the source of the patience
required to distil principles of construction from practice. In
general the superiority of art to craft and the concrete should not
be taken for granted. What at first looks like the unserious and
unfree expenditure of labour on material remote from mind
sometimes stands revealed as an immersion in the non-
instrumental which spiritualizes the material. What to begin with
looks like tinkering with a *perpetuum mobile* occasionally leads into
those realms which speculative aesthetics in their Hölderlinesque
heights called the calculable law of tragedy.

As an authentic Viennese, Schoenberg shared in a world which
one scarcely associates with him and which he was certainly
unconscious of. It is the world of Austrian popular music and of
those composers who spontaneously drew nourishment from it.
Nothing refutes the cliché of Schoenberg the intellectual – a

cliché which is mistaken in every respect – better than the realization of what he owes to that tradition and how many of the constitutive elements of the new music originated there. Of course it goes beyond the established language of a tonality which had been degenerating into a rigid routine. But its novel features represent the unconscious return of those aspects of the language of Austrian music that had outlasted the superficial rationality of the eight-bar period and all that that implied.

In its rejection of any allusion to popular music Schoenberg's music is more relentlessly consistent than any of his time. But what we may call the revolutionary features of his work spring from the marriage of pre-bourgeois rudiments with late bourgeois consequences. Thus Schoenberg's asymmetries are prefigured in the irregularities of rhythmic structure in Schubert which refuse to be forced into the straitjacket of even-numbered formations. Brahms was among the first to follow Schubert's lead here. In one sense Schoenberg's atonality could be thought of as the attempt to transfer to the realms of melody and harmony the 'organic' nature of a pre-rational musical form which had not yet submitted to the dominance of abstract numerical relations. Cutting across the official mainstream of musical history in a similar fashion is Schoenberg's tendency to prevent complexes and structures from leading into each other smoothly and to refrain from constructing schematic bridges in order to connect them. Instead he gives the inner form priority over an unbroken outer one. This too can be found in Schubert at points where he uninhibitedly introduces a general pause and breaks off where good musicianship stipulates continuous developments. Bruckner's caesuras are an analogous phenomenon. Only in Schoenberg's case the fear of mediations external to the internal logic becomes such a crucial part of his conscience as a composer that it divests itself of the enervated, chance elements that were still found in the earlier composers.

The spirit of a popular music that had not been totally penetrated by rationality to disintegrate and break up into a diffuse set of juxtapositions is recuperated by Schoenberg into the space of an integrated compositional practice. Ultimately such a process can even be discerned in its impact on melody. Popular Austrian music is familiar with large intervals from the yodelling tradition. Mahler had exploited them from his early songs in order to extend the melodic space beyond the good old octave. Schoenberg's large intervals, which end up permeating the entire texture of the music, may take their lead from him. Schoenberg often writes 'schwungvoll' [with verve], for preference on themes which make use of large intervals. This verve is unmistakable in waltzes by Johann Strauss, such as 'Wiener Blut'. Schoenberg, Berg and Webern have written arrangements for some of these waltzes.

Of all such connections perhaps the greatest paradox of all is that the anti-culinary element in Schoenberg, his hostility towards pleasant, sensuous sound, itself points back in one of its meanings to the sensuous culture of Vienna, an intense delight in pleasure. There is an affinity between a certain luxuriant lushness of harmonic feeling, a sense of letting the sounds melt on the tongue, and the enjoyment of dissonance. The chord is the more acutely felt the more it appears to have something profound and three-dimensional about it. It attracts through its dissonant arpeggiation. Consonance and dissonance are not simply opposites, but mutually condition each other, just as the gourmet's pleasure in a delicacy thrives on the knife's edge of disgust. As psychoanalysis will confirm, an element of regression is always associated with any refined pleasure and the choosiness of the Viennese School, its fastidiousness towards the banal and the hackneyed, does not derive simply from its liking for the distinctive, an ideal of Art Nouveau and its later Viennese variant, the Secession.[6] It goes back to that very much more ancient stratum which had not been eradicated by the taboos of bourgeois musical rationality. The dissonant chord, which, despite the element of fourths, was nourished predominantly by irregularly stacked-up thirds, came to the rescue of that Viennese love of thirds which Schoenberg consigned to hell.

---

6. The Vienna Secession was founded in 1897 by Otto Wagner, Joseph Hoffmann and Josef Maria Olbrich under the presidency of Gustav Klimt.

The tradition of popular music is perhaps inherent in the innermost recesses of the new music. An example is in its relation to the bass. Austrian popular music – admittedly it is not alone in this – does not have any sense of clear harmonic steps in such forms as the *Ländler* and the march. It does not require momentum of its bass line, but oscillates between a few harmonic steps, in the basic instance between the tonic and dominant, or even the tonic triad and its alteration into the six–four chord. In Mahler's early works the suspension of a 'bass' consciousness was not confined to the explicit use of popular musical models: he himself originally heard music as if without the bass and only gradually acquired a sense of harmonic progression, only to relax it again later on, with the greatest possible artistic sophistication, in *Das Lied von der Erde*.

Schoenberg, in contrast, began as a disciple of Brahms. He paid scrupulous attention to progressions in the bass and their relative weight, their strengths and weaknesses, even in the *Treatise on Harmony*. It was he who reminded us again about them after Riemann had discredited the entire concept. The extent to which such a reinforcement of the harmonic steps contributed to atonality is well known. But this contribution, too, is ambiguous. As progressions in the bass become independent the problem of the function of the bass increases. It may be questioned whether this should be ascribed to Austrian popular music or to an even older tradition, namely the unconscious memory of the monodic chants of the Jewish religious service.

The melodic integrity of the bass and above all the pervasive ambiguity of harmonic reference to a 'lowest note' in atonality make it questionable, in any chord progression, whether anything remotely like a bass effect really takes place. This is because of the ceaseless turnover of lowest notes. In free atonality the progressions and the harmonic connections can scarcely any longer be heard in terms of a bass, but hover, sustaining themselves by virtue of their own power, independently of the gravitational pull of a lowest part which derives its authority from a system that regulates the harmonies from the outset. An authentic bass consciousness probably only exists where progressions in the bass and with them the entire range of harmonic and contrapuntal relations are assigned their rightful place a priori. Otherwise, harmonies progress as a whole, each part according to its voice-leading tendencies, not relative to the lowest notes [*Grundtöne*]. To this corresponds Schoenberg's practice of invertible counterpoint, which effectively negates the traditional status of the bass line, since every theme can virtually be put into every part. This would result, through the extreme sublimation and differentiation of the new music, in the restoration of something which preceded tonal organization genetically, but which under its hegemony merely maintained an apocryphal existence.

In Schoenberg all that is latent, far beneath the manifest shape of the works. But as early as Berg and Webern the Austrian element surfaces once more. In disposition, in the way in which the voluptuousness and rapture punctuate the construction, Berg is self-evidently Viennese in every bar. In a sense this reveals the link between the Schoenberg school and Mahler. This is particularly marked where Berg spoke his unspoilt musical Viennese with the vocabulary of atonality and twelve-note technique, above all in the passages where the dramatic or poetic intention permitted it. An early instance is the great scene in the inn in Act II of *Wozzeck*, especially in the introductory, degenerately mournful *Ländler*.

The same may be said of the first movement of the Chamber Concerto and sporadically in the *Lyric Suite*. The idiom was used consciously in the second movement of the Violin Concerto, all of whose themes are in the Austrian manner. Anyone who has been sensitized to this language is unlikely to feel that the inclusion of a Carinthian song in the scherzo and its recurrence in the variations shortly before the end is anything like as stylistically inconsistent as the difference between tonal melody and the twelve-note context might suggest at first sight. In its original state that folksong is sung to a crude and silly text, one for which Berg – a faithful reader of the *Fackel* – would have felt nothing but scorn.[7] But that melody made a decisive entrance into the musical structure of his last work and there found the expression for a leave-taking more moving than any words – all this appears in retrospect like an allegory of the relationship between the new music, which had distanced itself from the earth, and its home.

Berg's last completed work reflects the hidden origins of the new Viennese school. Things that are modern do not just sally forth in advance of their time. They also recall things forgotten; they control anachronistic reserves which have been left behind and which have not yet been exhausted by the rationality of eternal sameness. When set beside the 'up-to-date'[8] the advanced is always also the older. Of course this has a fatal social implication: the ageing of modernism itself in the face of an indiscriminately expanding rationality. Anything which consistently trusts in its own truth to enable it to survive a confrontation with the powers which control culture as well as everything else is hopelessly naive.

Thus the shift away from Vienna as the capital of the new music is something that cannot just be explained in external terms. Its Viennese and Austrian component was authentic in its remoteness. Viennese new music was never directly at one with its own milieu. From the outset it pressed beyond the boundaries of its place of origin. Even before the First World War Schoenberg had already spent two extended periods in Berlin, which for a Viennese like him in itself constitutes a sort of emigration. According to Schoenberg, Berg had for years abhorred the very idea of travel and felt that even Imperial Germany was a place of exile. Despite this he contemplated following his brother to America in the early 1920s. If we have to have technical civilization, he argued, let's have the real thing. Artistically such ideas were by no means so bizarre.

The new Viennese music did not piously conserve its Austrian component, but consumed it as a living force. The more

7. *Die Fackel* [The Torch] (1899–1936) was the satirical magazine published by Karl Kraus who himself wrote most of the articles in it. It was required reading for the Viennese intelligentsia.
8. In English in the original.

rigorously it developed in contradiction to the official music of Europe, the more European it became, and the less Viennese. When Vienna had ceased to be the world metropolis it had been before the First World War, the West opened its arms to the advances of the Viennese school, particularly after the sterility of neo-Classicism had begun to make itself apparent in the Stravinsky imitations of the 1930s. If Stravinsky had been the Picasso for whom he was so often mistaken, if his neo-Classicism had been no more than an episode and if he had remained true to his instincts, Parisian eyes might never have strayed as far afield as Vienna. But now it became necessary for Paris to take note of what had been taking place here, if it were not to subside into provincialism. This in turn brought about the deprovincialization of Vienna. The integral method of composition, which was so profoundly in harmony with specific components both of the overt tradition of Beethoven and Brahms and with the latest Viennese tradition, was revealed as being of one mind with the drive towards rationalization and thus with the entire trajectory of musical development in the West.

The musical dialect of Vienna suddenly became the musical language of the world, not by dint of imitating suggestive stylistic models, as in the era of Stravinsky's international hegemony, but through the sheer power of musical logic. The critic Albert Schulze Vellinghausen recently noted an astonishing convergence in the painting of various countries, at the expense of national distinctiveness. What was true of painting applies with even greater force to music. But despite the ineluctably levelling effect of its rationality, the musical language of radically worked-out construction has absorbed into itself the Vienna which first gave it the cold shoulder and on which it then turned its back. Even at a purely personal level there are far more connections than is generally known. But the situation is one in which the best-known serial composers of the younger generation re-enact the traditional drama of the father–son conflict and so prefer to stress their remoteness from Schoenberg, rather than to promote a *recherche à la paternité*. Top of the list would be René Leibowitz, a pupil of Webern's, who through his performance,

his writings and his own compositions, indefatigably and un-
waveringly promoted the cause of the Viennese school in Paris
and even did so illegally during the German occupation. He
brought it into contact with the Parisian nose for the avant-garde,
which in the long run was not to be satisfied by any neo-Baroque.
Boulez was not just Messiaen's pupil; he was Leibowitz's too, and
thus a direct descendant of the Viennese tradition. He expresses
that himself in his attitude to Webern. Just as tangible is the link
with two of the principal exponents of Italian modernism, Nono
– who was Schoenberg's son-in-law – and Maderna, who studied
with Scherchen.

Structurally the most recent music has scarcely any essential
links with any other contemporary school but that of Vienna. But
its elective affinity with Schoenberg's work and that of his friends
cannot be wholly defined by the idea of integral composition, nor
even as a continuation of specific techniques from Webern's last
works. Beyond the processing of the material – and the common
denunciation of compositional alchemy – their unity is established by the accent and quality of the musical texture. Thus the
highly sensuous but also extremely non-naturalistic declamatory
style of Boulez's vocal writing is obviously modelled on Webern's
Second Cantata. The musical textures of the Viennese and the
[new] Serialists are similar, not just in the tendency to aim for the
greatest possible determinacy, in the desire to spin everything
out of a common core, but also in the way the music manifests
itself. Nothing is allowed to remain as mere matter, unformed
and unarticulated. In both total organization implies the
thorough working-over of the musically sensuous elements. In
both the principle of filigree detail, which stems from the
Viennese Classicism of around 1800, and which French music
had resisted hitherto, is omnipresent. The dissolving of the
music into the most minute motivic units was one aspect of this, as
was the dismantling of the sound-surfaces, in analogy to analyti-
cal Cubism in France. For both the Viennese and the New
Serialists dissolution and dissociation are the necessary prerequi-
sites of integration. The classicistic categories of simple, easily
graspable line, homogeneous sonorities, and settled appearance

are rightly frowned on. Vienna is responsible for the entry into the musical thought of the West of something which is roughly comparable to the impact of Proust on Cartesianism. The reception of this element, which may be called German, reflects at an extreme spiritual level the real fact that the age of individual European nations is over. The easy-going informality [*Gemütlichkeit*] which can only survive where life has not been seriously disrupted, has come to an end for good and all.

In the new serial music, too, wherever it really works, every moment is as highly charged as in the Viennese school. Over-zealous critics have taken exception to the expressiveness of Stockhausen's *Gruppen*. Wrongly, because expressiveness cannot be separated from the technical procedure, any more than the Viennese technique could have come into being in the absence of the need to express something. The hatred felt by the most recent composers for the soothing construction of specious façades is identical with the earlier hostility of the Viennese towards academicism. The fact that they compose settings for revolutionary texts, the diaries of anti-fascists under sentence of death, or surrealist shock verses, is appropriate to the music, just as the dreamlike convulsions of *Erwartung* can be said to fit what is admittedly a comparatively harmless text. The renunciation of the clichés of Latin form, which have long since become as hackneyed as their counterpart, the inwardness and idealism on this side of the Rhine applies – and here again the analogy with the Viennese school is evident – not just to the hedonistic provision of entertainment but also to the asceticism of a mechanical objectivism. The relentless insistence on objectively shaped form seizes hold of the subject and takes possession of it, while the more arbitrary form of the neo-Classicists wrongly laid claim to general validity by virtue of its violent expulsion of the subjective. Only constructivity, and not a heartless game, can envision that reconciliation with the subject proscribed in the pre-fascist and National Socialist periods and usurped by an imposed collective order. Boulez's *Marteau sans maître* is a modern *Pierrot Lunaire*, forty years younger, not just because of its assembly of brief forms, the colourful contrasts of the chamber orchestra and the plenitude of thematic figures, but above all because it achieves expressiveness through an articulation oblivious of self.

With its reception, and with what might be called its systematic work on models like the *Pierrot Lunaire*, the most talented exponents of recent music also come to form a contrast to the Viennese school, a contrast created by the sheer fact of the passage of time. It is obvious that with its shift to the West the new music has absorbed certain Western characteristics: above all, the sensuous sound, which admittedly was not wholly alien to the Viennese; a sort of painterly pleasure in orchestral timbre; and even a number of qualities associated with Stravinsky, such as Boulez's use of percussion. We are not talking here of some cheap synthesis of East and West, but rather about productive criticism. Its point is not the elimination of all sorts of traditional features taken over by the Viennese school – features which were not simply in the air, but which fulfilled a definite function, certainly in the case of Berg and also in a certain element of formal conservatism in the later Schoenberg.

The point is rather that a particular feature is being eradicated. What I have in mind here is that provincialism which did so much damage and not just in Schoenberg's choice of texts and in the late Webern. While the best of the young composers serve notice on the comfortable doctrines of sheer objectivism, the concept of the musical subject undergoes a change. It loses some of its private nature, of that petty-bourgeois mustiness that surrounds the image of Strindberg, that patron saint of the Viennese composers, with the aura of decaying old age. In the Viennese pathos of personality something naively Wagnerian had been immured, something which affected not only their attitude but also the tone of the music.

This pathos is now on the point of disappearing. In his study of the problems of teaching art, Schoenberg, the great technical innovator, polemicized against the conception of technique which the New German composers had dubiously made autonomous. Instead he called for pure expressiveness. From a certain distance we might define the present state of musical consciousness by asserting that it refuses to content itself with the antithesis of expression and technique. The two categories have now merged completely – and this time consciously so, in contrast to their spontaneous commingling in the practice of the Viennese. The French concept of *métier* now comes into its own, where previously German idealist metaphysics of art had looked down its nose at it. A self-confident sense of *métier* proves itself to be just as effective at creating musical substance as the need to express themselves had inspired the Viennese concern with technique [*Technik*].[9]

This does away with the primitivism which lay at the foundations of the new music, even in its most complex projects. Inwardness ceases to presume to defend a protected area against technology [*Technik*]. The protest of art against the dominant culture can only acquire authority by making use of technology. The entire complex of gestures becomes transformed. It becomes more intransigent thanks to the ruthless complexity which arises from the principle of construction. But at the same time it becomes more sophisticated. It is undeniable that this deprovincialized new music thereby runs the risk of becoming worldly in the bad sense, as is suggested by the journalistic slogan of 'art in the technological age'. Much of the most illuminating works of serial music would remind us of Debussyesque '*mondanité*', were it not for the fact that that quality had been condemned by history, so that the memory of it tends to salvage a past phenomenon rather than suggest an act of reverence towards the salons which have already become mere pictures from the past.

But we shall only be fair to the new gesture which is of equal importance to both old Viennese and New Western serialists, if we understand its social necessity. Many people rebuke the young musical generation for their eagerness to make their views felt, and criticize their strategies and in general their relations to public institutions, contrasting all this unfavourably to the purity

---

9. It should be noted in this passage and elsewhere that Adorno assumes (musical) 'technique' to be closer to 'technology' than might be expected in English. This is encouraged by the fact that the German word *Technik* contains both meanings.

of the Viennese. But in the administered world[10] anything which is not administrative by nature can only survive, and indeed only make its voice heard, by using administrative methods. In a culture whose universal law is that of particularism, there is something hypocritical in the indignation felt towards so-called cliques. Even unworldly artists who are in earnest about their own work have not been as completely helpless as ideology – both their own and the vulgar variety – would have us believe. Richard Wagner would be the most important, albeit the most problematic instance of this. Whoever accuses others of cliquishness almost always belongs to a clique himself.

Today we are witnessing the emergence of a type of composer in whom the processes of production and marketing are intermingled to a point which in earlier days was not acknowledged. This phenomenon is more than just a symptom of decay – such talk of decadence is a characteristic of the many spokesmen for what is historically doomed. It is also the reply of the musical forces of production to their incarceration in monopolistic institutions. The dubious aspect of this process is quite obvious. It is the tendency to let the business of marketing divert attention from the composition itself, paralyse the process of production and dilute the quality of the music. But a society which inexorably smokes out the bolt-holes which had been left for artists down to our own day, and which were particularly plentiful in Vienna, inevitably dictates a different relationship to practice, to the business of realizing the artist's intentions, as well as to that of maintaining his actual existence. Anyone who waxes indignant about the way in which modern art and the modern artist seek to support themselves – a process in which the works too are functioning parts – takes sides with a reactionary view which would be well suited if those who take the risks were to starve to death and hence would have nothing left to risk. And for its part the practical gesture of the intransigent artist corresponds to the

10. *Die verwaltete Welt* (the administered world) is an important concept in the later Adorno. It encapsulates his vision of a totalitarian world, whether dominated by monopoly capitalism or Stalinist communism. Within it the individual is imprisoned, deprived of his humanity and condemned to lead a 'damaged life'.

fact that the spheres of musical production and reproduction, which hitherto had pointed in opposite directions, have now objectively been brought together.

What is symptomatic here is the increased sensitivity towards modernity, towards those phenomena for which the time is ripe. The Viennese had pretended to regard such factors with arrogant indifference, and Schoenberg, not without rancour, was proud of his hostility to fashion. In this, of course, he was not so far removed from the academic musicians who castigated his 'obsessive desire to create something unprecedented'. He concludes his comic opera[11] with the words, 'Mummy, what are modern people like then?' Such questions make the legacy of the Viennese an oppressive one. They can scarcely be in much demand today, and that applies both to the texts and to the entire cast of mind.

The reaction of Stockhausen and Boulez is to insist that only the latest and hence by definition ephemeral thing can be certified as permanent. They are radical in that they provoke the compact majority with a musical practice that remains faithful to that maxim at every moment. For the first time music comes to incorporate in itself something which formerly only came to exist objectively and, as it were, independently of the works: it is the historical value of aesthetic truth, which is not embedded in time, as historicists insist, but is an integral part of time itself. Up to now this idea of modernism existed only in painting and the lower forms of music – that is, light music. Now, the most advanced kinds of music are emancipating themselves from the taboo on fashion, the ephemeral moment without which Picasso's greatest *trouvailles* would never have come into existence. It is foolish, therefore, to mock the tempo of change which make the changes of the first half of the century look like the stage-coach, and to ridicule the hectic succession of slogans in which the latest trends eagerly rush to consume themselves.

Art of high quality now seems to be divesting itself to a certain extent of the fetishistic ambition to last for ever. Its pace

---

11. I.e., *Von heute auf morgen.*

constitutes a kind of self-criticism. The residue of arbitrariness, of elements which are not wholly subject to the logic of the music itself but are imposed from outside, elements which had come to the surface with the systematization of the new music and the introduction of twelve-note technique – this residue is decontaminated, now that the system no longer solemnly proclaims its validity, now that the system is disintegrating and even accepts its own disintegration. It virtually becomes identical with Cubism, that other great system of modern art: not a self-sufficient system in itself, but a disciplinary bottleneck for the unbridled consciousness. The composers who incorporate chance into the law are now sorely tempted to break the spell of the law yet again.

(1960)

Sacred Fragment:

Schoenberg's *Moses und Aron*

For Gershom Scholem

Statt offener Gemeine sing ich Gesang.
Friedrich Hölderlin,
'Der Mutter Erde'[1]

'Brave men are those who accomplish deeds that surpass their courage.' The opening of Schoenberg's Four Pieces, Opus 27, whose title contains the suggestion that everything is in pieces, fragmentary, like the Tables of the Law which Moses smashed, proclaims not just Schoenberg's own basic attitude, but also one of the fundamental experiences which give life and soul to his great unfinished biblical opera. At the start of the scene in which he is summoned, Moses complains:

O God of my Fathers, God of Abraham, Isaac and Jacob, who hast reawakened the thought of them within me; My God, do not compel me to proclaim it. I am old. Let me graze my sheep in peace.

Even his courage is not equal to the task he cannot refuse. For to act as the mouthpiece of the Almighty is blasphemy for mortal man. Schoenberg must have touched on this theme even before *Die Jacobsleiter*, when he composed a setting for Rilke's poem in the songs of Opus 22:

---

1. 'Instead of open community I sing a song.'

Alle, welche dich suchen, versuchen dich.
Und die, so dich finden, binden dich
An Bild und Gebärde.[2]

Thus God, the Absolute, eludes finite beings. Where they desire to name him, because they must, they betray him. But if they keep silent about him, they acquiesce in their own impotence and sin against the other, no less binding, commandment to name him. They lose heart because they are not up to the task which they are otherwise enjoined to attempt. At the end of Act II of the biblical opera, in the final sentence which has become music, Moses breaks down and laments, 'O word, O word which I lack'. The insoluble contradiction which Schoenberg has taken as his project and which is attested by the entire tradition of tragedy, is also the contradiction of the actual work. If it is obvious that Schoenberg felt himself to be a courageous man and that he invested much of himself in Moses, this implies that he advanced to the threshold of self-knowledge about his own project. He must have grasped the fact that its absolute metaphysical content would prevent it from becoming an aesthetic totality. But by the same token he refused to accept anything less.

Important works of art are the ones that aim for an extreme; they are destroyed in the process and their broken outlines survive as the ciphers of a supreme, unnameable truth. It is in this positive sense that *Moses und Aron* is a fragment and it would not be extravagant to attempt to explain why it was left incomplete by arguing that it could not be completed. But such an explanation would have little to do with that notion of the tragic, the insoluble conflict between finite and infinite inherent in the subject matter Schoenberg chose. The impossibility which appears intrinsic to the work is, in reality, an impossibility which was not intended. It is well known that great works can be recognized by the gap between their aim and their actual achievement. The impossibility we have in mind is historical: that

---

2. 'All who seek you, tempt you. / And those who find you, bind you / to image and gesture.' Rainer Maria Rilke, 'Das Stundenbuch' [The Book of Hours].

of sacred art today and the idea of the binding, canonical, all-inclusive work that Schoenberg aspired to.

The desire to outdo every form of subjectivity meant that he had subjectively to create a powerful, dominant self amidst all the feeble ones. An immense gulf opens up between the trans-subjective, the transcendentally valid that is linked to the Torah, on the one hand, and the free aesthetic act which created the work on the other. This contradiction becomes fused with the one which forms the theme of the work and directly constitutes its impossibility. Theologians have complained that the designation of monotheism as 'thought' — that is, something which is only subjectively intended — diminishes the idea of transcendence in the text, since every thought is in a sense transcendental.

Nevertheless, a truth manifests itself in this, however clumsily it is expressed: the absolute was not present in the work other than as a subjective intention — or idea, as the philosophers would say. By conjuring up the Absolute, and hence. making it dependent on the conjurer, Schoenberg ensured that the work could not make it real. But it does the Absolute the honour of not pretending that it is present, a traditional reality that cannot be lost, but instead, of defining it as accessible only in the work, even if it thereby negates it. Around the time of the First World War Schoenberg asked Richard Dehmel to compose a text for an oratorio which he was ultimately reduced to writing himself. He spoke of the religiosity that was still possible for a modern man. Even his last texts, which he left incomplete at his death, are called *Modern Psalms*. This suggests both that he had an intuition of the link between the possibility of sacred works and the actual historical situation and that objectively the notion of a theological art which the individual wrests single-handed from an uncongenial age is highly questionable.

The impossibility of the sacred work of art becomes increasingly evident the more the work insists on its claim to be one without invoking the support of any outside authority. With the modesty characteristic of the greatest emotional integrity Schoenberg ventured into this realm. The objection that the individual is no longer capable of the subjective piety which the biblical story calls for misses the mark. Bruckner was presumably a believer in an anachronistic sense and as musically inspired as any composer can be. Yet the Promised Land remained closed to him, and perhaps even to the Beethoven of the *Missa Solemnis*. The impossibility we are speaking of extends right into the objective preconditions of the form. Sacred works of art – and the fact that *Moses und Aron* was written as an opera does not disqualify it from being one – claim that their substance is valid and binding, beyond all yearning and subjective expression. The very choice of canonical biblical events implies such a claim. It is certainly implicit in the pathos of the music of *Moses und Aron*, whose intensity gives reality to a communal 'we' at every moment, a collective consciousness that takes precedence over every individual feeling, something of the order of the togetherness of a congregation. Were it otherwise, the predominance of the choruses would scarcely be imaginable. Without this trans-individual element or, in other words, if it were merely a case of what is known as religious lyric poetry, the music would simply accompany the events or illustrate them. The compulsion to introduce into the music a sense of its own intellectual situation, to organize it in such a way that it expresses the underlying foundation of the events described, in short, its high aesthetic seriousness forces it into a collective stance. It must of necessity extend a hand to the sacred if it is not entirely to fail its own intention.

But cultic music cannot simply be willed. Anyone who goes in search of it compromises the very concept. The cultic is, in Hegel's term, 'substantial' – that is to say, it is upheld both in form and content by the society which it addresses. Yearning, even need, do not suffice: a secular world can scarcely tolerate any sacred art. Schoenberg's greatness is that he faces this fact squarely and refuses to fudge the contradiction. Instead he unhesitatingly follows it through to the end. He scorns mere citations of the past, traditionalist gestures, in a situation in which tradition no longer holds sway. By renouncing an 'as if' attitude which his antipode Stravinsky adopted in order to achieve what he never aspired to, Schoenberg remains consistently matter-of-fact, a strict functionalist, even as the composer of sacred music. He places his trust blindly in the autonomous aesthetic structure, and does not let himself be driven from the only standpoint that is appropriate to his music. No bar must be allowed to stand if the composition cannot justify it in its own terms. By this means it attempts to achieve what it disdains to usurp.

Its implicit Kantian question would be radical, without any ontological pseudo-radicalism: how is cultic music possible in the absence of a cult? Its method is one of determinate negation; what is negated is every subjective ingredient. Productive criticism of the latter interlocks with constructivism. A cultic action is one which obeys a law that goes beyond the mental capacity of those involved in the cult, in accordance with the idea of something which is not just surmised, but is actually revealed in the language of truth. In the same way the musical construction, for which the subject requires nothing but its own powers and the preformed material, shall transcend the sphere of the subject from its own impetus. The purity of the procedure aims to eliminate whatever the individual has added to it externally.

This is the inner and, it is almost superfluous to add, the objective intention of the work, one which is concealed from the composer himself. The inhumanity which great music comes closer to, the further it is removed from the chance nature of individual expression, makes this intention into something superhuman, or rather, the image of something superhuman. For the purity of construction free of any intention is itself the product of subjectivity and intention. It is this purity which creates that absence of expression which it takes for theological truth, and it does this by developing the means of expression and going beyond them. If the text creates the theological scandal of speaking of the One God as the idea [*Gedanken*], then this is a scandal that is duplicated in the texture of the music, though rendered almost unrecognizable by the power of the art. The absolute which this music sets out to make real, without any sleight of hand, it achieves as its own idea of itself: it is itself an image of something without images – the very last thing the story wanted.

The Jewish prohibition on making images which forms the centre of the text also defines the approach of the music. Another chorus from Opus 27 begins 'Thou shalt make no graven image'. Music is the imageless art and was excluded from that prohibition. That is no doubt the key to the relationship between Judaism and music. But at the historical stage of *musica ficta, stile rappresentativo* and of expressive music which makes sensuous something other than itself, music had become interwoven with the pictorial arts throughout Europe. The progressive unity of the arts, which stems from their rationalization, the increasing mastery of their materials, raised a protective zone around them, as the preserve of that mythic sphere which was condemned by rationalism as much as by the ban on images. Music learned to imitate.

By a profound irony Schoenberg was forced unconsciously to pay his tribute to this process. Aaron, the man of images and mediation, has to sing in the opera, but makes use of language without images. Moses, on the other hand, who represents the principle of the ban on images, does not sing in Schoenberg, but just speaks. The only way in which he can dramatize the Old Testament taboo is by making him communicate in a manner which is not really possible according to the biblical story. Such a change – and it is not the only one – would be of no significance in an ordinary text. Here, however, where the subject matter dons the authority of a sacred text, it verges on heresy. It highlights the crisis of an art which makes use of this text purely as art and of its own free will. But the intractable task of the music to provide an image of the non-pictorial could well overcome the master's matter-of-factness.

To that extent matter-of-factness is his metaphysics. Music should not be an ornament, he once wrote, it should be true, and it may well be thought that in his eyes the pictorial character of music finally succumbed to Loos's verdict that ornament is a crime.[3] Despite this he did not violently do away with the

---

3. Adolf Loos (1870–1933) was an architect and an influential theorist associated with the Secession. His pamphlet *Ornament and Crime* first appeared in 1908.

expressive side of art which history had had branded into it and which it could no longer rid itself of. The pathos which swirls through the entire work and which vividly proclaims what its true goal would like to be had its source in the expressive needs of Schoenberg's own past. It stamps its imprint on countless details, as was also true, incidentally, of the authentic sacred music of earlier periods – Bach's, for example. But in Schoenberg's case the expressive aspect is peculiarly discontinuous, since what is expressed is not the composer who stands behind the score and expresses himself through it, but the *dramatis personae*. This both relativizes it and incorporates it in a totality which crucially aims to go beyond expressiveness, at any rate beyond the artist's own expressiveness. Schoenberg's remarks about Mahler's Ninth Symphony could equally well define the canon of his own works:

> In this symphony the author hardly speaks any longer as a subject. . . . This work no longer speaks in the first person. What it offers is what might be called objective, almost dispassionate statements of a beauty which is only perceptible to those who can dispense with animal warmth, and feel at home in an atmosphere of cool intellectuality.[4]

A third factor – the operatic form – has occupied the space between composer and composition. Schoenberg may have been influenced in his choice of form by the consideration that subjectivity cannot be sidestepped musically and that it is inappropriate for a sacred work. It is reduced to something of secondary importance, a medium. It is no longer the composer who expresses himself, but protagonists and antagonists. In the interplay between them the musical objectivity of the whole comes to life. This is why the most sensuous of all musical forms has been used for a project devoid of sensuousness. The opera *Moses und Aron* is *musica ficta*, but elevated to a different plane

---

4. Arnold Schoenberg, 'Gedenkrede über Gustav Mahler', Prague 1913. The most complete version available is printed in *Forum* 79/80, Vienna 1960, pp. 277 ff. (Quoted by Walther Vetter, 'Über ein Spätwerk Gustav Mahlers', *Deutsches Jahrbuch der Musikwissenschaft* 6, Leipzig 1962, p. 21.) [Adorno's note.]

[*aufgehoben*]. The pictorial aspect of music from which the idea of the non-pictorial work recoiled, is now shifted on to the individual figures, as if the non-pictorial might result from their demise. As if – for the success of such a manoeuvre is itself a fiction.

We may legitimately ask what produced the conception of this work in the light of such immense difficulties, which may be compared to those experienced twenty years before in connection with *Die Jakobsleiter*. It is not the product of that misconceived monumentality, that unlegitimated gesture of authority which marks so much of the pictorial arts of the nineteenth century, from Puvis de Chavannes down to Marées. Of course it was Schoenberg's own individual make-up that provided the critical impetus. His parents do not seem to have been orthodox in their beliefs, but it may be supposed that the descendant of a family of Bratislava Jews living in the Leopoldstadt, and anything but fully emancipated, was not wholly free of that subterranean mystical tradition to be found in many of his contemporaries of similar origins, men such as Kraus, Kafka and Mahler.

The Enlightenment displaced the theological heritage, shifting it on to the plane of the apocryphal, as we can infer from Schoenberg's own autobiographical remarks. In particular, superstition survived tenaciously in his life and he often reflected on it. It is doubtless an instance of secularized mysticism. The experience of pre-fascist Germany, in which he rediscovered his Jewish roots, must have released this repressed dimension of his nature. *Moses und Aron* was composed directly before the outbreak of the Third Reich, probably as a defensive reaction to what was about to sweep over him. Later, even after Hitler's fall, he did not return to the score. A central section of the work, the Dance round the Golden Calf, was performed for the first time a few days before his death. But the penetrating depth of Schoenberg's music, the limitless intensification of its claims to truth, have latent theological implications that go well beyond such biographical data.

In the Quartet in F-sharp minor of 1907/8, a work which Schoenberg may never have surpassed, the ascent to the breakthrough, above all in the finale with its message from 'another planet'[5] has a power and authenticity which is equalled only by Mahler. Schoenberg's own need to express is one that rejects mediation and convention and therefore one which names its object directly. Its secret model is that of revealing the Name. Whatever subjective motive lay behind Schoenberg's choice of a religious work, it possessed an objective aspect from the very outset – a purely musical one in the first instance. Many years ago an essay by Heinrich Jalowetz, a former student of his, who is now dead, but who during his lifetime was one of the most perceptive connoisseurs, made the point that Schoenberg's works, as the only relevant *œuvre* of his age, comprehended all the genres and that this is connected in an essential way with their substance.

In this respect too Schoenberg is the opposite of Stravinsky who linked the significant with the specialized in furtherance of his policy of permanent refusal. Schoenberg's works exploded and melted down all the formal categories from which traditional music had hoped to create a self-contained, rounded totality that denied the existence of anything outside its own cosmos. But it is no less true that despite his destructive tendency, he always had a totality in view. For its sake he left to one side everything that merely laid claim to totality, instead of creating one. His relation to the tradition of Viennese Classicism is that he remained faithful to the idea of totality and defended it tenaciously against imitations, behaving as if the aim of his compositions was to recreate the language of music in toto. The call for internal consistency in each individual work, to a degree that went far beyond anything previously achieved, the ideal of integral composition, was that of musical totality. Self-contained and free-floating, it tended towards the absolute, like the philosophical systems of a bygone age. And as in these the theological legacy becomes fused with the task, inherited from the past, of creating that absolute just once more, but this time in freedom and within

---

5. 'I feel the air from another planet', from Stefan George's poem 'Entrückung' [Rapture], which is used in the fourth movement of the Quartet.

man himself. Every music that aims at totality as a simile of the absolute has its theological dimension, even if it is unaware of it and even if it becomes anti-theological by virtue of presenting itself as a creation.

At the end of the history of musical integration this theological dimension emerges into the full light of day. But the compulsion to do so is purely musical. If music is to satisfy its own norms of logic and stringency – norms which have acquired their shape in the course of its tradition of rationalization – it must strive to achieve complete consistency, to become a seamless web, in short a totality. Anything which could not be integrated would be an artistic flaw. The denser the texture, the less able it is to tolerate protest and auditory distraction and the more authoritarian it becomes. The absolute determination of every detail makes it resemble willy-nilly the manifestation of the absolute, and this remains true even when, in accordance with Schoenberg's theological convictions but contrary to the great philosophical tradition, it denies that essence can become manifest.

This internal musical compulsion is joined by a further one, the thrust of stylistic tradition. This exerts pressure on the content of expression. The intention of Schoenberg's music is that each bar should be made substantive by means of the musical concretion of what transpires within it. This runs parallel, as has been repeated *ad nauseam*, for the most part with pharisaical disapproval, to the reduction to the isolated individual existing purely for himself. In fact the more zealously the late phase of individualistic society to which Schoenberg belongs collectivizes its individuals, the less that individualism is overcome. The spiritual content available at such a stage of consciousness cannot be anything else but that of the individual expressing himself. Hence the definition of Schoenberg's music as an extreme example of musical Expressionism, a description which ac-companied it to the threshold of twelve-note technique. It is this, rather than his personal contacts, which were certainly not lacking, that established him as the musical Expressionist *par excellence*.

But even though the stance of being-for-oneself immeasurably strengthens the power of the individual, it is also a curse that he cannot shake off, because it has its source in an objective fact – namely, the solitude which is inscribed in society as a whole. Authentic expression probably only exists as the expression of negativity, of suffering. In music one would only have to compare the quality of sad pieces and the impotence of joyful works of whatever kind. The more inexorably the overwhelming might of the world forces the subject back on to himself, and on to his detached being-for-self, and the more he is forced to postulate himself, then the more painful the substance he expresses and the more he becomes a negative being in his own eyes.

Like the Expressionists, Schoenberg discovered this in the sphere of his most intimate experience – namely, in love. For the unhappy consciousness love becomes a misfortune.[6] The climax of despair in the Quartet in F-sharp minor coincides with the words from George's poem, 'Take love from me and give me thy happiness'.[7] Schoenberg was decisively influenced by Strindberg. It was in his spirit that he composed the setting to those words and it is from him that his expressiveness and his sense of form drew their sustenance. This reveals that the difference between Strindberg and neo-Romanticism, on whose lyric poetry Schoenberg drew for inspiration, is by no means as great as it appeared in the disputes between the rival schools. An instance may be found in the way in which the poems of the conservative Rudolph Borchardt, who detested everything connected with Strindberg, nevertheless reverberate with the battle of the sexes. Something of this, as well as of the attitudes of Weininger, accompanied Schoenberg throughout his life.[8] The man who

---

6. The 'Unhappy Consciousness or the Alienated Soul' is Hegel's term for the religious man in the Judaeo-Christian tradition, who can neither fully embrace earthly existence, nor entirely separate himself from it. See G.W.F. Hegel, *The Phenomenology of Mind*, Chapter IV.

7. From the poem 'Litanei' which Schoenberg uses in the third movement of the Quartet.

8. Otto Weininger (1880–1903), was the author of a rabidly misogynist treatise *Geschlecht und Charakter* [Sex and Character] which appeared in 1903, the year in which he took his own life.

celebrated free love in his youth later developed repressive sexual attitudes. These colour *Moses und Aron* in which mono-theism's hostility to polygamy is emphasized and the idea of the One Spirit places a taboo on a plurality of instinctual drives which for their part are regarded as part of the amorphousness of nature.

This is not the least of the reasons for classifying the work as belonging to that part of the artistic tradition which, hardly to its credit, always applauded the historical power of a victorious status quo. In Schoenberg's development, as in Strindberg's, this negative version of expression, this personal suffering, gets carried away to the point where it becomes negative theology, a conjuring up of that objectively all-embracing, conciliatory meaning which is denied to an absolute subjectivity for which there is no escape. In authentic artists this dialectic in the object is no mere external matter of attitude, a question of a conversion. The harsh Expressionist visions of loneliness, which Schoenberg painted, literally, around 1910 also resemble phantoms of transcendence. Ghostly, disembodied figures appear like ter-rifying emissaries from another world. In the Quartet in F-sharp minor the individual, bereft of hope, breaks down and, without any transition, the imago of his ecstasy answers him.

Schoenberg's conversion to theology means that he would like to negate the message of negation which the historical con-juncture proclaimed to him. The element of truth in this is that by defining itself as negative, his approach implicitly postulates the positive. But the existence of that positivity is not guaranteed by a mere postulate. The latter is simply a reflex reaction to a false reality, its inverted mirror-image in the mind. It is not anything which exists in and for itself. Since it is a chimera, it remains marked by the false. This is no less evident in the positive language of music than in the leap from negative to positive theology. Schoenberg's sacred opera is unable to eliminate the autonomous individual whom it aims to supersede.

The integrative power of the work does not resolve the contradictions inherent in the situation. At first sight its most striking feature is its peculiarly traditional effect, for all its reservations towards the tradition. In theory the only person able to meet the challenge posed by *Moses und Aron* would be the one who could separate out and then piece together again what is traditional about it and what is not. The reluctant Classicism, the harmony of the whole, scarcely harmonizes with the musical means which are deployed. Nor indeed does it chime in with the idea of something sacred which only comes into being by force, rather than being present as an ontological given, confronting mere appearance as an immovable essence. In Schoenberg's comic opera, which technically paved the way for *Moses und Aron*, a gulf had opened up between the ineluctably tragic methods he deployed, which were dissonant in a double sense, and the serenity he aspired to. In the biblical work, in contrast, the stylistic principle, the method of objectification, had a moderating effect. It draws the sting from the individual dissonances and piles up everything which speaks of suffering as if it were made of stone.

The simplest way to describe the general effect is to say that the music is dissonant from the first bar to the last, but that it does not sound dissonant for a single second. Even though Schoenberg's transposition of the expressive vocabulary into musical material is magnificent, there can no doubt that it is neutralized in the process. This is achieved technically by an unprecedented art of disposition which distributes the complex sonorities so as to eliminate any friction between them. By establishing sound relationships vertically, he does away with what used to be achieved through harmony with the result that the distinction between consonance and dissonance is deprived of its *raison d'être*. A total constructivism creates a lapidary style which is not all that far removed from neo-Classicism in its effects, even though its formal consciousness operates at an incomparably higher level. The pacifying, distancing effects inherent in twelve-note technique are elevated to a formal principle in the Old Testament opera. Without resorting to clichés it sometimes recalls the oratorio of the age of Bach and Handel, simply by virtue of its musical stance and the logic of its approach. An instance is to be found in the arioso-like melody of the Priest at the beginning of Act II, Scene 1: 'For forty days we have been lying here'. There are even echoes of the choral double fugue, as in Act I, Scene 2, 'Do ye bring an answer, a message from the new god?'. All that contributes to a certain overall static effect, not to mention the undisputed primacy of the whole over the parts, which are held fast in the composer's iron grip.

The paradoxical traditionalism of a work which would like to eliminate everything which it cannot fully derive from its components is not created by the occasional quotation but by its general characteristics, the very things which are not affected by the process of integration. Here, where the composer's imagination apparently enjoys unlimited scope, the traditional elements stored up in his mind come to the fore: emphatic declamation, the contrast between a *cantus firmus* and its counterpoint, the oratorio-like autonomy of the chorus and, finally, the trajectory of the singing parts. We should also include here expressive tempo modifications – ritardandi, stentato, accelerando and the like. They are handled in familiar ways and serve the same functions as in the past; they guarantee the comprehensibility of the music. From them we may learn what inspired the younger generation of composers to integrate temporal relationships in their works: despite its liberation, it was precisely the element of time that was still unfree in twelve-note music, the vestige of a musical language which was still burdened by a meaning incompatible with the new constructivity. But in *Moses und Aron* the archaic element is the consequence of mastery. We are no longer shocked by the virtuosity with which Schoenberg dominates his music, cutting away all unruly elements, smoothing it over and ensuring that he has total control. This is why the eruptive, expressive passages become images, metaphors of expression in a double sense. They are put in their place by the overall plan, domesticated and made inauthentic.

The same is true of timbre which is integrated into the construction of *Moses und Aron* to a greater degree than almost any other of his works. Timbre is not just completely emancipated so as to become one available resource among others. Here Schoenberg, who was one of the greatest orchestrators, liberated it from the sense of strangeness which had characterized its use in many of his earlier works. This work tempts one into heretical speculations about the concept of skill itself. In his Expressionist phase Schoenberg did not regard the idea of skill with any favour and wrote that it was necessary to free oneself from the belief that technique was the sole road to salvation. Later, however, he reinstated the concept of musical technique in all its rigour. And with reason: without technique conceived as something other than the essence of what is realized in the components of the music itself, music can never be valid. But alongside this the concept of skill also contains the idea of being able to do it the way it has to be; and by making the work the way it has to be it becomes something else. To have to be this particular thing would imply transcending every apparatus of compulsion. It would be a truly realized freedom. The a priori impossibility of sacred art today and the problematic nature of skill regarded as something which aspires to perfection form a perfect fit in the *Moses* opera.

The knowledge of the way something should be also influences the style of a work. With the vestiges of a naivety which is perhaps indispensable he puts his trust in proven methods. Not that he is tempted to resort to formulae in order to revive or renew sacred music. But he does strive for a balance between the pure musical development and the desire for monumentality, much as Wagner had done. He too extended his critique of the musical theatre to the bounds of what was possible in his day. But at the same time he wanted the larger-than-life as evidence of the sacred. He deluded himself into believing that he would find it in myths. They are inaccessible to the subjective imagination that aspires to the monumental while suspending the traditional canon of forms which alone would create it.

Moses und Aron is traditional in the sense that it follows the methods of Wagnerian dramaturgy without a hiatus. It relates to the biblical narrative in just the same way as the music of the *Ring* or *Parsifal* relate to their underlying texts. The central problem is to find musical and dramatic methods whereby to represent the idea of the sacred – that is to say, not a mythical but an anti-mythical event. The Wagnerian realm of the passions, however, is not that of the theology in which *Moses und Aron* has its being. Schoenberg's aim in transposing the work into the sphere of passion was to rescue it from statuesque illusion. But in so doing, he humanized that superhuman element which alone legitimated the monumental style.

On the other hand, the musical and dramatic style was less advanced than the most radical Schoenbergian works. Curiously, the *Moses*, like the earlier humorous opera, ignores the fact that in *Erwartung* and *Die glückliche Hand*, Schoenberg had dismissed the constituents of the Wagnerian music drama. The non-repeatability of atonal cells is essentially hostile to the architectonic and the monumental. The literal nature of the musical expression rejected the stylization which acts as a filter to expressiveness in Wagner and brings about a reduction in scale. But if the white-hot language of Schoenberg's musical Expressionism really did become musical substance in the integral construction of the *Moses*, it is no less true that the vocabulary of expression which is required by his musical ideal has retreated into the distance.

The traditional cut of the individual components is dictated by such dramaturgical calamities. Because the drama retains what the music can no longer spontaneously give, whether as expression or as construction, the expressive components of the music drama are infiltrated and taken over as conserves from the tradition. The new language of music, entirely renovated to its innermost core, speaks as if it were still the old one. This is particularly true of the pathos which is extracted from the specifically Jewish inflection and the patriarchal nature of the principal figure. The posture of command, which is as alien to the expression of suffering as to the distanced construction, has to be introduced into the substance of the music from outside, as a reminiscence of the pathos of the traditional music drama.

It is inspiring to see with what overwhelming power Schoenberg has succeeded in overcoming the recalcitrant nature of his material in order to accomplish this at the very moment when such pathos had become an anachronism. Today our sensibilities rebel against this because it seems forced and affected – that is the price he paid for using such conserved material. It is not unlike the biblical pictures from Chagall's late period, in which the theological symbols have ceased to have substance, to represent the truths of the objective spirit. Instead they depend on the subjective imagination to dredge them up, as if from the collective memory, luminous like fairy tales and yet with a slightly decorative aftertaste, as with a picture of childhood bathed in nostalgia. These aspects of Schoenberg which – inevitably – share in this amount to a negation of the over-specific idea of the work as a whole. The aesthetic drive towards sensuous expression works to the detriment of what that drive brings into being.

In a very striking fashion the principle of the music drama cuts across the overall plan of the work. The Wagnerian pattern and identity of the musical language which is doubly sustained throughout the work by the method of construction, cannot accommodate what the subject matter requires above all: the strict separation of Moses's monotheism from the realm of myth, the regression to the tribal gods. The pathos of the music is identical in both. This indicates how closely the problems of style and of the realized shaping of the work are intertwined. Both factors point back towards the content. In Wagner's case the unified vocabulary and construction, like that of epic narrative, was appropriate, since the events all took place in the realm of guilt and of entrapment in the coils of myth, from which there is no escape. In Schoenberg the vicious circle was to be broken: the caesura was to be decisive. The rupture was to become music. The undifferentiated unity from which the ruthless process of integration allows nothing to be exempted, comes into collision with the idea of the One itself. Moses and the Dance round the Golden Calf actually speak the same language in the opera, although the latter must aim to distinguish between them.

This brings us close to the source of traditionalism in Schoenberg, an issue which has only started to become visible in recent decades and especially since his death. In his eyes the idea of musical vocabulary as the organ of meaning was still instinctive and unquestioned. This vocabulary imagined itself able to articulate everything at any time. But this assumption was shaken by Schoenberg's own innovations. The radical separating out of all the features and elements of the composition no longer allows them direct access to that kind of universality which had accompanied the tonal system and its quasi-conceptual treasure house of forms for so long. But this implies that the quasi-linguistic configurations which presuppose the universal validity of the stock of tonal forms can no longer go unquestioned. It is as if a language were to continue to be spoken with its long-accustomed intonations despite fundamental changes of its core. This introduces a fictional element into the actual construction which so energetically opposes one.

The situation points back to an illusion from which the bourgeois spirit has never been able to free itself: that of the unhistorical immortality of art. It forms a perfect complement to that decorative stance from which the Schoenbergian innovations had effected their escape. The belief in genius, that metaphysical transfiguration of bourgeois individualism, does not allow any doubt to arise that great men can achieve great things at any time and that the greatest achievements are always available to them. No doubt can be permitted to impugn the category of greatness, not even for Schoenberg. A justified scepticism towards that belief, which is based on a naive view of culture as a whole, is to be found in that specialization which Schoenberg rightly opposed on the grounds that it acquiesced in the division of labour and renounced that extreme of the aesthetic, the sole legitimation of art.

In Schoenberg's fragmentary main works – the term 'main work' is itself symptomatic – there is something of the spirit that Huxley castigated in one of his early novels. The greatness, universal validity, totality of the masters and masterpieces of yore – all this can be regained if only you are strong enough and have the genius. This has something of the outlook that plays off Michelangelo against Picasso. Such blindness about the philosophy of history has causes rooted in the philosophy of history itself. They are to be found in the feeling of an inadequate sense of authority, the shadow-side of modern individuation. To overcome this blindness would mean relativizing the idea of great art even though great art alone can provide the aesthetic seriousness in whose absence authentic works can no longer be written.

Schoenberg has actually rendered visible one of the antinomies of art itself. The most powerful argument in his favour is that he introduced this antinomy, which is anything but peculiar to him, into the innermost recesses of his own *œuvre*. It is not to be overcome simply by an act of will or by virtue of the power of his own works. The fallacy that it is necessary to depict or negotiate the weightiest subject matter in order to produce the greatest works of art – a fallacy which puts an end to the Hegelian aesthetics – derives from the same misconception. The elusive content is to be captured by chaining it to the subject matter which, according to tradition, it once inhabited. A futile endeavour. The prohibition on graven images which Schoenberg heeded as few others have done, nevertheless extends further than even he imagined. To thematize great subjects directly today means projecting their image after the event. But this in turn inevitably means that, disguised as themselves, they fail to make contact with the work of art.

With all this the crucial question about *Moses und Aron* is what Schoenberg made of the work despite everything. It is the question about the possibility of the impossible, of the salvation of the work, to use an outmoded term. To discover what could be achieved it is necessary to turn to the work's specificity, its inner construction. Schoenberg's aversion to the concept of style, his liking for concrete shape is vindicated by such a scrutiny. However much *Moses und Aron* was plagued by the idea of the *chef d'œuvre*, it actually is his masterpiece, a masterpiece *quand même* and for the last time. The traditional concept of mastery has been undermined, but the opera satisfies its conditions. What it lacks as unprecedented achievement is compensated for by the fact that the music is in command of itself as never before and achieves the identity of intention and composition with unwavering assurance. All his energies come together at once: his most fundamental inspiration and his most complete articulation,

articulation of the kind that had crystallized out in his orchestral works, that ability to go all out which was not just the legacy of Beethoven, but his own musical reflex, the form which distinguishes him from all other music of his own age.

In *Moses und Aron* it is necessary to imagine the symphonic *élan* of *Die glückliche Hand* and *Die Jakobsleiter* as being combined with the polyphonic organizing power which he had honed in the twelve-note works that preceded the biblical opera. This led to a monumentality of tone over and above the pathos of the actual declamatory style. It arises directly, probably most compellingly, in the final scene of Act II and the last scene to be composed: the scene of Moses's return. This monumentality of tone, however, as it is to be found in the last section of that scene, accompanied by a single instrumental strand, does not fit the convention of great simplicity. At the risk of creating a primitive misunderstanding, it could be said rather that such monumentality is concerned with everything which is gathered together in this music and which occupies the musical space. The attentive ear must behave much like someone entering a church who finds his gaze jerked upwards towards the roof. This would suggest that monumentality is synonymous with extreme polyphony, a pure consequence of the internal compositional method, independently of the accompanying gesture.

Complexity is achieved early on. In the first scene it is already present with the entry of the chorus on '*dem einzigen Gott verbunden*' ['joined to the one God'], but this is immeasurably increased in Scene 3, the Annunciation. This complexity can be heard undiminished, undisguised, but it does not announce itself as such. It is this perhaps that points to the true secret of monumentality. Like everything of musical significance, it has its technical aspect and this is manifested in a variety of procedures. The simplest is the gradual increase in polyphonic density, in line with the intensification of the dramatic conflict. In no other work does Schoenberg so consistently and with such facility follow the rule that the compositional effort – that is to say, in the first place the sheer quantity of simultaneous events – should correspond to the content of the music, of the events to be represented. In *Moses* he takes this to extremes. Nowhere else is there so much music, almost in the literal sense of so many notes, as here *ad majorem Dei gloriam*. The sheer density of the construction becomes the medium in which the ineffable can manifest itself without usurpation. For it is this that can be wholly and convincingly created in the material by Schoenberg's own musical consciousness.

The formal energy matches the wealth of ideas. Organized through to the last detail, the whole work is articulated in such a lucid manner that the overwhelming complexity is made to appear quite manageable, thanks to the clear, internal dividing lines. In contrast to the tradition of continuous setting *Moses und Aron* leans towards the intermittent and segmented. In later phases of twelve-note technique this approach was extended to orchestral works. The division into scenes and into often very brief segments which are sharply distinguished from each other, and above all the relative autonomy of the choral sections, is not ordained from above. It follows directly from the structure itself. In the form in the narrower sense, too, in the organization of time, the overall structural principle and the autonomous vitality of individual detail are in perfect equilibrium.

In an unmistakable and deliberate way the declamatory sequences resemble the old-style oratorio. It is an astonishing *tour de force* to see how, despite the Wagnerian dramaturgy, the score eliminates the unending melody in favour of a compositional saturation, without casting a nostalgic glance back to the number opera. This mode of articulation is strengthened by a procedure Schoenberg had tried out in *Von heute auf morgen*. This was the alternation between quasi-recitative and less open-ended forms. Even in Wagner, beneath the surface, something of this division can be discerned. It would seem that over very long stretches it is simply not possible to ensure that every bar is equidistant from the centre, the product of an equal rigour, as had once been Schoenberg's ideal. For such compositional saturation would tend towards monotony.

It goes without saying that the recitatives are not set apart from the overall structure; the row makes sure of that. Even its independent elements are given shape. Nevertheless, the tension between expression and construction, which is the source of the vitality in Schoenberg's music and which is thematized in *Moses und Aron*, if we may put it that way, actually creates the form by means of the contrast between the recitative and the coherently organized sections. Within the totality the recitative parts seem to function as a reminiscence of the vocabulary of the expressionistic Schoenberg, where they represented the expressive element, while the coherent complexes represent the constructivist side. The alternation between the two does more than create a breathing space; it enables the music to get to grips with whatever cannot be subsumed in any smooth unity by turning it into the principle governing the musical flow.

The unity of *Moses und Aron* is created by its strictly sustained dualism. The organized complexes are rounded off not just by their use of polyphony, but by their rhythmic structure. They are frequently built over sharply defined rhythmic models like the one in 6/8 time from the Dance round the Golden Calf. They are then drawn in their turn into the developing variation. The more homophonous, recitative segments, however, follow old Expressionist traditions and remain free of repetitions. The more formal movements too vary. There is no lack of relatively simple and even, at the beginning, chordal complexes. The function of the orchestra as a whole is that of an accompaniment, apart from the dance pieces of Act II, which are again segmented. Schoenberg's preferred method is to divide the orchestra into a main, polyphonic section and a supporting one.

The other side of the coin is the very full use made of tonal space. As in all his vocal works, the voices are always main parts. It is out of consideration for them that the independent orchestral melodies tend to be placed either high up, above the singing voice, or else as low as possible, so that however dense the orchestral texture, the singing voice can always penetrate through their instrumental doublings. Characteristic, too, are both the jagged and elongated contours of the violin melodies. In *Moses und Aron* Schoenberg's orchestral technique shows him to be the disciple of Mahler, with whom he has nothing in common from the point of view of musical idiom. The concern with clarity, with what might be called the effect, becomes productive for the composition as such. The unmistakable tone of the opera is created by his concern that everything that takes place should be audible, by that unprecedented transparency of even the most complex sounds, thanks to the use of every available register. It is infinitely differentiated and yet at the same time a unity. It is as remote from the monumentalizing mannerism of baldly contrasted segments and sound families as it is from the diffuse sounds of the Neo-German and Impressionist schools. The fairly modest orchestral forces generate unsuspected energies in the hands of the master, since they are led by profound experience to meet him halfway.

Their productive clarity serves to enhance the melody. Indeed, in harmony with an undisputed tradition, its primacy is maintained. Schoenberg's compositional ideal is no more willing to sacrifice the substantiality of melody to stylistic considerations than it would abandon the primacy of thought. But the warmth and expansiveness of the melodic line, which flows more freely in *Moses und Aron* than at any time since his youth, is controlled in a completely novel way. How he does so has yet to be analysed. The melody appears to develop from the rhythm of language and its asymmetry. Basic rhythmic figures are thematized in the row, bursting with energy to discharge themselves in the form of melody. Once the initial vivid models have been formulated, the line of development never falters. It continues without eroding the distinction between initial statement and development. The adoption of the prose-like language rhythm, together with the necessity of discovering characteristic figures which are especially well defined rhythmically, gives particular prominence in *Moses und Aron* to this language rhythm as a means of articulation. But Schoenberg never confuses rhythmic primitiveness, emphasis of accents, with rhythmic imagination. Above all else the Dance round the Golden Calf simply had to ignite his imagination. Without any percussive monotony, it hits home with maximum force.

By conceptualizing this we have probably arrived at the full

247

measure of Schoenberg's success in his biblical opera. It is intensified by what seems at first to stand in its way: the inordinate
complexity of the music. This leads to the liberation of Schoenberg's supreme talent, his gift for combination, his precise grasp
of distinct but simultaneous events. The idea of unity in diversity
becomes a sensuous musical reality in him. He was able not just to
imagine, but actually to invent complexes of opposed extremes,
which yet occur simultaneously. In this respect he represents the
culmination of the tradition in which every detail is composed.
This talent reveals his metaphysical ingenuity. The unity of what
he had imagined truly does justice to the idea which forms the
subject of the text. The striking effect and the unity of the
disparate are one and the same. Hence the simplicity of the end
result. The complexity is nowhere suppressed, but is so shaped as
to become transparent. If everything in the score is clearly heard,
its very clarity means that it is heard as a synthesis.

In *Die glückliche Hand*, which comes the closest to *Moses und
Aron* as regards complexity, layers or bands were superimposed
upon each other. Here they are transformed into actual lines.
Instead of superimposed layers we now have an interlocking
totality. But the fact that the combinatorics are not, as the stereo-
typed criticism of Schoenberg would have it, intellectual excogi-
tations, but are instead sensuous realities, and the fact that they
live in the imagination, in the living idea, is something more than
a subjective, psychological aspect of the process of composition.
It stands in the profoundest relationship to the substance of the
music. When Schoenberg was once asked about a piece that had
not yet been performed, 'So you haven't heard it yourself?', he
replied, 'Yes, I have. When I wrote it.' In such a process of the
imagination, the sensuous is directly spiritualized without losing
any of its concrete specificity. What was realized in the imagination thereby became an objective unity. It is as if Schoenberg's
musical mind recapitulated that movement from the tribal gods
to monotheism, the story of which is encapsulated in *Moses und
Aron*. If our epoch refuses to vouchsafe to us a sacred work of art,
it does at its close give birth to the possibility of something under
whose gaze the bourgeois age was ushered in.   (1963)

248

Music and New Music

In memory of Peter Suhrkamp

> What is best in the new responds to an ancient need.
> Paul Valéry, *Rhumbs*

In one of my last conversations with Peter Suhrkamp he remarked on the titles of a number of the pieces in my *Klangfiguren* and commented, 'Why do you still keep on talking about new music? People have long since abandoned such terms in the world of painting, whereas you cling desperately to this one in music.' I should like to reply to my late friend as best I may. Of course, I shall hardly be able to confine my comments simply to the question of nomenclature. It is clearly necessary to reproduce some of the complex considerations which the question raised, in the hope that I shall be able to get to the heart of the matter. To begin with, a term so well established inevitably becomes suspect. It presumably came into being in connection with the German title of the Internationale Gesellschaft für neue Musik [The International Society for New Music] which had begun from the early twenties to foster every trend in music which was making efforts to distance itself from the New German school, from Impressionism and from the vestiges of other nineteenth-century tendencies. Just how adventitious that name was is revealed by the English title of the very same organization, the International Society for Contemporary Music (ISCM), which replaces the polemical 'new' with the neutral, chronological 'contemporary'. It is the latter term which more aptly described its programmes.

If we were to review today what was performed at those festivals, only a very small proportion of it would be included in what we may nowadays think of as new music. There were countless concerti grossi and suites, wind serenades and other mechanical productions which would sound, once the superficial glaze of dissonance had been breached, just as old-fashioned and perhaps even more boring than anything by Raff or Draesecke. The only works to have retained any of the aura of strangeness, of something essentially different, which attached itself even to timid and compromised compositions forty years ago, are those which seemed eccentric at the time. This means the works of the Viennese school and the youthful pieces of Stravinsky and Bartok.

As a concept 'new music' seems to share the fate of growing old which has so often been its destiny in the past. The fact that people continue to use the term as if it referred to something self-contained and unrelated to what had gone before and what continues to fill the opera houses, concert halls and the ether, tends to erect a wall around the music itself and to neutralize it instead of promoting its cause. The expression actually provokes the idiotic question, 'Is this really music at all?' This is the question which enables the outraged listener to unburden himself of his own indignation by classifying the object of his hatred as a special case which may indeed have its own legitimacy, along with so much else that has stood the test of time, but which really only concerns the experts because it does not come into the category of music proper.

The concept of 'new music' simply confirms the way it is institutionalized in studios, special societies and concerts. Such organizations inadvertently negate its claims to truth and hence universal appeal, even though without them its cause would be hopelessly lost. We are reminded of the American division of musical programmes into 'popular' and 'classical', which serves up to the 'fans' what they want,[1] while relieving them of the trouble of making any choice other than between those simple

---

1. Adorno used the English words.

alternatives. In the meantime most of what the ISCM attacked has died a natural death, at least this side of the Iron Curtain, and no one imagines any longer that he ought to compose in the style of Bausznern and Hausegger, or Georg Schumann and Max Trapp, or even to include their junk in the concert repertoire. This suggests that the term has lost its point. Its emotional force no longer has an enemy to strike and its own usage cannot remain unaffected by its harmlessness.

Despite all this it is no accident that the epithet 'new' has survived in music and not in painting. It marks the fact of an abrupt, qualitative leap, whereas analogous changes in painting are distributed over a longer period and go much further back in time. Even in its most recent development music has proved to be a belated art, a 'latecomer'[2] who runs through the different phases all the more briskly. But the prime fact about the new music was that it signalled a change in the tonal system.

Painting has no direct equivalent to tonality. In painting the relationship to an object-world which is to be represented, a relationship which has been disrupted by the modern move-ment, goes back well beyond the age of tonality in music. Moreover it is not directly connected with the forms and colours which constitute the material of painting. It would appear that a musical language which renounces those features that have become second nature – the triads, the major and minor scales, the distinction between consonance and dissonance, and ulti-mately all the categories that spring from these – is far more exacting than the innovations in painting. It is doubtless true that these developments in music did not come about overnight and can be traced back over a hundred years, to *Tristan*. It is no less true that the elements and problems of the new music are all rooted in the musical tradition.

But none of this alters the fact that for the majority of people, thanks to their experiences ever since their early childhood, their education and the overwhelming predominance of everything that inundates them in the name of music, the new music is

---

2. Adorno used the English word.

experienced as something which deviates from their fixed notions as to what constitutes music. Their listening habits, which suffice in their view to enable them to deal with everything from Monteverdi to Richard Strauss, do not give them access to Schoenberg, Webern or Boulez. The changes which have taken place in music are not simply a matter of style, content or the specific character of the works. There is really no comparison with earlier innovations, such as those of the Mannheim school, Viennese Classicism or Wagner.

This explains why, when confronted with the new music, the reductive argument that everything is subject to the historical process and that every new phenomenon was rejected at first, seems so impotent, hackneyed and self-serving. Even Strauss, whose boldest strokes were genuine caprioles which unquestionably dealt the system a severe blow, finished by reinforcing it all the more powerfully. The closing section of his otherwise brilliant *Elektra* is a case in point. The same may be said of Max Reger's pan-chromaticism, whose ceaseless modulations deprived the fixed key concept of its structural meaning. Nevertheless, in the construction of individual sonorities and their immediate relationships he maintains the traditional system and nowhere violates the sacrosanct taboos imposed by the listener's expectations.

It is doubtless the case that of all the works that have sailed under the flag of the new music, through its different phases right down to its latest manifestations in Darmstadt, only a few will have wholly satisfied its ideal of a language purified of the vestiges of tonality and organized exclusively in terms of its own elements, without regard to the traditional system. Apart from the products of the Viennese school, all the works which passed for the new music for forty years turn out to be permeated with the residues of tonality and to this day it is not yet clear whether music can or should even wish to divest itself of it entirely, if only as its negation, as long as it clings to such concepts as octave equivalences.

Nevertheless, it is not entirely wrong to have included in the canon of new music the compromising and especially the neo-Classicist works of the successors and imitators of Hindemith and Stravinsky. People felt that tonality was only vegetating, leading a sort of shadow existence, without any of the vigour of its former self. It often seemed to be appealed to by a consciousness that was looking for something to hold on to, an order inaccessible to itself. In this it was not unlike that deceptive similarity to models of the world of objects which Picasso made use of, and not just in his few neo-Classical years.

The irrevocable change continued to have its repercussions, even where people were unwilling to admit to its existence. Difficult though it may be to point to a particular year or a particular work as marking the end of tonality, it is nevertheless quite mistaken to insist, as well-intentioned and naive musicians frequently do, on the essential unity and continuity of all music and even on an unending dialogue of geniuses down the centuries, from Bach to Schoenberg.

Schoenberg and Berg rejected the word 'atonal' as defamatory. And indeed if it were interpreted literally, as music without tones, it would be utter nonsense. Yet Schoenberg's peculiarly conservative naivety may have played a role in leading him to repudiate a term which has as much to be said for it as a slogan as the Gueux in the remote past[3] and Dada almost fifty years ago. 'Atonal' registers with some precision the shock-waves caused by the new music. This shock was in fact an integral part of it and was moderated the instant that people began to replace atonality with twelve-note music, as if that were a completely new musical system. This aside, it may be said in Schoenberg's defence that he was also opposed to this reification of technique. After all, the reification only aimed to come to the aid of the ear which was drifting around helplessly on an ocean of new sounds, the discovery of which Webern ascribed to Schoenberg some fifty years ago. To speak of atonal music is still to express something more than the affirmative and dogmatic belief that the rows are

---

3. Les Gueux or ragamuffins. This was the nickname assumed by the first revolutionaries in Holland in 1665. When the Duchess of Parma asked Count Berlaymont about them, he told her they were 'the scum and offscouring of the people' (*les gueux*). This having been made public the revolutionaries took the name in defiance. See Motley, *Dutch Republic*, vol. 2, p. 6.

the source of a new feeling of security whose dubious nature has meanwhile become all too evident in philosophy.[4] Much recent music, especially the music that has been influenced by John Cage, could undoubtedly be called atonal rather than dodecaphonic.

The sociological merits of the term 'new music' also merit some scrutiny. For whereas there is scarcely any new musical production which has contrived to elude the pressure set up by the new music, the realms of reproduction and consumption have remained loyal to the tonal tradition, apart from those carefully segregated enclaves which are reserved for the new. It is this quarantining of the new music, this astronomic distance between its fully fledged idiom and the traditional language that promotes the ossification of the allegedly eternal language of music. It may be supposed that, with the division into highbrow and lowbrow music and its immediate continuation, the official world of music, rather less new music slips through the net than was the case before the different stages of the history of music had been compartmentalized.

Nor is this situation changed by elevating the classics of modernism to the pantheon where they are now the subject of occasional acts of worship. Such formal institutionalization only serves to distort their achievement. The all-powerful culture industry says, Stop! and confines itself to its unvarying constants, as in its non-musical media, above all the film. Thus the circle is closed. With the whole system tending towards encapsulation and rightly mistrustful of the truth, the culture industry is terrified of any unregimented sound, however impotent, just as in the Third Reich the authorities trembled at Marquis Posa's call for a modest freedom of thought.[5] The more problematic the overall situation has become in the light of the vast increase in

4. Adorno uses the term *Geborgenheit*, safety or security. In his eyes the term is questionable because of its central position in the existential philosophy of Martin Heidegger.
5. The Marquis von Posa is the idealistic hero of Schiller's *Don Carlos*. Although the Nazis attempted to promote Schiller as a German nationalist, his resounding calls for more freedom frequently had to be censored.

technical and human forces, the more it comes to constitute a threat to the very people who compose it. The more systematically every chance to improve matters is wasted and compromised by usurpers, then the greater are the efforts made to hammer into a helpless mankind the conviction that nothing can be other than it is and that the basic categories of present conditions are those of life itself, true and immutable.

This tendency extends its tentacles into the innermost recesses of cultural politics, even though individual organizations and responsible people may remain quite unconscious of what is happening. It is only too easy to justify this by reference to the intellectual opinions of the majority whose only desires are for the things with which they are being force-fed and who regard any attempt to unmask the deception as a threat to the very comfort in which they do not even wholeheartedly believe. The new music may continue to assert its own newness, but only as long as it refuses to join this vicious circle. Hence its critical and aesthetic self-understanding also has an objective social dimension.

But society's response also has a bearing on its content, regardless of whether its reception be thwarted or calculated in advance. It might easily be imagined that the mere fact of its nonconformism, of its inaccessibility to the mass of the population, is too abstract to tell us anything about its specific nature. The non-representational nature of music, a quality arising from its non-conceptual material, and its resistance to handy theses, allow free rein to even its more wayward products, and it has every reason to be grateful for this. Moreover, this is a defect it shares with every articulate art which refuses to allow itself to be reduced to the ignominious common denominator known as a 'statement'. But this does not at all imply that its content is neutral. The reactionaries of every kind who set up an organized protest in the years before Hitler and who are now once again emerging from their bolt-holes, have understood this better than those friends of art who imagine that they are disseminating important insights into the new music by counting rows and other equally innocuous clerical services.

The new music suffers from the practised and the all-too-familiar, from which it differs so profoundly. It impotently takes up arms against the way of the world; its posture is aggressive. In its desire to submit only to its internal law and to mutiny against the law of demand, its subject, its potential being, which is concealed even from itself, expresses itself in highly concrete form. Its qualities become manifest in what it prohibits. This did not escape the notice of Schoenberg who would have been only too delighted to be a great composer like the predecessors he revered. When a Hollywood film mogul wanted to give him a contract to write some background music and greeted him with a compliment about his '*lovely music*', Schoenberg is said to have shouted at him in fury, 'My music is not lovely'.[6] He was not given the contract.

The aggression which the new music directs against the established norms even now, after thirty years, an aggression in which something of the violence of surrealist onslaughts still survives, has its own specific tone; it is a tone of menace. It has ceased to be the tone which expresses individual feeling. On the contrary, it has been brought about by bracketing out the subject. It is not for nothing that indignant readers' letters associate many compositions with catastrophes and panic. Among the more advanced scores today there are a number which sound literally as if they were 'out of this world',[7] as the Americans would say. This aggressive tone intensifies with the rigour with which an integrated construction refuses to communicate the homely traces of the humane. It stems from a correct perception of the reified alienation and depersonalization of the destiny imposed on mankind and of the inability of the human sensibility to modify that destiny.

The tone of the new music expresses its horror that even fear is no longer able to intervene between the subject and what is done to him: that destiny has become monstrous and overwhelming. Only through the imageless image of dehumanization can this music retain a hold on the image of humanity. Wherever it

---

6. In English in the original.   7. In English in the original.

follows the phrasemongers and sets out to serve mankind, perhaps by allowing man to speak directly, it puts a false gloss on the existing state of affairs and debases itself. Only with this mute utterance can it articulate itself. Only by taking the odium of dehumanization upon itself can it redeem the precept of autonomy, of the pure elaboration of the material in hand in all its aspects which has accompanied music throughout its subjective phase ever since it liberated itself from ritual. Only by ceasing to be 'lovely'[8] can it provide an intimation of beauty. Its gesture of menace is unmistakable when it discards its internal logic as a mere semblance [*Schein*] and throws itself on the mercy of chance. John Cage's Piano Concerto, whose only meaning and internal coherence is to be found in its rejection of every notion of coherent meaning, presents us with catastrophe music at its most extreme.

This change in social function has utterly transformed the nature of music. Bourgeois music was decorative, even in its greatest achievements. It made itself pleasant to people, not just directly, to its listeners, but objectively, going far beyond them by virtue of its affirmation of the ideas of humanism. It was given notice to quit because it had degenerated into ideology, because its reflection of the world in a positive light, its call for a better world, became a lie which legitimated evil. The effect of cancelling its contract reverberates in the most sensitive sublimations of musical form. Hence the right to speak of new music.

Nevertheless, it has its limitations. We become conscious of them when confronted by that hydra-headed question, 'Is that really music at all?' For the only way to answer it is with an emphatic, Yes. Nor does this answer need to confine itself to a tactical retreat to physical or psychological definitions, such as the assertion that new music, too, makes use of musical sounds, and not just noises, and that although these sounds are differently arranged, the arrangement has its own order. For in the meantime, the noises which had always acted as a yeast in the production of musical effects have been absorbed into the sound

---

8. In English in the original.

257

relationships by a continuous series of transitions and to an extent hitherto undreamed of.

This notwithstanding, the new music is still music because all its categories, though not identical with traditional categories, are in a sense identical with them – because in all of its refusals, in everything which it denies itself, the force of what is forbidden is stored up. It is mediated by professional expertise [*Metier*], a concept which ranks highly among its contemporary exponents, sometimes to the point of fetishism. Nothing is tolerated unless it is articulated down to the last note. If it is true that quality in music depends on whether a composition is exhaustively composed out, without any crude, unformed remnant, then it may be said that the new music satisfies this criterion in full measure.[9] And it cannot even take the credit for it. The disappearance of all syntactical and grammatical paradigms, of all lexical tokens, forces it unremittingly to generate connections from within itself, connections which no longer emanate from elsewhere, and if they did they would be dismissed as alien. For this reason it is only possible to do justice to the situation by dint of the most rigid technical control, technique being understood here in the radical sense of realization, not in the comfortable sense of the manipulation of allegedly tried and proven means. Nevertheless the strength to accomplish this is derived from whatever forces had organized all older music, frequently from behind the façade of tonality.

Equally important as this commitment to technique is the allergic reaction to even the remotest derivatives of traditional music. Nothing from the past is absorbed without first being deconstructed. This is most clearly demonstrated in electronic music, whose most consistent adherents eschew everything reminiscent of the usual sound effects and who strive to extract from the new material sounds that are peculiar to it and qualitatively different from the traditional instruments. But this

---

9. Cf. the radio discussion on Music for Young People broadcast by North German Radio in April 1959. In addition to Adorno Doflein, Oberborbeck, Vötterle and Warner took part. [Adorno's note.]

allergy towards the residue of the traditional musical language is the starting point of a new idiom. Nowadays we react incomparably more sensitively to anything false in the new music than we did thirty years ago. There is general agreement about this.

Riegl's thesis about the decay of the power to form a style is doubtless obsolete, in music as in painting. The growing convergence of all modern music, regardless of its country of origin, is a consequence of the situation. The more consistently an artist allows himself to be guided by this, without resolving to compose his music according to a preconceived general idea, the closer he will come to the idea of the style which extends beyond individual artists. Even today a canon of what is possible and what is impossible may already be discerned. Admittedly it is one which is no longer validated by society, but is hostile to social validation itself. The organization of time as space now becomes a serious preoccupation, whereas in Stravinsky it had still manifested itself as an 'as if', perhaps as the troubled dream of what was to come. Now serial manipulation is to make time malleable, to take it captive. No longer open-ended, it seems to have been made space-like. This is not the consequence of a violent process. But nor should we pass over in silence the profound difficulty that the time continuum is not literally 'simultaneous', as the rational organization of time would suggest. We can scarcely imagine it in isolation from its development from below, from its birth in the impulse of the moment.

This points objectively, in terms of the material of music, to the necessary place of the subject in music and hence the factor with which it has to come to grips in the present. We might speculate whether the integral rationality to which music aspires is at all compatible with the dimension of time, and whether rationality, as the power of the equal and quantitative does not actually negate the unequal and qualitative from which the dimension of time cannot be separated. It is not for nothing that all rationalizing tendencies, those in the real world even more than in aesthetics, aspire to the abolition of traditional procedures and hence, in effect, of history as well. The integration and total elaboration of time may well destroy it, as is not unfitting in an

259

age whose subjects increasingly relinquish their control over their memory. However that may be, these trends have their effect on what might be called the ontology of art. Whereas music comes closer to painting, Tachist painting draws nearer to music, right down to the plethora of individual significances – equivalent to the groups of notes or tones – and to the dynamic element, all of which was alien to traditional painting.

The new musical language is encoded as the positive negation of the traditional one, but it cannot be reduced to the triviality that composers simply wanted to do something new and different – a critical platitude that applies to everything and nothing and amounts simply to the tautology that in the history of art early developments are succeeded by later ones. What is meant, rather, is that the new music constitutes a critique of the old one. Its enemies are well aware of this and this is why they raise such a hullabaloo about the undermining of tradition. Hence anyone who identifies with the new music should stand by this critical element instead of striving for acceptance.

This is not a matter on which Schoenberg has given us his reflections. But he detested such famous nineteenth-century melodies as the stretta in *Trovatore*, because you know the main rhythmic motives after the first four bars and because it is an insult to the musical intelligence to repeat them so complacently. In responding in this way he intuitively revealed not just an attitude which implicitly informs every note of the new music, but also an objective state of affairs. For the ideological element in traditional music, its affirmative aspect, affects not only its general stance, its assertion that this is what music is and how it should be, but it also betrays itself in constant stupidities and incongruities. The works of the past, at least since the end of the Rococo, gain in importance in proportion to the resoluteness with which they give shape to their own negation, instead of concealing it behind the smooth surface of their sensuous flow. This is the basis of the greatness of Beethoven's last works.

It was as impossible to synthesize the tonal system and the individual musical impulse as to harmonize the bourgeois order with the interests and passions of its subjects. This has left its mark on every piece of traditional music that lays claim to such unity. The compulsion to establish a form by repeating entire complexes, the rigid, thing-like nature of the recapitulations, even in Brahms and Reger, is only the most obvious symptom of a failure which goes well beyond the will and the capacities of individual composers. The law of affirmation has long since ceased to provide standards of musical quality. Again and again composers of the stature of Schubert, Chopin, Debussy and Richard Strauss were seduced into sacrificing integrity of structure to the need to conciliate. The repugnance aroused by these insinuating, ingratiating gestures, which have wormed their way into even the greatest works, forms part of the pathos of a qualitatively new music.

The bourgeois musical tradition had always contained an element of incongruity. It offered an internal musical explanation for the discontinuity of music history, something which of course also has social implications. This discontinuity increased with rocket-like rapidity. More and more mediating historical links were consumed in accordance with the principle of an intensified rationality. But the discrepancies that arise from relinquishing control of the historical tendency, on the one hand, and the possibility of appropriating it through living experience, on the other, should not be misused in order to provide a vindication of those works which have not survived. Today the tradition has been definitively disrupted, but it was never free of internal fractures. This is why an account of the history of music since 1600 in terms of *Geistesgeschichte* [history of the spirit][10] is so inappropriate.

It is not the case that, starting from that caesura, music blindly progressed in an organic fashion. In fact, in harmony with the rationalizing tendencies of the bourgeois era, it strove at the same time to obtain control of itself. There is a programmatic strand proclaiming the primacy of the new which runs from Caccini's

---

10. *Geistesgeschichte* describes the way in which cultural phenomena become subsumed under a single spirit of the age [*Zeitgeist*], such as Gothic or Baroque, and are viewed as its direct manifestations. In consequence it tends to underplay, if not ignore, contradictions and conflicting tendencies.

Nuove Musiche right through to Wagner's art-work of the future. And even the Middle Ages played the Ars Nova off against the Ars Antiqua. This may suggest an explanation of the curious combination of autonomous composition and pedagogic exercise that characterizes some of Bach's most powerful instrumental works. They were conceived not simply as compositions, but also as exercises which would enable the composer to get such a grip on the musical material that the difference between it and the musical subject might one day vanish.

To the extent to which the new music, unlike the old, pursues this aim in full consciousness, it makes a reality of something of which traditional music could only dream. Though irreconcilable with that tradition, it yet keeps faith with it; though different from it, a link is preserved. The new music may well be understood as the effort to do justice to all that the sharpened ear of the composer finds unresolved or antinomial in traditional music. Tradition is not imitation, regression or straightforward continuation, but the ability to gain insight into challenges which remained unresolved and which left flaws behind in the music. The new music faces up to these challenges. It remains open whether its idea of music can be realized in an antagonistic reality, or whether by virtue of the totality of its logic it will simply reproduce the contradictions it has inherited, and whether this supreme reproduction of the contradictions is identical with the crisis of musical meaning. On its own music has no power over this.

That the new music is still music does not remove the inevitable doubt about whether it will ever gain such a wide audience as traditional music and whether its idiom and style have any prospects of becoming second nature as was the case with tonal music. Of course this assumes that this second nature was a piece of good fortune and not just a childish one. Such considerations, which place their trust in a philosophical god of history and leave future generations to take the decisions that we are evading in the here and now, are unworthy. They act out the attitude of the contemplative, neutral observer who believes that the truth resides in the historical moment and is spontaneously revealed to us.

Whether the new music should be gratified by the slow progress it makes in gaining acceptance is uncertain. It must doubtless fear and desire it in equal measure. But there can be no doubt that the anxiety about whether it will ever be able to compete in general popularity with the traditional music as it is now administered by the culture industry is sheer hypocrisy. It is based on the idea of an unbroken historical continuity and a linear progression of consciousness which is refuted by the new music's very existence, as indeed by the entire history of music. The very notion that tonality is natural is itself an illusion. Tonality did not exist from the outset. It established itself in the course of a laborious process which lasted far longer than the few centuries during which the hegemony of major and minor has prevailed. The music that preceded it, the Florentine Ars Nova, for example, is just as unnatural and just as alien to contemporary ears, as are the works of the late Webern or Stockhausen in the proud ears of the normal listener. The semblance of naturalness which serves to disguise historical relationships inescapably attaches itself to the mind that insists that the rule of reason is unimpaired while surrounded by a world full of persistent irrationality.

Tonality is probably as ephemeral as the order of reality to which it belongs. But on the other hand, the relationship between music and society should not be thought to be as static and harmonious as was imagined in the age of High Liberalism. It is not permissible to equate quality with social acceptance, on the model of a market society which rewards socially useful labour with success and even defines it. The substance of the new music is determined to a certain extent by its hostility towards the administered society. It is idle to prophesy whether it could be released from this antagonistic situation and safely transferred to the future. Even if that were not possible, it would not in itself constitute a judgement on it. The fetish of an artistic value that endures through the ages is itself a piece of ideology.

No less questionable, however, is whether history will continue as before and whether true worth will survive for posterity, as the common belief would have it. Just as traditional music has culminated in the synthetic illiteracy of the culture industry, it may well turn out that the extraordinary efforts which the new music makes and which it imposes on its audiences will come to grief on the rocks of barbarism. Its fate is not wholly in its own hands, but depends on whether it is possible to break through the fatedness of society, a fatedness before which every bar of its music stands as if hypnotized.

However, the solution is not to call – patiently or angrily – for an existence beyond society and its tensions, in line with the familiar market-based division into mass media and ivory tower. Music must not allow itself to be terrorized by the popular sociology which, with index finger raised in admonition, gives it to understand that its sense of responsibility is really an irresponsible *l'art pour l'art*. Nor should it let itself be intimidated by the more valid fear that it might relapse into Art Nouveau. The shadow of the antiquated, the splenetic mood of dogged blindness with which it burrows into a world of its own, is something that overwhelms all art nowadays which bears witness to the absolute negativity of the world, the world of Auschwitz. Whereas the truth is that it cannot bear witness to anything else except by making itself into an absolute. The theologians above all should be the first to be on their guard against a pharisaical attitude towards the new music, unless what they are secretly after is some sort of organizational glue.

When, as in Bach and Webern, music is offered up to God, should it not be perfectly self-contained rather than compliant in its commerce with men? Purely as a phenomenon music is much more than itself. Its transcendence is not externally preordained, but secreted within itself. Schubert's doubt that there is such as thing as cheerful music remains valid. The truth-content of music tolerates no positivity and it is only now that it incorporates this into its own intentionality, as a possible self-annulment. Music's ideal is finally to rid itself of the semblance [*Schein*] of the positive, as of the mythical web of delusion; but even to say this is perhaps over-positive. Nevertheless, that ideal is also perfectly practical. The alleged esotericism of the new music desires not only to help articulate its social content, which the language of society suppresses. It communicates through non-communication; it aims to blast away the things blocking mankind's ears which they themselves hasten to close once more. A loss of tension makes itself apparent as soon as it renounces that explosive factor which, to use Brecht's term, we may call 'distanciation' [*Verfremdung*]. The fact that it does not aspire to acceptance, and is unwilling to join the universe of consumer goods does not imply that it relinquishes a relationship with an audience. But that relationship is not infinitely adaptable. It is instead the permanent, albeit Sisyphean effort to open people's ears, to penetrate the anthropological sound barrier. Not even the alienation [*Entfremdung*] between man and music may be taken as plain fact, or be dialectically hypostatized. It contains the potential for the abolition of the alien.

Alienation becomes a provocation in electronic music. It is a veritable incitement to revive all the phrases about the evils of mechanization, the destruction of personality and dehumanization which have accompanied the new music ever since it did away with the tried and tested clichés for the tried and tested feelings. Every self-righteous appeal to humanity in the midst of inhuman conditions should be viewed with the very greatest suspicion. There are no words for the noble, the good, the true and the beautiful that have not been violated and turned into their opposite – just as the Nazis could enthuse about the house, its roof resting on pillars, while torture went on in the cellars.[11] The positive values have degenerated into a mere device to prevent anyone reflecting on the fact that none of them has been made real in practice. Anyone who is truly concerned about them feels unable to express them in words and feels compelled to deconstruct them when others venture to do so. He thereby puts himself in the wrong and gains a reputation as the foe of all that is noble, good, true and beautiful, thus strengthening the

---

11. Adorno points to the Nazi appropriation of German culture by alluding here to Mignon's song in Goethe's *Wilhelm Meister's Apprenticeship*, '*Kennst du das Land, wo die Zitronen blühen?* [Knowest thou the land where the lemon trees blossom?]. Its second stanza begins, '*Kennst du das Haus? Auf Säulen ruht sein Dach* [Knowest thou the house? On pillars rests its roof].

hegemony of evil. Anyone who wishes to speak of electronic music must draw attention to this vicious circle. Otherwise the whole ethical machinery will be set in motion and he will be sucked into it.

Nor should he be astonished to hear in tones of utter conviction that everything depends on people themselves, tones that set out to make us forget the extent to which people have become objects – namely, the objects of 'human relations'.[12] Needless to say, the public interest in electronic music is obscurely mixed up with the hobby element it contains. It profits from the ubiquitous replacement of ends, even spiritual ends, by means: by the pleasure taken in machines that work, the predominance of the how over the what. But even such assertions as this require caution. No art, not even the highly rationalized art of the present, is entirely transparent. It must be remembered that the products of purely unspiritual technical efforts may well be a proving ground for the cunning of reason, that is, the rationality of objective spiritual tendencies which would never be made real if pursued simply by the conscious subject rather than in terms of the concrete material.

More plausible is the suspicion that electronics, which after all developed as a technology independently of music, is external to music and that it has no internal relationship with the immanent laws of music. I have not myself worked in the realm of electronic music and so am not qualified by my own experience to pronounce on the relationship between electronic music and musical meaning. Moreover, I find the scientific aspect of art quite alien and am unable to forget that chief among the impulses underlying the new music was the onslaught on the stubborn power of a self-perpetuating reason, ambitious to control the whole of nature. Admittedly, its no less stubborn insistence on the immediacy of living creativity was not able to realize itself aesthetically. The greatest example of the tension between these two poles is to be found in the works of Webern.

But so much seems to me to be beyond doubt: electronics and

---

12. Adorno used the English expression.

internal musical developments are converging with each other. No idea of a pre-established harmony is called for by way of explanation. The rational control over the musical raw material and the rationality of the production of sound by electronic means both ultimately obey the identical basic principle. The composer has at his disposal – at least in theory – a continuum consisting of pitch, dynamics and duration, but up to now, not of timbre. As far as timbres are concerned, even in their most comprehensive array, in the orchestra, they tend to occur independently of each other and sporadically. Their anarchic origins continue to have their effect.

Even today there is no scale of timbres comparable to those of intervals or dynamics. Electronic music promises to make good this defect which is familiar to every musician. It is an aspect of the tendency in the new music to integrate all the dimensions of music in one continuum. Stockhausen has explicitly erected this into a programme. Admittedly, according to his statements in the sixth issue of *Die Reihe*, the electronic timbre spectrum does not seem to be identical with the range of all possible timbres and so does not automatically include more than a selection of the non-electronic vocal and instrumental timbres. For this reason the committed electronic composers, those who fully exploit the constructive potential of the medium and are not just interested in its technical novelty, demand that their music should satisfy the specific conditions of the electronic continuum and should be appropriate to its material. Given the fact that composers have only seriously experimented with it over the last few years, no blame can attach to them for failing to go beyond the initial stages – Stockhausen's *Jünglinge* being the most striking instance hitherto. The same may be said of the fact that electronic music is still shot through with the reminiscences of other sound media, notably the organ and the piano. The criticism that many electronic pieces lack consistency and modernity is much too convenient a pretext for those who want to nip the modern movement in the bud. There is no call to fall into ecstasy over the products of electronic music like jazz fans. But the emergence of electronic music does answer a need which existed in new instrumental music from the outset, above all in the idea of timbral melody [*Klangfarbenmelodie*].

Thus the new music has two extreme tendencies. On the one hand, it is emancipated expressiveness; on the other, there is electronic music whose material laws seem to preclude the subjective intervention of the composer, just as they preclude that of the interpreter. The fact that these extremes actually meet confirms the objective trend towards unity. In the final analysis it leads to the liquidation of the concept of new music. This is not because the new music is simply absorbed into a larger *musica perennis*, but because music in general will be absorbed into the new music. The latter brings to fulfilment the idea contained in all traditional music. It is for this reason that the new music is obsolete as a particular category; it is a suspect subheading. The concept has become irrelevant because by the side of the new music all other music production has become impossible. It has degenerated into kitsch. The distinction between new music and music in general becomes the distinction between good and bad music as such.

(1960)

Vers une musique informelle

In memory of Wolfgang Steinecke

Dire cela, sans savoir quoi.
Beckett, *L'Innommable*

Anyone of my age and experience who is both a musician and who thinks about music finds himself in a difficult quandary. One side of it consists in the attitude 'so far and no further'. In other words, it consists in clinging to one's youth as if modernity were one's own private monopoly. This means resisting at all costs everything which remains inaccessible to one's own experience or at least one's primary, basic reactions. This had once been the attitude of confirmed Wagnerians when confronted by Strauss, and the Straussians adopted it in their turn as a defence against the new music of the Schoenberg persuasion. We are perfectly modern ourselves; who are they to offer us tuition? Sometimes, of course, my narcissism, which asserts itself even though I can see through it, has a hard task persuading itself that the countless composers of music that can only be understood with the aid of diagrams and whose musical inspiration remains wholly invisible to me can really all be so much more musical, intelligent and progressive than myself. I frequently find myself unable to repress the thought that their system-driven music is not so very different from the false notes arbitrarily introduced into the neo-Classical concertos and wind ensembles of the music festivals of thirty or forty years ago. Musicians are usually truants from maths classes; it would be a terrible fate for them to end up in the hands of the maths teacher after all. The speculative artist above

269

all ought to cling to the vestiges of common sense which would remind him that music is not necessarily more advanced just because he has failed to comprehend it. It may indeed be so primitive and uninspired that he failed to consider it an option in the first place. This explains why the products of laborious mindlessness are sometimes not seen through at the outset. Because the musical material is intelligent in itself, it inspires the belief that mind must be at work, where in reality only the abdication of mind is being celebrated.

The other side of the dilemma becomes visible when we see how many members of the older generation feel compelled to go along with the latest trend in order to avoid being thrown on the scrapheap. The works they produce are greeted for the most part with well-earned disdain by the young. At best they are tolerated for their propaganda value. It is essential to overcome these equally unpalatable alternatives. They are too abstract and operate solely at the level of the subjective judge where nothing counts but the content of the judgement and the motives underlying it. Nor is the prehistory of musical judgement, the judge's own intellectual pedigree, decisive here, although that is undoubtedly an important factor in the formation of his thought. I would not wish to claim that my membership of Schoenberg's Viennese school confers any particular authority on me or to assert that as an initiate I had easy answers to these questions.

What we have to contend with in the development of music since 1945 did not simply appear from a clear blue sky. It can be seen to have been haunting everything that is included nowadays under the rather suspect title of 'classical' twelve-note technique. I have been very favourably impressed by works of the Kranichstein or Darmstadt School such as Stockhausen's *Zeit-maße, Gruppen, Kontakte*, and *Carré*, as well as Boulez's *Marteau sans maître*, his Second and Third Piano Sonatas and his Sonatina for Flute. I was also deeply moved by a single hearing of Cage's Piano Concerto played on Cologne Radio, though I would be hard put to define the effect with any precision. Even at the best of times precise definition is anything but straightforward with works of this kind.

Nevertheless, my reaction to most of these works is qualitatively different from my reaction to the whole tradition down to, and doubtless including, Webern's last works. My productive imagination does not reconstruct them all with equal success. I am not able to participate, as it were, in the process of composing them as I listen, as I still could with Webern's String Trio, which is anything but a simple piece. But what I am tempted at first to register as my own subjective inadequacy may turn out not to be that at all. It may well prove to be the case that serial and post-serial music is founded on a quite different mode of apperception, in so far as music can be said to be based on apperception at all. In traditional listening the music unfolds from the parts to the whole, in tune with the flow of time itself. This flow – that is to say, the parallel between the temporal succession of musical events and the pure flow of time itself – has become problematical and presents itself within the work as a task to be thought through and mastered.

It is no accident that in his theoretical essay 'How time passes'[1] – easily the most important one on this topic – Stockhausen should have dealt with the central issue of how to achieve unified parameters of pitch and duration in the context of partition, that is to say, from top to bottom rather than from bottom to top. My first reaction to *Zeitmaße*, in which I relied exclusively on my ears, involved me in a strange interaction with his theory of a static music which arises from a universal dynamics as well as with his theory of cadences. Actual acoustic listening may not provide the ultimate in musical criteria, but it is certainly superior to the far-fetched and idiotic commentaries with which scores are often provided nowadays – the more fulsomely, the less they contain that stands in need of commentary.

In the best modern works there is a unity of theory and practice. Listening to actual performances is likely to be the best way of determining whether a musician whose own assumptions lie some way behind the latest developments will thereby be debarred from an adequate appreciation. The recognition of

1. *Die Reihe*, no. 3, 1957, p. 13. [Adorno's note.]

271

frontiers implies the possibility of crossing them. It is just as urgent for musical theory to reflect on its own procedures as it is for music itself. It is the bitter fate of any theory worthy of the name that it is able to think beyond its own limitations, to reach further than the end of its nose. To do this is almost the distinguishing mark of any authentic thinking. It is in this spirit that these pages, which are not the product of the most recent ideas, venture to speak of one of the most advanced concepts – namely, that of an informal or, to use Metzger's term, an *a-serial* music.

Given the prestissimo of recent years, the time is perhaps not unfavourable for such an attempt. The developmental lines of composition themselves seem to converge with the postulate of musical emancipation which I find so appealing. I have coined the French term *musique informelle* as a small token of gratitude towards the nation for whom the tradition of the avant-garde is synonymous with the courage to produce manifestoes. In contrast to the stuffy aversion to 'isms' in art, I believe slogans are as desirable now as they were in Apollinaire's day. *Musique informelle* resists definition in the botanical terms of the positivists. If there is a tendency, an actual trend, which the word serves to bring into focus, it is one which mocks all efforts at definition, just as Nietzsche, no bad authority on musical matters, once remarked that every historical phenomenon eluded semiotic attempts at definition.

I am not able to provide any programmes for athematic music or any statisticial law governing the incidence of marks on the writing paper, or anything of the sort that might clarify my vision of informal music. Nevertheless, I should like at least to attempt to stake out the parameters of the concept. What is meant is a type of music which has discarded all forms which are external or abstract or which confront it in an inflexible way. At the same time, although such music should be completely free of anything irreducibly alien to itself or superimposed on it, it should nevertheless constitute itself in an objectively compelling way, in the musical substance itself, and not in terms of external laws. Moreover, wherever this can be achieved without running the risk of a new form of oppression, such an emancipation should also strive to do away with the system of musical co-ordinates which have crystallized out in the innermost recesses of the musical substance itself.

Of course this gives rise to the difficulty that in the absence of such residual forms, musical coherence appears to be quite inconceivable, while their survival as foreign bodies inhibits the integrated elaboration of musical events. This contradiction highlights most clearly the problems facing music at a stage when an unconstrained musical nominalism, the rebellion against any general musical form, becomes conscious of its own limitations. Just as in dialectical logic, so here too in aesthetics the universal and the particular do not constitute mutually exclusive opposites. If informal music dispenses with abstract forms – in other words, with the musically bad universal forms of internal compositional categories – then these universal forms will surface again in the innermost recesses of the particular event and set them alight. This was the greatness of Webern's music.[2] However, a universality and cohesion achieved by means of specificity must be as hostile towards the same qualities as borrowed from the tradition, as it would be towards a pure mathematics of objective reality which remains neutral towards individual phenomena.

Such informal music had been a real possibility once before, around 1910. The date is not irrelevant, since it provides a demarcation line, dividing the age from the vastly overrated twenties. The beginnings can be seen in the period when Schoenberg wrote *Erwartung, Die glückliche Hand* and *Herzgewächse*, and Stravinsky the *Three Poems from the Japanese*. But this age, the age of synthetic Cubism, soon drifted into other directions. Quite early on, in *Die glückliche Hand*, we find Schoenberg making use of all too palpable surface structures, together with a sort of recapitulation – a notable contrast to *Erwartung*, although doubtless with good reason. These surface

2. Cf. Theodor W. Adorno, *Der getreue Korrepetitor. Lehrschriften zur musikalischen Praxis*, Frankfurt am Main 1963, *passim*, especially pp. 102 and 129. [See also *Gesammelte Schriften*, vol. 15, Frankfurt am Main 1976, pp. 252 and 179.] [Adorno's note.]

structures contribute greatly to the articulation of the work as drama, but represent a regression when compared to the ideal achieved in *Erwartung*, in which everything strives forward to a coda without a recapitulation. And the *Pierrot Lunaire*, above all, cites a myriad of traditional individual forms, albeit with irony. Looking back on it today we can see that Schoenberg comes quite close to Stravinsky. The *Pierrot Lunaire* became a so-called popular work because of these unmodified basic forms and the familiar configurations they gave rise to, configurations which contrasted markedly with *Erwartung*, the song with celesta and also the Four Orchestral Songs, Opus 22. As with the twelve-note technique later on, Schoenberg is running for cover.

What stopped the development of the 'free musical style', as Alois Haba termed it over thirty years ago, was not anything inherent in the music, as Schoenberg may well have imagined, but sociological and ideological factors. We have to link the revisionism in musical structure with such statements by Schoenberg as the one contained in a letter he wrote to Richard Dehmel in 1912, asking whether he would be willing to provide the text for 'a work that would fill a whole evening':

> I have long wanted to write an oratorio on the following subject: modern man, having passed through materialism, socialism and anarchism, having been an atheist, but still retaining the vestiges of his ancient faith (in the form of superstition), wrestles with God (see also Strindberg's *Jacob Wrestling*). He finally manages to find God and become religious. He learns to pray.[3]

In this naive quotation the need to return to theological authority is combined with the renunciation of political radicalism. But in an artist like Schoenberg such a change in attitude had to have repercussions in his music. The element of violence and rupture in the transition from the experiences of free atonality to the systematization of twelve-note technique, and the conception of religiosity as return, together with the finger-

---

3. Arnold Schoenberg, *Briefe*, selected and edited by Erwin Stein, Mainz 1958, p. 31. [Adorno's note.]

wagging admonition about learning to pray, all come together, not just historically, but also in terms of musical substance. In both dimensions order is derived from the need for order and not from the truth of the matter. The vulgar notion that twelve-note technique has its origins in the longing for order does contain a grain of truth, however, despite its blindness towards the role played in its emergence by the logic of music itself. In the light of the pretended objectivization of music the task is to resume the process which Schoenberg throttled at the very moment when his brilliant innovation appeared to give it fresh impetus.

A *musique informelle* would have to take up the challenge posed by the idea of an unrevised, unrestricted freedom. But not a repeat of the style of 1910. It is not possible to carry on composing undeterred in the manner of the most daring works of that period, Schoenberg's most productive one. It is no doubt true that the phrase about the irreversible nature of history, the wheel of time which cannot be turned back, says everything and nothing. The psychologists are familiar with the alacrity with which people hold time responsible for matters which they do not wish to examine too closely or for which they want to disclaim all responsibility. But the impossibility of a revolutionary restoration is a concrete reality. Once the new principles of construction have crystallized out, they entail total and pure consequentiality, even when the principles themselves are subject to dramatic change. Hangovers from the past, such as chromatic relationships within free atonality, can no longer be tolerated as they were at a time when the immanent requirements of the musical means had not yet made themselves fully felt. Valéry has noted that anyone who looks at the achievements of the avant-gardes of the past – and the musical avant-garde of 1910 is now fifty years old – will be constantly struck by their timidity. Or, as Cocteau put it, although they went too far, one is astonished to see by how little they did so. But in fact this timidity is more apparent than real. Every art contains elements which appear natural and self-evident at the moment it is brought into being. Only the course of further developments makes clear that they have come into being and are therefore transitory, so that their naturalness stands revealed as a 'second nature'.

But this discovery changes everything. It is to Stockhausen that we owe the insight that in a certain sense the whole rhythmical and metrical structure of music, including atonal and twelve-note music, has remained within the bounds of tonality. This insight can no longer be forgotten; the contradiction it points to can no longer be tolerated. The fact that since then the relationships between all the dimensions of musical composition have been thoroughly ploughed over, that each one inevitably affects the others, has now become as deeply pervasive as any compositional technique of the past. Even thematic work, in the broadest sense, nowadays displays a tonal aspect, if the word is taken in its truest sense. Admittedly, the significance and the greatness of the works composed just before the First World War can no longer be divorced from their own illogicality. Their effects were so profound simply because of the friction produced by their interaction with something they still felt to be alien, something with which they had not become identical. But even friction coefficients cannot be preserved artificially.

Over the last fifty years there has been a huge growth in the productive forces of music, that is to say, in technique, in the simple ability to exercise control over right and wrong. This does not imply that a stubborn belief in progress should lead us to ascribe a higher value to what is written now than to the products of the past. The point is rather that the advances in control over the material of music cannot now be reversed, even though the results, the actual compositions, do not show the same progress. This is one of the paradoxes of the history of art. No consciousness can assume a greater innocence than it actually possesses. Any attempt to ignore recent developments and to become fixated on the musical modes of the past in the belief that the technically less advanced is capable of achieving a higher quality, is doomed to failure.

The most powerful argument in favour of the authenticity of the historical development is provided by the compelling immediacy, despite all actual mediations of the differences in quality of the most recent compositions when presented in live performance. In general this immediacy is all the greater, the more rigorously the logic of the construction is followed through. Laxer methods, such as can be seen, for example, in electronic music, are recognizable by their liking for 'attractive sonorities' [*Klangreiz*], to use an old-fashioned Impressionist word, and they are betrayed by their peculiarly ineffectual speculativeness, which seems both cunning and stupid at the same time.[4]

The dilemma of a situation which calls for a truly informal music can be summarized in the recognition that, on the one hand, the more urgently the structural arrangements insist through their own shape on their own necessity, the more they become guilty of acquiring contingent matter, external to the composing subject; while, on the other hand, the composer who strives to resist this paradox sinks to the level of the ephemeral and the arbitrary, even though the rules he is confronted with are administrative prescriptions. Almost inevitably new music's supposed freedom of scope is forced back to that condition which was the starting point for the entire movement. Here too we become conscious of an acute antinomy.

Up to now every composer who has insisted on his own integrity and refused to compose in any way other than that suggested by his own spontaneous reactions, or who has rebelled against the constraints of the principles of construction, has failed miserably in his attempt to break fresh ground. Instead,

---

4. The false emphasis on the idea of sonority [*Klang*] in the new music is the sign of the dilettante and of those people who place arbitrary interpretations on what they have failed to understand. The dimension of sonority is perhaps the most prominent element in the new music, having been liberated by it and, though newly discovered, it is less in conflict with older listening habits than anything else. However, in works which count it is never an end in itself, but instead is both functional in the context of the work and also provides an element of fermentation. Schoenberg always stressed that sonority [*Klang*] was a means to achieve the adequate representation of the musical idea. If the new music is at all incompatible with what preceded it, it is in the absence of sonic attractiveness [*Klangreiz*] as a categorical concept. This is still the most popular way into mis-hearing it. This has been confirmed by the most recent development, in which sonority has been integrated into the overall construction as one of its parameters. [Adorno's note.]

without suspecting it, he simply repeats the attitudes of those contemporaries of free atonality who proudly claimed not to be snobs, but who only succeeded in producing rubbish instead of works that were unmistakably their own. If, on the other hand, a composer wilfully ignores the pattern of his own reactions and succumbs to the illusion that he can roll up his sleeves and labour away at the material to hand he will find that he has surrendered to the philistinism of reified consciousness. The strategic task facing an informal music would be to break out of this double bind.

In his actual practice Schoenberg himself never committed himself fully to the idea of the totality of relationships, of panthematic composition. From his Opus 10 on his entire production oscillated between the extremes of the totally thematic and the athematic. With an iron nerve he refused to seek a compromise, but instead held the two modes apart in sharp opposition to each other. In the third movement of the Quartet in F-sharp minor, the variations, he uses tonal means to bring about a concentration of the thematic and motivic relationships in a way that does not recur until his serial compositions. The last movement of the same work, however, comes close to non-thematic music, despite the presence of rather vague motivic reminiscences and a drastic articulation following the recitative-like and arioso-like codas, both of which are repeated. The sequence of Schoenberg's revolutionary works forms a rhythmic alternation between freedom and organization, like that between a concentrated breathing in and out.

The Three Pieces for Piano, Opus 11 move in the direction of the athematic; the final one actually achieves it, while in the second a developing variation shrivels into the bald reiteration of motifs and segments. As if by way of compensation, the large-scale architectonics are traditionalist in the first piece, a three-part song-form, with a repetition of the first section [m 53] which is disguised by its rhetoric and hence difficult to hear. In the second piece the outlines of an extended recapitulation are unmistakable. The majority of the Five Orchestral Pieces, Opus 16, on the other hand, are thematic; the dense orchestral texture sets up thematic relationships between the different parts almost

278

involuntarily. Here too there is a compensatory element. The forms are altogether freer: in the first piece, thanks to the *ostinato* idea which exercises an almost magnetic attraction on the direction of the piece; the second, because of the consistent use of the prosaic principle. In the middle pieces three-part forms are also evoked, in the rapid fourth, for example, the scherzo is reconceived in terms of the moment of eruption. Then the following work, the monodrama *Erwartung*, is again athematic, like a premonition of automatic writing, while the *Pierrot* is thematic and the Wind Quintet takes thematicism to an extreme. Lastly, the String Trio leans once again towards the athematic, at least in its rhythmic articulation: coherent or even comprehensible themes are scarcely attempted. Schoenberg's conception of a fully constructed totality overlaps with the opposing impulse. He rebels against the principle which he himself established, perhaps just because it is established, and he longs simply to let himself go.

Today this tension would have to be released in each individual work. It is by no means the case that the expression of the subject, which alternates in Schoenberg with constructivity, has made way for a musical order of existence, an ontology. It is doubtless true that serial and post-serial music and the radical Western experiments of the young Stravinsky and Varèse have rendered the Expressionist ideal irretrievably obsolete. In the case of the latter, however, the discontent with expression can be reinterpreted as the positive wish-fulfilment of a musical cosmos in which the individual subjects who are expressing themselves are balanced against each other to the point where the individual's power to express himself becomes unnecessary and irrelevant. The contemporary rebellion against subjectivity has nothing in common with the reactionary anti-subjectivity which has been under way for over forty years, apart from the conviction which has received the seal of approval from official ideology that man no longer stands in the centre of creation.[5] But this loss is not glorified as a new, higher stage of development.

---

5. A reference to Hans Sedlmayr's *Verlust der Mitte* [The Loss of the Centre] 1957, which popularized this thesis.

The new rebellion sacrifices no nuance, but in tendency at least, it raises each nuance from the realm of expression onto a less malleable technological plane. It retains a firm hold on the achievements of subjectivity; its exponents all maintain the tradition of the Schoenberg School rather than that of neo-Classicism. It is worlds away from the recuperation of the pristine, and hence from any tendency to make a cult of its objectivity. But it does represent a response to the progressive expropriation of the individual to the point where it threatens to overwhelm the totality with catastrophe. Because of this recent history has reacted by coating every direct expression of subjectivity with a layer of vanity, inauthenticity and ideology.

In the tradition of Western nominalism art had always imagined that it could locate its enduring core and substance in the subject. This subject now stands exposed as ephemeral. While it behaves as if it were the creator of the world, the ground of reality, it turns out to be what the English call a 'fake', the mere trappings of someone who gives himself airs, sets himself up as something special, while scarcely retaining any reality at all. The events that have taken place in the world, which are repeated daily and can get even worse, have contributed effectively to the undermining of art in which subjectivity asserts itself as a positive good, just as they have devalued every would-be pious community art. Impossible though it be to conceive of music, or indeed any art, as bereft of the element of subjectivity, it must nevertheless bid farewell to that subjectivity which is mirrored in expression and hence is always affirmative, a form of subjectivity which Expressionism inherited directly from neo-Romanticism. To that extent the situation is irreconcilable with the position of classical Expressionism in which expression and the individual were unproblematic features of music.

With the increasing mastery of the material the events at the subjective pole of music inevitably unsettle the opposite pole, the musical material itself. Misunderstandings arise because of the tenacious resistance of the concept to any abstract designation. But this resistance is historical in form. The sound material available is different at different times and it is not possible to overlook these differences in considering the concrete shape of the work. Material cannot be thought of except as the stuff with which the composer operates and in which he works. And this in turn is nothing less than the objectified and critically reflected state of the technical productive forces of an age with which any given composer is inevitably confronted. The physical and historical dimensions mutually interact.

In Viennese Classicism, for example, the material comprises not just tonality, the tempered tuning system, the possibility of modulation through the complete circle of fifths. It also includes countless idiomatic components which add up to the musical language of the age. One might say that music operates *within* that language, rather than *with* it. Even typical forms such as the sonata, the rondo, the character variation, or syntactic forms like those of the antecedent and consequent, were largely a priori givens, rather than forms actively chosen.

What Schenker calls the fundamental line [*Urlinie*] is in reality probably the essence of that idiom expressed as a norm. When he reproaches Wagner with having destroyed the fundamental line, he speaks no more than the truth in the sense that in Wagner for the first time the form-creating function of musical idiom was being eroded by the process of evolution of the musical material.

Schenker's lasting achievement as an analyst is and remains the fact that he was the first to demonstrate the constitutive importance of tonal relationships, as understood in the widest sense, for the concrete shape of a composition – an achievement which stands in curious contrast to his cult of genius. Imprisoned in his dogmatic approach, however, he failed to perceive the countervailing force. This was the fact that the tonal idiom does not just 'compose' of its own volition, but that it actually obstructs the specific conception of the composer as soon as the moment of the classical unity of both elements has vanished. Dazzled by the idiom, he hypostatized it and, notwithstanding insights into structure which have affinities with Schoenberg's practice, he strove to establish for a reactionary aesthetics a solid foundation in musical logic which tallied all too well with his loathsome political views.

In contrast to his formulae, whose sterility is not eliminated by his habit of pointing to them as if to a sublime and unalterable norm, the composer's relationship to those features of the tonal idiom which have freed themselves from their original context has resulted in egregious difficulties whose effects are still with us. In Kranichstein I once accused a composition, which in intention at least had managed to unify all possible parameters, of vagueness in its musical language. Where, I asked, was the antecedent, and where the consequent? This criticism has to be modified. Contemporary music cannot be forced into such apparently universal categories as 'antecedent' and 'consequent', as if they were unalterable. It is nowhere laid down that modern music must a priori contain such elements of the tradition as tension and resolution, continuation, development, contrast and reassertion; all the less since memories of all that are the frequent cause of crude inconsistencies in the new material and the need to correct these is itself a motive force in modern music.

Of course musical categories are probably indispensable to achieve articulation, even if they have to be wholly transformed, unless we are going to rest content with an undifferentiated jumble of sounds. The problem, however, is not to restore the traditional categories, but to develop equivalents to suit the new materials, so that it will become possible to perform in a transparent manner the tasks which were formerly carried out in an irrational and ultimately inadequate way. This would be the prime task of the material theory which I am envisaging here.[6] But if the materials of music are not static, and if to work with the available materials is to mean more than contenting oneself with a craftsmanlike approach which aims at no more than the skilful manipulation of the means available, then materials themselves will be modified by the act of composition. The materials will emerge from every successful work they enter, as if newly born. The secret of composition is the energy which moulds the

---

6. Cf. Theodor W. Adorno, *Mahler. Eine musikalische Physiognomie*, Frankfurt am Main 1960, pp. 124 ff. [Now also in *Gesammelte Werke*, vol. 13, *The Musical Monographs*, second edn, Frankfurt am Main 1977, pp. 239ff. [Adorno's note.]

material in a process of progressively greater appropriateness. Anyone who refuses to take cognizance of such a dialectic will fall victim to the sterility of the New Sobriety [*neue Sachlichkeit*]. This transferred to music requirements which were already encountering resistance in architecture from where they originated, even though they had a greater justification in the practical exigencies of architecture than in music.

The risk I am alluding to manifests itself in what I have heretically termed the loss of tension. The real social emasculation of the individual, which everyone feels, does not leave the artist unscathed. It is scarcely imaginable that in an age when the individual is so diminished and is conscious of his impotence and apathy, he should feel the same compulsion to produce as did individuals in more heroic epochs. Given the anthropology of the present age, the call for a non-revisionist music is to expect too much. Composers tend to react to it by renouncing any control of their music by their ego. They prefer to drift and to refrain from intervening, in the hope that, as in Cage's *bon mot*, it will be not Webern speaking, but the music itself. Their aim is to transform psychological ego weakness into aesthetic strength.

Something of the sort may be said to have been anticipated by their antipode, integral twelve-note technique, if we view it as the attempt to free the ear from the obligation of ubiquitous immediacy, permanent presence, by normalizing and institutionalizing that obligation. But the very relief this brought resulted in an important shift, a quite concrete and specific shift of emphasis in the material itself. I mention just one example. One of the crucial impulses of twelve-note technique, one recently confirmed in Webern's posthumously published lectures, was the prohibition on repeating any one note before all the others had appeared. A work like Webern's Bagatelles for String Quartet, Opus 9, which does not yet embody the principles of dodecaphony, obeys this injunction more purely and more rigorously than anything that came later. One argument in favour of the thesis that systematization brings about a qualitative change, is that the moment the four basic row shapes were fixed, music abandoned the experience which gave rise to them. If a composer writes less ascetically than Webern in the period of the works from Opus 9 to Opus 11 – if, in other words, he uses more notes, and if he attempts, legitimately, to create not just intensive, but also more detailed music – he will find himself violating the prohibition on repeating notes. The combination of different row transformations, the use of a second basic shape to accompany a melodic row, merging rows harmonically or combining them contrapuntally – all these are incompatible with that requirement. Such methods easily result in that fatal preponderance of an individual note which triggered off the original dodecaphonic rebellion. The entire situation is a textbook model of musical dialectics.[7]

Illuminating for the present controversy is the confrontation of a possibly apocryphal statement of Schoenberg's with utterances of very different musicians like Eimert and Cage. When Darius Milhaud visited Schoenberg in Brentwood after the Second World War and told him of the universal triumph of twelve-note technique, Schoenberg is said to have been less than delighted, a reaction with which it is easy to sympathize. Instead, he asked, 'Indeed, and do they actually compose with it?' This tallies with the cumbersome, but stubbornly defended description he gave of twelve-note technique, namely, 'composition with twelve notes related only to one another'. Everything in him resisted the idea that the notes somehow composed themselves,

---

7. The sensitivity towards repetition which, according to *The Philosophy of Modern Music*, is one of the motivating forces of twelve-note technique, is less ambiguous when viewed from a distance than when it was discussed there. Its dialectic is one of the architectonic features of music as such. As a developmental structure music is an absolute negation of repetition, in accordance with Heraclitus' assertion that no one ever steps into the same river twice. On the other hand, it is only able to develop by virtue of repetition. Thematic work, the principle which concretizes the abstract passage of time in terms of musical substance, is never more than the dissimilarity of the similar. A development which leads to something new can only do so thanks to its relationship to the old which is assumed a priori in such a relation and is repeated in however sublimated and unrecognizable a form. There can be no articulated music in the absence of this highly formal constituent of similarity; identity in non-identity is its lifeblood. In serial music this dialectic is taken to extremes. Absolutely nothing may be repeated and, as the derivative of One thing, absolutely everything is repetition. The task of informal music would be to rethink this dialectic and incorporate it into its own organizational structure. [Adorno's note.]

or even that their pure essence is the meaning of music and must manifest itself in the composition: they were there to be composed with. In contrast to this Eimert, in his essay 'The Composer's Freedom of Decision' (in the third issue of *Die Reihe*), asserts very succinctly, 'The notes' – the context is Messiaen's celebrated short piano composition *Mode de valeurs et d'intensités* – 'do not function, they exist. Not that psychology in music is to give way to physics. The sums don't work out as neatly as that. The acoustic process is the product of the intercourse between perception and the state of the object.'

The contrast here is profound. Schoenberg's 'Indeed, and do they actually compose with it?' contains in the 'with it' a residue of unresolved externality. Composition is understood in a traditional sense; the composer composes with raw material which he works on thematically, establishing motivic connections which in Webern, thanks to their extremely condensed nature, develop into an all-embracing canonic system. Material and composition remain alien, opposed to each other. Ways of mediating between them have not been worked out. This alienness becomes manifest in the decline of the element of idiom. Previously the problem of reconciling composition and material was not the least of its tasks. But the more complete the composer's control of his material and the more vigorous his rejection of established musical categories as conventional, then the more abrasive his encounter with his material tends to become.

In consequence the composer's traditional way of making use of the notes becomes tinged with something anti-traditional, something comparable to an industrial form of production: a ruthlessness in the treatment of the material which was inconceivable when the musical subject was in its prime. Nor is the situation affected by the fact that the composer's material, the row, is preformed – or, as many would not hesitate to assert, manipulated by him. The twelve-note row is treated far more uninhibitedly than was earlier the case with interval successions, chords and the idiomatic elements of tonality, without any great concern being shown about the connections between *what* is composed and the *materials* of composition. But the objection to twelve-note practice is no less problematic. This approach simply accepts as realities in themselves what are actually a subjective set of sound materials which have been preformed by history. The note is hypostatized, as it were. This is the basis of the concept of the parameter. According to this concept all musical dimensions of the entire piece of music should be deducible from the properties of individual notes.

In a strange way this leads here, and not only here, to a resurgence of certain motifs of *Jugendstil*. Following the demise of aesthetic Victorianism, with its obsession with copying other styles, *Jugendstil* hoped that it would be possible to create a new formal idiom solely from a pre-existing set of materials. The result was that plethora of refined and spiritual structures which were still causing such mischief in 1920 in such activities as rhythmic gymnastics, expressive dancing and the arts and crafts. The confusion here lay in the idea that the purely subjective work could be avoided by fetishizing the subject matter, as if it were as pure as the driven snow. Absolute qualities were attributed to it in the hope that they would speak. But these materials, the idea of the world as a precious jewel, only become what they are by virtue of their relationships, if not to the individual subject, then at least to the collective subject that negotiates with them. It is doubtless true that the idea of the selfhood and absolute identity of the material used in advanced music has been purified of *kitschig* associations. It would not occur to any half-way intelligent theoretician of Serialism to talk of noble sounds in the way people used to talk of rough or unsmoothed material, and so forth.

But there is an echo of that ideology in the credo that the raw material, the note in itself is more than simply just there and actually enjoys a real existence. If this ideology is eradicated from the whole conception, then nothing remains of the much-vaunted material to which the composer submits, except for natural, physical qualities. As such, however, they are pre-artistic, crudely factual and incapable of guaranteeing anything of aesthetic worth. Whatever you do you get it wrong. The first task is to establish an awareness of the limitations. Schoenberg's dictum, 'Indeed, and do they actually compose with it?' opens the door to the abuse of operating with the twelve notes as if they still belonged within the scheme of tonality. But the hypothesis that the note 'exists' rather than 'functions' is either ideological or else a misplaced positivism. Cage, for example, perhaps because of his involvement with Zen Buddhism, appears to ascribe metaphysical powers to the note once it has been liberated from all supposed superstructural baggage. This destruction of the superstructure is conceived along botanical lines, in the sense that either the tone's basic acoustic material is scooped out from it, or else the composer relies on chance, placing his trust in probability theory.

Eimert underscores the distinction between science and the work of art, but as far as I can see, even he has failed to take the distinction to its logical conclusion and follow through its physical and aesthetic implications. He postulates that 'the musical calculus must harmonize with the fundamental musical material'. Less mathematically, and couched in the language of Hegelian philosophy, this would become the ideal of a musical subject–object. The only question is whether such a harmony is possible. Does not such an a priori requirement beg the question of the identity of subject matter and 'manipulation'? And does that not imply that the subject, which has only been removed after huge efforts, will now return by virtue of the preformation of the musical material? Or alternatively, does it not entail the ascription of an occult quality which mysteriously creates an objective musical meaning to an already prepared material to which the composer has only to adjust himself? In the absence of such explanations an adequate relationship would be nothing but the miracle of a pre-established harmony. Adherents of communication theory will find that hard to swallow.

Conversely, the fundamental material – and Eimert is in the right on this point – is not simply the subject in its own right; it also contains the element of what is alien to the subject, the element of otherness. Every musician who comes into contact with physically pure sounds is aware of the shock he experiences. But if what Eimert calls the fundamental material [*Grundstoff*] really cannot be reduced to the subject, then there can be no identity between it and the 'musical calculus' or the process of composition. In that event, however, it would correspond to the idea of doing justice to the material; to the efforts of art really and truly to be what it is, without the ideological pretence of being something else. Or rather, to admit frankly the fact of non-identity and to follow through its logic instead of covering it up by an appeal to the almost Romantic concept of a seamless identity.

This might well be the way in which Stockhausen would see the matter. At least, it says quite literally in his essay 'How Time Passes' '. . . should he not' (the composer, that is) 'accept the contradiction and resolve to compose from out of the dialectical relationship, since it frequently appears more fruitful to start from a contradiction than from the definition $2 + 2 = 4$'. Yet the context in which this sentence occurs is so difficult that I hesitate to appeal to it without further qualification. Nevertheless, he too refers to the antinomy of material and composed music. Stockhausen becomes conscious of it in the context of the problem of the relationship between physically measurable and authentically musical time.

That identity, the congruence of the composition and its preformed material, was also the ideal of classical twelve-note technique. Musical totality should also be at one with the set of internal musical relationships. But the problematic nature of that ideal makes it necessary to go beyond the dodecaphonic, as well as beyond the old tonality. Webern called on composers to establish as many interconnections as possible. Alban Berg, and Schoenberg too for that matter, would have agreed. This postulate can scarcely pass unchallenged today. I may perhaps be allowed to reminisce. When one comes across such things as a very young and somewhat naive man, one occasionally gains insights which are easily overlooked because they seem all too obvious, once a certain familiarity with a subject has been attained. When I was not yet twenty, I heard Webern's Five Movements for Strings, Opus 5, for the first time at a music festival, and studied the score. I then wrote an essay on it for the Leipzig *Zeitschrift für Musik*, which published my first pieces of music criticism.

In this essay I contrasted Webern with Schoenberg, especially the Schoenberg of Opus 19 and Opus 11. My reservations about Webern would perhaps take a different form nowadays from what they were even ten years ago. I maintained that tendencies which in Schoenberg derived from the need for self-expression and which arose spontaneously and, as it were, irrationally, were given a rationalized and systematic form in Webern. This was already evident in the exhaustive motivic development of the Five Movements, Opus 5. Compared to the unprotected openness of Schoenberg which I so greatly admired, I found the Webern reactionary. I scented reification in his postulate of a maximum of interconnections. It was comparable to what happened later on, in classical twelve-note technique, where the density of organization was intended to make good the loss of the tonal system of relations. In this respect Webern was to be classified among the exponents of traditional, that is, thematic music. Eimert points out that although 'he was the first to abandon the merely linear dimension of the row, he did not do so by integrating the row within a three-dimensional sound world', but that he had gained 'space by splitting up the row into motivic particles and by inserting, as it were, the flat surfaces into each other, thus creating a relief-like network set fast in the sound material, a structure whose material nature and modes of interlocking have only recently become fully transparent'.

In an analogous way, in 1957, I interpreted the function of counterpoint as a device for reconstructing the musical space that had been lost. There can be no doubt that that too was what was meant later on by the totality of the relationships distilled from the individual note. Webern did not think in parameters; what he did was to intensify motivic and thematic music in a way that surpassed Schoenberg and he did so in order to eliminate what may be thought of as the fortuitous residues which survived into both atonality and twelve-note technique. But we should add that this greater concentration of the relationships and the tightening up of technique does not necessarily make the musical end-product, the composition, denser and more compelling.

There is quite a simple explanation for this. As an instance of this canon-like interlocking of the row shapes, Webern's Concerto for Nine Instruments is undoubtedly one of his most authentic works. However, the last movement has nothing like the intensive and compelling effect to be expected from his musical method. It resembles a joyful conclusion. The traditional march accompanies the departure of the nine musicians; it is almost consciously archaic in fact. Instead of the universality of the serial relationships putting their stamp on the material, we find ourselves reminded rather of eighteenth-century cassations, which are scarcely in keeping with the times. There is a wide chasm between the means and the end result.

This calls for closer scrutiny, not in order to find fault with Webern, but because of its aesthetic and technical implications. How many relationships should be looked for depends on the character of the work, the nature of what is to be composed, the simplicity or otherwise of what is to be represented in the composition. The totality of relationships as such, their profusion or absence, are not indispensable features of the work's truth-content. They have no merit in themselves, nor do they automatically provide guarantees of musical meaning.

The realization that this is so has made itself felt in the counter-reaction against the totality of relations as expressed in the aleatoric principle. In the *Lichtspiel* music, Opus 34, a relatively straightforward piece which, incidentally, Schoenberg himself undervalued, we find the work pointing away from the ideal of density of texture. All the serial relations are treated in a consciously primitive fashion, whereas in an ambitious work of paradigmatic importance, the Variations for Orchestra, Opus 31, they are gathered together in an extreme of concentration. Contemporary constructivism, likewise, has a graduated scale, according to the aim of the composition, much as there used to be a continuum between sonata and fantasy from which the composer might make his choice.

It is on such choices that the importance of the concept of coherence [*Verbindlichkeit*] may be said to depend. Not everything need be equally coherent, nor need everything aspire to the same kind of coherence. The antinomy of freedom and coherence cannot be overcome by consigning coherence to the realm of mere method and striving for what is traditionally called 'lawfulness', without reference to content. Compared to the new material, the old thematic work and many of its derivatives were external in the extreme, but the same could be said of conformity to the laws of physics and that fantasy of the *Ding an sich* in art.

The misunderstandings about the relationship between coherence and freedom in art date back to Erwin Stein's celebrated essay of 1924 on the new principles of form, which Schoenberg had authorized. He justifies twelve-note technique by arguing that the methods of free atonality did not permit the construction of the large-scale forms of absolute music. They would have stood in need of the text as a crutch, and they only became possible once more with the advent of twelve-note music. Large-scale atonal works, however, existed much earlier.[8] The oldest, boldest and most important stems from Schoenberg himself, namely the last Orchestral Piece from Opus 16. In this work there is no thematic unity in the usual sense. Instead, symphonic unity is established by a completely different method: the migration of the main line from one voice to the next. Here already the technique of putting things together comes to determine the form. This is only one of the infinite number of organizing principles which can be read out of the conception of the piece and which render superfluous any appeal to systems external to the work.

I have never understood the so-called need for order which has led, if not to the invention of twelve-note technique, at least to the current apologias for it. It is also worth reflecting on the reasons which lead people, no sooner have they reached open ground, to create the feeling that it's time for order to be restored, instead of breathing a sigh of relief that such works as *Erwartung* and even the *Elektra* could be written, works which are incomparably closer to the actual conscious and subconscious of contemporary listeners than any artificially imposed style. Scarcely any artistic movement has escaped the toils of such

---

8. Cf. p. 182 above. [Adorno's note.]

impositions. Even the development from Fauvism to neo-Classicism confirms this, as is borne out by Cocteau's slogan '*L'ordre après le désordre*'. I am unable to discern any guarantee of truth in this eternal recurrence of the need for an order based on known systems; on the contrary, they seem rather to be the symbols of perennial weakness. They internalize the social compulsion oppressing them in their supposed kingdom of freedom, the realm of artistic production, and on top of that they confuse it with the innate vocation of art.

The immanent, transparent laws that spring from freedom and the capitulation to an invoked order are mutually incompatible. The contradiction between the power of order and the impotence of human beings cuts them off from their own yearnings, yearnings for which art could assume responsibility. For all the oppressiveness of the actual and spiritual world, they do not really want things to change. They continually reproduce the authoritarian mechanisms within themselves, in the belief that you cannot dispense with the conventions, even when their validity has long since been exposed and even though culture fails to generate anything remotely similar to them any more. This is the dark secret of the Classical ideal, the authentic formalism. In Stravinsky this attitude is atoned for to a certain extent, because he lets the cat out of the bag, naming the conventions for what they are, instead of claiming any musical substantiality for them by false pretences. It is where that is done that the rot sets in.

Categories like order should be scrutinized under the microscope so as to destroy the illusion of their unity. It is illuminating that after the collapse of the tonal schemata, which fell apart because they were unable to create the form which was their *raison d'être*, music should stand in need of organizing powers so as not to lapse into chaos. But the fear of chaos is excessive, in music as in social psychology. It results in the same short-circuiting as is found in the schools of neo-Classicism and twelve-note technique, which in this respect are not all that far apart from each other. Order simply has to be imposed on freedom, the latter must be reined in – so the argument goes –

whereas the situation is rather that freedom should organize itself in such a way that it need bow to no alien yardstick which mutilates everything that strives to shape itself in freedom. Perhaps one day people will be astonished at music's failure to rejoice in its own freedom and at its short-sighted commitment to ideas that were disastrous philosophically, as well as in other respects. People will be astonished, in short, at music's masochism.

The discomfort shown by emancipated music when faced by a situation in which anything goes, is handed down from one generation to the next, like the violent order of the world itself. The shadow of that order weighs on all musical construction, all structured composition, to this day. From the standpoint of the composing subject informal music would be music which liberates itself from fear of reflecting it and radiating it back, instead of being governed by it. It would learn how to distinguish between chaos, which in reality never was such a great threat, and the bad conscience of freedom, in which unfreedom can blossom and thrive. Concepts like logic and even causality, which the passion for order necessarily avails itself of, but which even the conception of *musique informelle* cannot entirely dispense with, do not operate literally in works of art, but only in a modified way.

To the extent to which works of art share some of the features of reality, logic and causality also intervene, but only in the way in which they function in dreams. If someone invents novel techniques and attempts to justify them, he can easily fall into the trap of naturalizing them, treating them as if they were directly subject to the laws of the phenomenal world. This is demonstrated as much by the pride with which Schoenberg imagined that the twelve-note technique established a lasting control over the material of music, as by the most recent enthusiasm about the supposed origin of sound. It is as important to explode the illusion of naturalness in art as it is to dismiss the superstitious belief in the unambiguous aesthetic necessity which is grounded in that illusion.

In works of art there is no such thing as natural causality. When compared with causality in nature, causality in art bears an extra layer of subjective mediation. The illusion [*Schein*] that art is thus and cannot be otherwise must always be refuted by what art actually is. If works of art exaggerate their fictive necessity and convert it into a literal one, then their 'realistic' attitude will have led them to violate their own reality. The category of correctness, which has been used to supplant that of similarity in art, is no more suitable than the latter to serve as a philosopher's stone. Whatever is observably correct in art can all too easily turn into the false.

The benefits of emancipating aesthetic necessity from the literal variety can be profitably studied at an earlier stage of control of the material of music, namely in *Erwartung*. In this and other closely related works Schoenberg evidently felt that motivic, thematic work was somehow alien to the spontaneous flow of the music. That it was, in short, a form of manipulation, in much the same way as serial determinism appears to be today. Hence the athematic thread in Schoenberg's monodrama. However, it does not simply surrender to chance, but elevates [*aufhebt*] the spirit of motivic, thematic work in a positive assimilation. This brings about a change in the latter; it expands it. From now on this concept subsumes all music (including Webern's middle period) which integrates partial complexes of relative autonomy into a relationship which manifests itself cogently through its characters and their reactions to each other, without its being generally possible to point to motivic similarities and variations. Such things are not rigorously precluded; indeed they are discreetly hinted at on occasion. The impulses and characteristic relations of such music do not presuppose any system laid down in advance or superimposed, not even a principle like the theme.

Instead, they produce interconnections of themselves. To that extent they are the descendants of themes, although themes are not processed in them, or at most only in a rudimentary way, never repeated at intervals. Serial composition, in contrast, makes use on the one hand of the note and all its characteristics and, on the other, of the totality which is derived from it and before which all notes – and rests – are equals. Differentiation and integration are reduced to the same formula and the composition contains nothing qualitatively different to set against them. A thematic composition, however, is one in which the totality consists of autonomous elements which would be nothing without the totality and without which the totality would not exist.[9] Despite this serial music should not just be regarded as the antithesis of motivic, thematic composition. In actual fact serial music arose from the totality of motivic, thematic music – that is to say, from the extension of that principle to include time and colour. Both methods aim at total organization. The difference between them could perhaps be stated as follows. In serial composition as a whole unity is regarded as a fact, as an immediate reality. In thematic, motivic music, on the other hand, unity is always defined as becoming and thus as a process of revelation.

In each case this implies a different attitude towards dynamics and statics. The way in which music is encoded points to a contradiction it shares with literature. Both are dynamic – as the continuum of syntactic clauses, as mental process and as the temporal succession of mutually conditioning elements. Even in Stravinsky's stylized static constructs, the model cube at the start could not simply change places with one of its subsequent distortions; for in that event those constructs would sacrifice their own punctilious claims. An experiment with the opening march in *Raynard* demonstrates this quite clearly.

On the other hand, music and literature alike are reduced to immobility by writing. The spatial, graphic system of signs holds successive events spellbound in simultaneity, in stasis. In neither case is the contradiction superficial. The factor that defines music as a process – namely, the knitting together of themes so that one follows from another – only becomes possible thanks to the fixed pattern of notes. The complex forms by means of which succession is internally organized as such would be inadequate for any improvised, non-written music-making. In the age of

---

9. I owe the formulation of this distinction to a conversation with Rudolf Kolisch. [Adorno's note.] Kolisch, a prominent interpreter of the views of the Schoenberg Circle, taught Adorno the violin.

obligato composition[10] improvisation quickly died out, and memories of an improvising practice in many of the Fantasies from the age of Viennese Classicism are actually defined by the absence of motivic, thematic dynamics, using the term not in the sense of intensity, needless to say, but in the sense of musical development.

But in the contradiction between its congealed written state and the fluid state it signifies, music shares in the ambiguity [*Scheincharakter*] of developed art, even though it does not pretend to offer any other reality than its own – or if it does, then only intermittently. What is fixed in the sign and is really there, appears in terms of its meaning, as process. The language of words shares something of this quality. Just as all new art rebels against illusion [*Schein*], music rebels against this particular version of it. Looked at from this point of view, its most recent development should be seen as the attempt to discard fictive dynamism, that is to say, to make itself as static in its acoustic form as it always was in its written form. Aleatory music, in which successive sounds can be interchangeable, does in fact go as far as this. Conversely, the loosening of the notation to vanishing point envisages a music which really achieves a stasis to which it could only aspire in the past. This reduction to object status refuses to pretend to be process when in fact all is decided by the notation in advance. It is therefore left with the choice of either ruthlessly realizing the decision taken in advance by downgrading what follows, or else of transforming itself into an authentic process.

However, such a reduction still remains an abstract negation. The static nature of notation is only one side of the problem. The other side is what is heard, the temporal event. Unthinkable though this be without script, the latter is no less unthinkable without the former. Notes are of course more than just directions for performance; they are music objectivized as text. This is why they exert a gravitational pull towards being read silently. But what makes a text a text which coincides with its immanent

---

10. This term was introduced by Eric Doflein. [Adorno's note.]

meaning and which requires no performance is something which unfolds in time.

This fact condemns a thoroughgoing static music once more to the status of illusion [*Schein*]. The illusion is that a succession of pure sounds can in reality stand outside time, while what the notes signify in space is nevertheless to be deciphered in temporal sequence, however far the notation may have strayed from measuring time. A succession in time that denies its own progressivity sabotages the obligations of becoming, of process; it fails to motivate why this should follow that and not anything else. But in music nothing has the right to follow something else unless it has been determined by what precedes it or conversely, unless it reveals *ex post facto* that what has preceded it was, in reality, its own precondition.

For otherwise the concrete temporal unity of music and its abstract temporal form will break asunder. What demands to appear just now, neither sooner nor later, feeds parasitically on time, since it automatically enters the chain of succession. If a *musique informelle* is expected to absorb thematic, motivic composition into itself, despite its rejection of it, this only means that music should resolve the dilemma of how to reconcile temporal form and musical content. Paradoxically, however, for this to happen recourse must be had to relatively static segments which alone make it possible to generate some dynamism. For an absolute undifferentiated dynamism would of course lapse once more into the static. It is true that the congealed time contained in musical texts can be actualized in every performance or reading, and hence is not identical with empirical time, but is deemed to be distinguished from it. In this respect too the innermost essence of music as a temporal art participates in the aesthetic illusion. But even while distinguishing it from non-aesthetic time, it retains the character of time within itself, although modified by its general inclusion in the category of art. As soon as the notation is actualized – that is to say, the piece is played – it merges with empirical time and possesses chronological duration, even while appearing simultaneously to belong to another order of time, namely that of the work which is

297

immortalized, as it were, by being written down. One is reminded of Kant's point that numbers, which are thoughts devoid of all intuition [*Anschauung*], must necessarily progress through time and that in consequence logic and intuition must be linked after all.[11] Considerations of this kind should not be dismissed as belonging to the realm of philosophical aesthetics. They are rather a part of that direct process of accounting for its own preconditions which the most recent music aims to provide and on which it is based. They have not yet entered into its actual procedures, although they could well protect them from naturalistic misapprehensions.

The quarrel between motivic–thematic and serial music is resolved essentially by the concept of relation, which has undeniably been neglected in thinking about music over the past few years. The reduction to the note had its negative truth. It had obliterated the intentions of the subject which had threatened to atrophy because they were artificially inserted into the work. It pensioned off the entire range of established and worn-out configurations on the grounds that they were disruptive, stylistically impure and inconsistent,[12] although it could not prevent new ones from coming into being uninvited. But it would be wrong to believe in the critical function of the note as opposed to the configuration [*Gestalt*], as if it were an immediate good, as opposed to a superstructure, and to imagine that the note from which all meaning had been removed, could nevertheless supply its own meaning.

The bare note is a transitional element in the critical process of music's reflection on itself, an anti-ideological marginal value. For it to become music, it must needs have recourse to those configurations which it cannot discover within itself. Music is not composed simply of elements purified of larger structures. The idea, still widely prevalent among young composers, that the

---

11. Cf. Immanuel Kant, *Kritik der reinen Vernunft*. Newly edited by Raymund Schmidt on the basis of the first and second original editions, Hamburg 1952, p. 201 (A 142). [Adorno's note.]

12. In actual fact the terms style and stylistic purity do play a certain role in Stockhausen. [Adorno's note.]

basic givens of a single note could determine the totality of a piece of music, come into the category of what Stockhausen has scornfully called *Quanteln*.[13] Such an idea forgets something which is itself incapable of further reduction, namely relationships. This is the fact that music consists not just of notes, but of the relations between them and that the one cannot exist without the other. But this in turn makes necessary the transition to a *musique informelle*. As an aesthetic ideology the idea of elementary particles was criticized scathingly by Metzger in *Die Reihe*, no. 5.

However, the practice of serial music hitherto has consisted of stripping everything right down to the parameter of the individual note and then – the word bears witness against the thing – building the totality up from scratch. Informal music would signal a departure from this practice. Whatever manifests itself in music as immediate, ultimate, as the fundamental given, will turn out, according to the insights of dialectical logic, to be already mediated or postulated. This holds good for the individual note. No doubt, a certain immediacy is undeniable in such elements, as is the fact of a spontaneous, specifically musical experience. Of undoubted significance for music theory is Hegel's insight that although all immediacy is mediated and dependent on its opposite, the concept of an unmediated thing – that is, of something which has become or has been set free – is not wholly engulfed by mediation.

Reduced to an element of music the unmediated is not the individual note, but the individual configuration [*Gestalt*]; it should be seen as relatively flexible and distinct from contrast and progress. In comparison, in the actual piece of music, the notes are abstract; they would only be thought of as primary in an acoustic sense, not in the realm of composition. *Ce n'est pas le ton qui fait la musique.* Music is not simply an agglomeration of notes. We are reminded here of the trivial example from gestalt theory whose importance for music has recently been emphasized by Henri Pousseur: the universal possibility of transposition.

---

13. 'To quantle', i.e., to treat notes as individually valid particles rather than as components of a higher structure. [Note by Eric Graebner.]

299

Beyond that, it confirms the musical relevance of pitch relationships, since it makes clear that within limits, configurations retain
their identity even when their overall pitch level is altered.

Underlying this is the fact uncovered by the unjustly forgotten
Ernst Kurth, that notes in music are not physical or even
psychological data, but that they possess a unique suppleness,
'elasticity'.[14] Every note that comes within the compass of music is
always more than a note, even though it is not possible to say
precisely what that 'more' amounts to. In the first place, it must be
whatever the note becomes in relation to others. In the termin-
ology of Christian van Ehrenfels from the early days of gestalt
psychology, this was called 'gestalt' quality. Musical notes do not
form a quasi-physiological continuum, but at best one for which
Kurth chose the rather unfortunate and easily misconstrued
expression 'psychology'. It is misleading because the continuum
of notes is not at the mercy of the whims of the individual psyche,
but becomes crystallized in a second objectivity after being
mediated by the subjective mind. And it is misleading above all
because the elements that enter into that continuum include the
non-emotive lifeless, acoustic elements just as much as the
emotionally charged [*beseelt*] acts of the subject, and neither the
one nor the other can be wholly separated out. The purely
acoustic element becomes emotionally charged, whether it will or
not, as soon as it is absorbed into the composition; even the
unexpressive participates in expression, namely as its negation.

The emotive, however, cannot become music without acoustic
support. Not even the subject of musical composition is identical
with the psychological subject. The subjectivity at work in art is
not the adventitious empirical individual, not the composer. His
technical forces of production are the immanent function of the
material; only by following the latter's lead does he gain any
power over it. By means of such a process of exteriorization,
however, it receives back a universality which goes beyond the
individuation of the particular producer. Valid labour on the

---

14. Cf. Ernst Kurth, *Musikpsychologie*, Berlin 1931, Section I, especially pp. 10ff.
[Adorno's note.]

work of art is always social labour. It is this that legitimates the talk of artistic rationality. Where there are grounds for asserting that a composer has composed well such universal subjectivity will have proved itself, as will reason as a positive, a logic that goes beyond the particular by satisfying its desiderata. Such reason tends rather to be obscured by the psychological subject that leaves its imprint on the music.

The site of all musicality is a priori an interior space[15] and only here does it become constituted as an objective reality. It is to be numbered among those things for which over forty years ago a gestalt psychologist coined the rather unattractive name 'psychic object-world'. It is precisely the most subjective aspects of music, the imaginative, associative element, the idea content and the historical substance that is present in all music that point back to externals, to the real world. Music negates psychology dialectically. It is doubtless enacted in an interior space, in the imagination, and to that extent in the subjective mind. But by objectifying itself through its own logic, and becoming a formed gestalt, it also exteriorizes itself at the same time, becoming an objective reality raised to the second degree, and even a quasi-spatial reality. In it the external objectivity returns as the objectivity of the subject itself.[16]

This is why relations in their turn, as the incarnation of the subjective dimension, cannot be regarded as the primal material of music: there are no notes without relations, no relations without notes. Deception is the primary phenomenon. The hypostatizing of relations would be the victim of exactly the same myth of origins as the reduction to the naked note, but in reverse. Even that definition of twelve-note technique as 'a composition with twelve notes only related to one another' resists that reduction to primal elements. It contains both the concept of notes and the dimension of relations: each is to be strictly defined in terms of the other. Schoenberg's idiosyncratic use of language

15. Cf. ibid. pp. 116ff. [Adorno's note.]
16. Cf. Theodor W. Adorno, *Mahler*, *op. cit.*, pp. 98ff. (Also *Gesammelte Schriften*, vol. 13, pp. 218ff.) [Adorno's note.]

is a little in advance of contemporary developments. The latter no longer rest content with the straightforward alternative between the serial principle – the absolute note – and the motivic–thematic principle as the incarnation of the relational dimension. In the latter it is the subject that predominates; in the individual note what dominates is the opposing principle. This is then actualized in the tension between composition and material. Subjectivity is not just injected into the material or imitated by it. The post-Schoenberg development has exploded the familiar equation between subjectivity and expressiveness. The latter only stood out where the composition failed, temporarily, to match up to its material.

What was objected to as experimental in the formative phase of the new music was essentially its criticism of this discrepancy: particularly of the way in which idiom had degenerated into a sort of padding between material and composition. What was profoundly shocking was the fact that this very idiom had received its marching orders. This shock was rationalized away with the argument that whatever deviated from the established language and whenever the composer ventured too far into the unknown, the resulting music would be more prone to failure and more likely to be consigned to oblivion than would be true of the so-called tried-and-proven tradition.

In the upshot the music that has been forgotten was the music that played safe and hence simply reproduced the same thing over and over again. If anything has any prospects of survival, then it will only be music that is not concerned with safety. This has led to a shift in the meaning of the experimental. The need for security today, unfreedom and heteronomy, exhausts itself in tone-row and serial productions which conserve the timbre and the harmonics of the experiments of yesterday. It is imagined that whatever we have in black and white by way of contract and factually provable material will be ours to take away and call our own. But thanks to the discrepancy between the methods of proof and what is actually proved, it is precisely this that is lost at the outset.

The avant-garde therefore calls for a music which takes the

composer by surprise, much as a chemist can be surprised by the new substance in his test-tube. In future, experimental music should not just confine itself to refusing to deal in the current coin; it should also be music whose end cannot be foreseen in the course of production. In genuine experiments there has always been something of a surplus of that objectivity over the production process.

The idea that the composer was able to imagine every last detail in advance is a legend which every composer finds refuted when he hears his own orchestrated sounds for the first time. Schoenberg, who always insisted on the primacy of the imagination and whose own imagination was quite unique, nevertheless admitted that this was a possibility when he made it known that he had had to interrupt work on the Variations for Orchestra, Opus 31, for a long time because some jottings about some of the rows had been mislaid and he was 'merely a constructor' by nature. The tension between what is imagined and what cannot be foreseen is itself a vital component of the new music. But it is no more than a vital element, not an equation which can be resolved in one direction or the other.

Highly complex atonal or twelve-note scores have presumably always eluded a fully adequate formulation in the imagination, whereas important composers have always known from experience that the relevant passages would sound right, as they say, and would be able to judge in advance whether the sound would fulfil its proper function. To that extent the element of chance was already incorporated teleologically into the very music from which aleatory music occasionally distances itself. But productive though it is for the composition to adopt on principle the phenomenon that had previously taken place against its will, namely the surprise experienced by the ear when it first hears the sound actually produced, this does not mean that the composer's ability to imagine has been made redundant. The element of the unforeseen in its new and emphatic sense must not be allowed to escape. From this point of view *musique informelle* would be the idea [*Vorstellung*] of something not fully imagined [*vorgestellt*]. It would be the integration by the composer's subjective ear of what simply cannot be imagined at the level of each individual note, as can be seen from Stockhausen's 'note clusters' [*Tontrauben*]. The frontier between a meaningless objectification which the composer gapes at with open mouth and closed ears, and a composition which fulfils the imagination by transcending it, is not one that can be drawn according to any abstract rule. To make this distinction in each individual case would not be the least insignificant of the tasks facing any informal composition.

The intention is not to reinstate thematic–motivic composition as an indispensable prerequisite of informal music. The notion that the relational aspect, which exists only between notes and has no independent existence, should not be hypostatized corresponds to the composer's suspicion that thematic interconnections might act as the rudiments of tonality. Just as the note, when turned into an absolute, tends to degenerate into pre-artistic physical sound, the absolutizing of tonal relations leads to a mechanical clattering. It is as if once the relationships were established, the whole composition would be cut and dried. The reprehensible thing here is the need for security as such. The clattering of pure relationships probably stems from the fact that they do not have to prove themselves through any friction with something other, something unintentioned: they give shape, but nothing shaped results. If in certain phases of twelve-note technique the only themes have been rhythmic – that is to say, relations independent of tones and pitch – these rhythms soon degenerated into 'patterns',[17] abstract schemata.

In fetishism there is a convergence between the hostile extremes of faith in the material and absolute organization. A *musique informelle* rebels against both. The late Erich Itor Kahn has coined the expression 'robot music'. It is directed against reification; against art which from a hatred of intellectual falseness goes to the other extreme of pure factuality, and ends by submitting to the spell of what actually exists, just like any ideology. Needless to say, this is not the inevitable fate of serial practice; the qualitative distinctions to be made here are those

17. Adorno used the English word.

between music and robotics. Anyone who fails to perceive them should be reminded that the marks of the mechanical which cause such irritation to those monopolists of creativity who stroll in the forest by themselves and find things that have been found there for the past 150 years[18] – that these marks really have been deeply etched into traditional music.

Musique informelle is not cultural neutralism, but a critique of the past. It is probably true that the art of the authentic composers of earlier times, that is to say, up to the threshold of the new music, had a greater ability to make the listener forget the pre-fabricated forms, or else to breathe new meaning into them, than to escape from their clutches. Up to now all composition was a struggle against something alienated; music has hardly ever been at one with its own systems, but has instead celebrated its triumph in the illusion [*Schein*] of such unity. Eimert's astonishment at how much sensible music there is today, despite the proliferation of mechanical recipes, could be extended to traditional music. In Bach all this is a matter of record; the same holds good for Mozart and Beethoven. They all made use of mechanical topoi down to the most intimate inflection.

In many ways the process of composition of the classical type resembled a jigsaw puzzle. Its greatness lay in its powers of self-reflexivity which liberated the mechanical from its inflexibility and transformed the trivial. The idea of the robot makes explicit something that had been implicit throughout the bourgeois musical tradition – an element of reified rationality in general. This now desires to atone by refusing to conceal itself any longer behind the semblance [*Schein*] of the organic. This is why the integral constructivists might do well to adopt the term 'robot music' and turn it from a word of abuse into a positive slogan, much as had been done earlier with the 'atonal'. If the rational and mechanical principle that pervades the entire history of Western music is made explicit, it parts company with

---

18. An allusion to a poem by Goethe, *Ich ging im Walde / So für mich hin, / Und nichts zu suchen, / Das war mein Sinn.* (I was just strolling in the forest by myself, without any idea of looking for anything.)

the ideology of the unconscious. But only when that is done does it become possible to free itself from the mechanical spell that is secretly allied with that ideology. Today, in the presence of the culture industry, the age of topoi is over.

Like all antinomies in aesthetics, the antinomy of the organic, which turned the ideology of the unconscious into an idol, can no longer be concealed behind the façade of the work of art. Art as an organized object, quite literally resembles the organism in the relationship which obtains between the parts and the whole. But with the growing similarity to the living organism, it gradually distances itself from the artefact which, after all, it must remain. The virtually total organization, in which every feature serves the whole and the whole on its side is constituted as the sum of the parts, points to an ideal which cannot be that of a work of art – that is to say, the ideal of a self-contained thing in itself. It comes increasingly to appear to be something which it can never become, precisely because of its axiomatic character as semblance [*Schein*]. The more perfect it is as an artefact, the less it claims to be one. The new music falls victim to this antinomy as soon as it tries to escape it. For the new music – an artefact – to carry off the illusion of the organic, it would be necessary to eliminate quite unsentimentally every vestige of the organic that does not originate in its principle of artifice, its thoroughgoing organization.

But in large measure this illusion of the organic would be the creation of the traditional language of music, with a chromatic emphasis. The minimal, as it were effortless, transition of semitone steps is regularly associated with the idea of growing plants, since it appears not to have been manufactured, but seems as if it were growing towards its final purpose without the intervention of the subject. The very thing which ever since *Tristan* has seemed with good reason to embody the subjectivizing process of music, is an objective reality from the point of view of the language of music: it is the semblance of the organic as mediated by this language. With incomparable genius, Wagner succeeded in creating in *Tristan* an almost perfect unity between the subjective work, the specific musical achievement, and the objectivity of the musical idiom of chromaticism. This was the musical site of the phantasmagoria. What has been postulated and created, claims to be natural.[19] Young composers react quite allergically to this. But following the liquidation of the organic language of music, music once again, thanks to its immanent organization, has become the very image of the organic. There is an analogy here to certain striking thematic tendencies in contemporary painters like Schultze and Ness.

For music the organic ideal would be nothing but a rejection of the mechanical. It would be the concrete process of a growing unity of parts and whole and not their subsumption under a supreme abstract concept, together with the juxtaposition of the parts. But that concretizing process can never be guaranteed by the material alone. Proceeding from the material one cannot get beyond the subsumption of the details; that is not the route to a true process on the basis of the musical content. A synthesis of that kind is achieved by work on the different elements, since these will not synthesize of their own volition. But if the musical substance is to develop organically, the intervention of the subject is required, or rather, the subject must become an integral part of the organism, something which the organism itself calls for. If appearances do not deceive, it is upon this that the future of music depends.

For the subject is the only component of art that is non-mechanical, truly alive. Nowhere else can composers discover anything that will lead them to the living reality. Music may not resemble the subject – for as an objectification it has become qualitatively different from any subject, even a transcendental one. But by the same token, it may not become totally unlike it: for in that case it would become a wholly alienated thing without any *raison d'être*. It can only serve as a simile of such absolute alienation because ultimately its form makes it diverge from it. The ancient epistemological controversy about whether like can be known by like has its relevance for art. In both cases it must be

---

19. Cf. Theodor W. Adorno, *Versuch über Wagner*, Berlin/Frankfurt 1952, pp. 107ff. [See also *In Search of Wagner*, New Left Books 1981, pp. 85ff.]

resolved dialectically. Works of art move towards a neutral zone between things that exist in themselves and those which exist for us, because this 'for us' is a constitutive element of their existence in themselves. This also affects the relationships of works of art to language from which they distance themselves.[20] The more completely the work is organized, the more eloquent it is, since the idea of complete organization refers to the content of the organic and not to mathematical necessity. In its pure form the latter is always a compositional defect – as has been most reliably shown by Stockhausen. Anything which only seems right everywhere, cannot be right anywhere, particularly in its proportions. This is signalled by the need of the integral construct for the assisting subject.

Even the most gifted and advanced composers scarcely rise to the situation. Under the spell of serialism they commonly confine the intervention of the subject to retrospective corrections and to sounding out the determinate structure to test its legitimacy as a living work. Aleatory literary texts, such as those generated by cybernetic machines, behave in a similar fashion. The author attempts to establish something like a meaning or some sort of order through retrospective interventions. In music too such retouching operations seem to be indispensable. It would be pedantic to object to them. In art the way a work is produced is a matter of indifference. Hölderlin wrote prose sketches for even his most powerful hymns. What can be said, however, is that such methods do not appear to be wholly compatible with the aleatory principle. The latter hopes that something like organization will result from the strict operations of chance. If it breaks free of chance, it denies itself and the entire procedure, together with its meaning, becomes self-defeating. It should be recalled that in statistical surveys the results will only be valid if the random selection of the sample has been strictly adhered to. If art allows itself such departures, it may not at the same time grant itself a dispensation from the scientific discipline from which it has borrowed, whether justifiably or not, its ideal of objectivity.

---

20. Cf. above, pp. 5–6. [Adorno's note.]

To tackle the problem from a different point of view is prohibitively difficult because there can be no reliance on the subject as an organic consciousness – on his hearing or his musicality. The superannuated language of music has built up layers of sediment to a degree which cannot be overestimated. As early as Schoenberg the burden of this language was a major source of difficulty. He dealt with it with the aid of a peculiar polarity in the rhythm of his production. It swings between the extreme organic, as in *Erwartung,* and the anti-organic, such as the Suite for Piano, Opus 25. At the same time it was perhaps not yet possible to see how one could be transformed into the other without inconsistency. This possibility is only explored, if at all, in the late instrumental works, like the string trio and the Phantasy for Violin and Piano, Opus 47.

There is an ambivalent relationship between Schoenberg's twelve-note technique and the organic ideal. In this respect, too, it is a turning point. The organic aspect, which was still the idea behind Schoenberg's concept of the instinctual life of sounds in free atonality, referred to the close contact between different musical complexes, just as in tonality. Only what comes into direct contact gives the impression that it is growing organically. On the age-old model of the leading note the organic relationship was always conceived as that of two successive, neighbouring events, which merge without break. Wagner's doctrine of the art of transition is the aesthetics of the organic ideal.

That contact between neighbours was already severed in twelve-note technique. Subjectively, Schoenberg strengthened this tendency with his dislike of 'animal warmth'.[21] The challenge of the first twelve-note composition to ears schooled in free atonality lay in the way that it strictly related successive musical complexes to each other, without one terminating in the other as if that were its rightful goal. To that extent the element of chance, which is intensified with the growing tendency towards integral constructivity, is undoubtedly implicit in twelve-note technique. Initially it is the individual successions that sound

---

21. See p. 231 [Adorno's note.]

accidental. They are deprived of the necessity that once bound them together. This is ceded to the determinants from above, the totality, and returned by these to the individual successions, which as the manifest derivatives of the totality fit into each other without joins, but by the same token, without their former instinctual vitality.

In music, as elsewhere, isolation, atomization was associated with integration from the outset. This brought with it the potential for stasis. At the micro-level temporal sequence remains external to the sounds. The concrete musical composition of individual events makes itself independent of time. In Schoenberg the compositional methods retained from tonality, thematic articulation, and especially the 'developing variation', carry the listener over these hurdles. But their contradiction to the virtual isolation of the micro-complexes from each other, could not remain hidden. The radicalized constructivists that go beyond Schoenberg draw the logical consequence from this when they lose all interest in drive-like relations at the level of detail, and even resist them, not unlike the way in which free atonality recoiled from the false sound of any triad it discovered in itself. For preference they would like to do away with everything covered by the term 'tendency' in musical *peinture*, that is to say, the idea that a musical expression left to itself would like to proceed to the next and go on from there.

This may well explain the overall static complexion: the image of a music essentially alien to time. It attempts to make do without strong categories. But, against its own intentions, this just deprives it of objectivity and makes it incompatible with the medium of time to which as music it inevitably belongs. To neglect time means nothing less than that music is failing to concern itself with one of its specific material preconditions. This raises the question about the nature of a form of music whose concrete elements move towards each other, or collide with each other, like monadic cells, without becoming infected by the residues of organic idiom. And this affects not just its micro-cells, but also the overall form right up to and including the large-scale architecture. The latter can no longer be erected above the individual events on the basis of an abstract plan, nor can it be deduced from parameters which leave matters to a chance succession from one sound to the next.

This throws some light on the category which had a normative significance for the later Schoenberg, that of equilibrium, the generation of tensions and their resolution through the total form. This norm was the apotheosis of the traditional notion of the organic. In Schoenberg the totality becomes for the last time what the pure particularity of the dominant–tonic succession once was. In this strict sense it may really be claimed that Schoenberg is classical music, much as Einstein may be said to be classical physics in relation to quantum theory as a whole. A composition as a whole creates tension and resolution, just as used to happen in the tonal idiom with its primal model, the cadence. This shift to the totality, however, has stripped the parts of their power. In order to become equal to the task, then, which at present remains hidden, it would be necessary to construct down to the last detail the entire texture of the composition, as Schoenberg did in his day with larger forms, like the sonata and the variation, trusting that construction at the level of detail would be carried out by the twelve-note technique. Relationships have to be established between events which succeed each other directly and indirectly – and this applies to events within simultaneous complexes – relationships which themselves provide the necessary stringency.

A premonition of the limitless possibilities of this was supplied by free atonality. They were the possibilities of something organic which did not let itself be seduced into imitating the organisms of life which in actuality just disguise reification. If we wished to provide examples with one eye to the larger structures of free atonality, then informal music would be a third way between the jungle of *Erwartung*, on the one hand, and the tectonics of *Die glückliche Hand*, on the other. However, the sections should no longer just be juxtaposed, as is commonly done nowadays to the point of monotony; they must be placed in a dynamic relationship, comparable to the relationship of subordinate clauses and main clause in grammar. Boulez's work with so-called parentheses, an idea that goes back to Schumann, probably points in this direction. The reification of structural types of composition today takes the form of involuntary clichés at the very point where the rational creation of something completely unforeseeable would like to prevent them. An instance of such a cliché was the use of pointillist methods, which have now fallen into disuse; one of the most recent consists of sound surfaces organized in patches and separated from each other with exaggerated tidiness. These unified sounds and the pieces that deploy them are all as alike as two peas.

Such defects have their roots in the limitations of serial composition. The most obtrusive among them arises from the way in which pitch and duration have been merged under the general heading of time. Stockhausen, who took this identity more seriously than any other serial composer, was also the first to express his doubts about it. The objective time-factor in all parameters and the living experiential time of the phenomenon are by no means identical. Duration and pitch belong to different musical realms, even if in acoustics they come under the same heading. In the controversy on this point the concept of time is used equivocally. It covers both *temps espace* and *temps durée*, physically measurable, quasi-spatial time and experiential time. Bergson's insight into their incompatibility cannot be erased.

Long before him, even traditional epistemology, which he called causal-mechanical theory, made a distinction between phenomenal and thing-like time. But in experienced time like is not like. Logarithmic concepts do not suffice to calculate such likenesses. With the Weber–Fechner law experimental psychology has ascertained that the relationships between basic stimuli – that is to say, objective physical events and the subjective reactions to them – were only relative, and that there was no direct equivalence. This law was concerned with experiences that are far more primitive than those of music; it was concerned simply with the intensity of sensations. The pre-eminent complexity of music as music renders even such conjectures impossible. There is little prospect of deducing musical time and concrete music from objective physical data, even though music cannot be said to be the summation of psychological reactions either. For if it could, we would be unable to think of musical objectivity by virtue of which music is art and not an agglomeration of sensuous modes of behaviour.

In the context of these thoughts about time, current practice reveals signs of discrepancies which make a reversal of these procedures an urgent matter. Sick of the pointillist translations of Webernian patterns into chamber works in which there is no tangible connection between the different attacks, some of the most gifted young composers have returned to the large-scale orchestra. And in general a growing need has been felt for broader, internally coherent areas of sound, in contrast to the austerity of dissociated ones. In sound these pieces often strikingly resemble the flamboyant style for which Boulez had earlier criticized Schoenberg and Berg. Many of these compositions display great mastery of the orchestra; but they are lacking in the representation of sculptured compositional events such as the luminosity and density of sound might suggest. But neither does an orchestral style working with a spatula tolerate the Impressionist primacy of sound-events as such. The emphatic nature of the sound-image calls for something substantial, which would merit such emphasis, instead of the sound constituting the musical content in itself.

The sound offers itself up to musical interpretation in a direct way; but what is usually present, the texture, remains bereft of such immediacy, an incomprehensible inference from the system which sets the parameters. Sound and music diverge. Through its autonomy the sound regains a culinary quality which is irreconcilable with the constructive principle. The density of material and colour has done nothing to modify the dissociative character of the structure, which remains external. Dynamism remains as elusive a goal as it had done previously when the fashion was for an unconnected succession of jumpy staccato notes or segments simply strung up in sequence. This is the objection that should be levelled at the so-called neo-Impressionist features of the most recent music. If music is to liberate itself from the Stravinskian imitation of painting, a reshaping of composition as such is essential. Music must acquire a theme-like force, on the lines of the opening bars of *Le marteau sans maître*, without restricting the thematic to the melodic. The thematic can be articulated at any level. However, the pure course of events must perform what was once done by thematic work, even if its methods – identity, variation, surface connections between motifs – are ruthlessly cut away. Only with musical postulates which are as vivid as the configurations of thematic music once were, will it be possible to create that tension in which the musical consciousness of time can actualize itself.

The aspirations of Cage and his school have eradicated all topoi, without going into mourning for a subjective, organic ideal in which they suspect the topoi of maintaining an after-life. This is why to dismiss anti-art as pretentious cabaret and humour would be as great an error as to celebrate it. But such aspirations do not yet amount to a *musique informelle*. As a joke they hurl culture into people's faces, a fate which both culture and people richly deserve. They do this not as a barbaric gesture, but to demonstrate what they have made of each other. The joke only turns sour when it appeals to an exotic, arty-crafty metaphysics and ends up with an exaggerated version of the very positivism which it set out to denounce. This helps to explain why the joke, which I respect, has been neutralized in contemporary society. The latter defends itself ideologically by swallowing everything. A *musique informelle* should also take good care to protect itself against revivals of *Die Aktion* and Dadaism, against Alexandrian anarchy.[22]

However, in the last analysis nothing slips through the net of the de-individualized society; it integrates everything, even its polar opposite. This is why we do not need to worry overmuch about art's social effect and can devote ourselves uninterruptedly to the matter in hand or, if the word is preferred, to culture. One feels moved to say musically whatever comes into one's head; the

22. *Die Aktion*, edited by Hans Pfemfert from 1911 to 1932, was one of the leading Expressionist magazines. It was notable for its extreme revolutionary attitudes in both art and politics.

only limitations would be those of one's own head. At all events, Cage's work does approach that of an informal music in one respect: as a protest against the dogged complicity of music with the domination of nature.[23] He does not yield to the terrorism of the phenomenon which has come to be known by the phrase 'the technological age', an age which people fear may leave them behind. But just as art is unable to retreat from the tendencies of the age into enclaves of sensitive souls, so too it may not behave as if it could take the bull by the horns and escape from reification directly into a non-existent immediacy. Cage, and doubtless many of his disciples, content themselves with abstract negation in seances with overtones of [Rudolph] Steiner, eurythmics and healthy-living sects.[24] What is astonishing is their ability to translate the apparently vague signs in a decisive manner and the collective acceptance of irrational modes of behaviour. It is easier to ridicule the element of folly than to recognize the utopia for which the provocation to the senses provides a refuge, namely the hope of escaping from the lie of everything meaningful, where meaning is merely subjectively postulated.

A *musique informelle* will find it as hard to avoid an element of abstruseness, as it would to consciously plan for it. Wholly organized and transparent music eternalizes the compulsion of form. So while even an informal music cannot dispense with the abstruse, it becomes a warning against its own dubiousness. It is the blind spot in which it conceals the uncultured element of musical culture. In free atonality such blind spots can no more be eradicated than the white spots on the coat of Pierrot Lunaire. They even appear in the most uncompromising twelve-note constructions, such as the intermezzo of the Suite for Piano, Opus 25. Perhaps the reason for this most recent abstruseness is

---

23. Cf. Cage's aphorisms from the *Darmstädter Beiträge* 1959, p. 52; and on this point see Theodor W. Adorno, *Philosophie der neuen Musik*, second edition, Frankfurt am Main 1958, pp. 195ff. [Also in *The Philosophy of Modern Music*, Sheed & Ward, p. 67.] [Adorno's note.]

24. Rudolf Steiner (1861–1925) was the founder of anthroposophy, a mystical creed based on Goethe's ideas on education and on theosophy. He founded schools to promote a more organic style of education.

that in contrast to its Dadaist grandparents it degenerates at once into culture, and it cannot remain unaffected by this. The assaults of Dadaism could not be accused of abstruseness because they were both conceived and interpreted as hostile to art and culture. Abstruseness degenerates into ideology and to a vacuous craft where its actions remain on the aesthetic plane and thereby submit to the very criterion of meaning – and culture is for good or ill the embodiment of meaning – which they have challenged. However, this is dictated by the impossibility today of that politics on which Dadaism still relied. 'Action painting', 'action composing'[25] are cryptograms of the direct action that has now been ruled out; they have arisen in an age in which every such action is either forestalled by technology or recuperated by an administered world. This indicates the extent to which political practice influences aesthetic modes and it does so precisely at the point where the latter are at their most intransigent and at their furthest remove from normal cultural practice. The limitations of art proclaim the limits of politics.

As long as criticism concerning the subject in music does nothing to promote the reactionary cult of 'bonds',[26] it stands in opposition to aesthetic illusion. The moment where the latter becomes visible is that of the crisis of musical meaning. What is held to be meaning in traditional music is often nothing of the sort; it is simply an established idiom or at best the reflection of the subject who articulates it. Neither sustains anything anymore and this is why meaning has collapsed. No metaphysical meaning is laid down, nor is there any pre-existing meaning for art to imitate. This explains why art and especially music have placed a taboo on every likeness.

But meaning is inescapable insofar as it imposes itself on works of art against their will. This importunate, quasi-alien meaning, should not be left to itself, but should instead be recuperated

25. In English in the original.

26. *Bindungen* means ties or bonds and has close associations with extreme right-wing and Nazi thought since its connotations are those of family ties or commitment to the soil, a region or one's country. It stands opposed to deracinated, cosmopolitan city-dwellers.

from the subject so as to reconcile it. The meaning of the work of art is something which has to be produced, rather than just copied. It is what it is only by becoming itself. This is the element of action in informal music. The concept of a *métier* which contemporary theory cannot dispense with – it is of cardinal importance in Boulez – is its representative in the work of art. It is activity as long as it is realized convincingly. The idea of a *métier* calls a halt to the collapse of meaning.

The aesthetic illusion cannot be eradicated from art. Even art without illusion would not be directly identical with empirical reality. The illusion survives even when it no longer wishes to appear to be anything other than it is. The element of unreality in art is not identical with illusion and deception in the bad sense. In other words, even negated meaning is still meaning. It is not translatable into facts, for every work of art is always more than itself. This is confirmed by the fact that even works in which all interconnections have been as rigorously eliminated as in Cage's Piano Concerto, nevertheless create new meanings by virtue of that very rigour. Nothing could be further removed from traditional music. But even here there is no absence of affinities: the prohibitions of harmonic theory have long since been annulled where prohibited forms occur not just once, without consequences, but are immediately repeated – or at least emphasized as specific effects. The best-known example of this are the parallel fifths in Puccini,[27] which have been legitimized by persistent use.

On the matter of excessive factuality, the objectified elements of art, those which have, as it were, congealed into things, point back to the subject as to their objective correlative: subjective mediation appears to be an inextinguishable component of aesthetic objectification. Art as a spiritual phenomenon is neither the last bulwark of a faded intellectual history, nor the playground of an ad hoc metaphysic of art. What Kandinsky called 'the spiritual in art'[28] is not superstructure, but paradoxically, an

---

27. Adorno may be thinking of the start of Act II of *La Bohème*. [Note by Eric Graebner.]

28. Wassili Kandinsky's book *On the Spiritual in Art* appeared in 1912.

actual state of affairs. Its non-factuality is its principal fact. In Schoenberg as in Kandinsky, this fact has developed from something subcutaneous to something visible to all. It was this that gave rise to that credulity about facts, that positivistic penchant of the artistic consciousness which is the object of criticism today.

Schoenberg wrote a number of introductions to his chamber music for a series of programmes by Kolisch in Madison. In the note on the Second String Quartet the composer observes without a trace of irony that the George poem in the last movement, *Entrückung* (Rapture) – Schoenberg never surpassed the genius and freedom of this work – anticipated or foretold space travel. The violence done to the George poem by this description is unimaginable if we confuse the ecstasy it expresses with the very modest experiences of automatically guided astronauts. Nothing could be more 'down to earth'[29] than the impressive but measurable distance from it. The composer throws his own imagination to the unimaginative as a sop. The task of an informal music and a consciousness appropriate to it would be to rid itself of such contaminations in its own relationship with technology. It should be enough to recollect that there is no atmosphere in the cosmos and hence no air from the other planets, such as is felt so powerfully in Schoenberg's finale.[30]

Nevertheless, if art really desires to revoke the domination of nature, and if it is concerned with a situation in which men abandon their efforts to exercise control through their intellect, it can only achieve this through the domination of nature. Only music which is in control of itself would be in control of its own freedom from every compulsion, even its own. This would be on the analogy with the argument that only in a rationally organized society would the elimination of scarcity lead to the disappearance of organization as a form of oppression. In a *musique*

---

29. In English in the original.
30. Adorno alludes here to the first line of George's poem, 'I feel the air from another planet', a statement which he often cites, since it formulates his view of the effect of all authentic art.

informelle the deformation of rationalism which exists today would be abolished and converted to a true rationality. Only what is fully articulated in art provides the image of an undeformed and hence free humanity. The work of art which is fully articulated, thanks to its maximum control of its material, and which therefore finds itself at the furthest possible remove from mere organic existence, is also as close to the organic as is at all possible.

It is only now that we are in a position to appreciate fully the truth contained in the edifice of Kant's *Critique of Judgement*, which was constructed from a theory of art and a doctrine of living organisms, theories which are as antagonistic to each other as they are similar. It is not the case that the call for the control of artistic material, that is to say, the full working out of the composition – literally its organization – should make way for a laxer procedure. But as a reflex of the composing ear, control over the material must intensify itself self-critically until it ceases to rub up against any alien matter. It must become the ear's form of reaction that passively appropriates what might be termed the tendency inherent in the material. The logic of artistic technique is always authentic control and as such it is also its opposite, the education of the subjective sensibility to respond to the impulses of whatever is not the subject. It is comparable to the assertion that someone has mastered a language, an assertion which only possesses a meaning worthy of mankind if he has the strength to allow himself to be mastered by that language. In this respect music today is close to Karl Kraus's philosophy of language.

Musique informelle would be music in which the ear can hear live from the material what has become of it. Because what it has become includes and culminates in the rationalization process, this process is preserved. At the same time, however, it is deprived of the element of violence it contained, thanks to the non-arbitrary nature of the subjective reaction. If the subject was the embodiment of rationality, it is now both negated and salvaged. It renounces its surplus over the composition. It ceases to mould the material, nor does it furnish it with arbitrary intentions. But the acts in terms of which all this takes place remain those of a spontaneous listening. This would be the threshold of an informal music, marking it off from a thing-like alienated music, as well as from so-called communication.

The structure of musical objectivity *through* the subject and not *towards* the subject sets it off sharply from communication. This latter concept properly belongs in the culture industry, which calculates questions of artistic effects, as well as in applied market research, which tells us what intellectual products must be like if they are to find purchasers. To this informal music is intransigently opposed. It is concerned instead with the representation of a truth content and with a true consciousness, not with adapting to a false one. Within the all-embracing blindness and delusion the only things which inhabit their rightful place in society are those which have broken with communication, instead of seeking to discover its genuine or supposed laws. If communication, that is to say the intervention of art into the realm of the non-artistic, is desirable today, it would be necessary to fly in the face of communication and to flout its rules. This was what was meant by Kolisch's apology for paper music. The norm of possible effects is as false as the norms of abstract mathematical or physical correctness.

The concept of the musical subject should be differentiated. It has absolutely nothing to do with potential listeners, and everything to do with the human right to what Hegel termed 'being there' [*Dabeisein*]. It is the right of subjectivity to be present in the music itself, as the power of its immediate performance, instead of being excluded from it once it has been launched. This right does not involve the hubris, the superstition, that the subject can create the music on his own and can reproduce it in himself, while in reality it is brought into being at every moment by the music to which the subject is at his most obedient when he most exerts himself. The musicality which a *musique informelle* would require for this would both carry the constituents of the old music in itself, but would also recoil from the demands of the conventions. In this it would resemble the musicality of the performer whose views and structural insights purify the score of that sullied layer of tradition, to trust in which passes for the seal of musicality.

In the course of such a process the concept of musicality undergoes a profound change. It would emancipate itself both from projections which are purely subjective and from thing-like objectifications. It would legitimate itself in terms of its adequacy to its own material if the most progressive ears could respond to it at every moment as if it answered their own desires. All of this appeals to aesthetic theory as a reaction to the plight of the actual experience of artists; a conversation with Boulez showed that we agreed on this. The contempt for aesthetics, whose spokesman was Schoenberg himself, had its day as long as aesthetics lagged behind actual developments to which it had remained external, and as long as it loudly proclaimed false, static rules. Neither these nor its purified taste, nor its eternal laws are capable of being restored now. A true aesthetics would have to start where all that fell silent. It can neither be inferred from philosophy, nor can it be an empirical descriptive science of art. Its medium would be the reflection of musical experience upon itself, but in such a way that it would present itself not as an object to be described, but as a force-field to be decoded. Its immanent dynamics contains the latent pointer to what is musically right here and now.

The trend that can now be felt everywhere is the renunciation of a false reliance on both an alien necessity and an alien chance, the surrogate for freedom. If the time is really ripe for this, then the old peasant's question about the toad he had eaten does call for an answer: why was this really necessary? However, the problem is not whether to repudiate these experiments, but how to bring them into line with living musical experience; much as the rules of counterpoint were appropriated and modified by contrapuntal practice. For example, one of the most plausible criticisms of classical twelve-note technique is that the rhythmic and metrical structure still remained tonal in the broadest sense even after the abolition of tonality. It is essential to the ideal of an informal music that this should become part of the composer's experience. Similarly, the spontaneous ear, conscious of itself, should resist not just tonal symmetry, but also its most sublime derivatives — the predominance of an abstractly maintained pulse, the strong beat, and its negative retention in syncopation.

Informal music could augment rhythmic flexibility to a degree as yet undreamt of. In this, as in all other respects, it would be the image of freedom. What the musician longs for, because it would be the fulfilment of music, has not yet proved capable of achievement. Impossible as it has been to discover what music authentically is, it has been no less impossible to bring wholly authentic music into being. It is better to admit this than to bar the way to it by choosing one type or the other and claiming that it embodies the ominously positive musical ideal. Informal music is a little like Kant's eternal peace. Kant himself thought of this as an actual, concrete possibility which is capable of realization and yet is nevertheless just an idea. The aim of every artistic utopia today is to make things in ignorance of what they are.

(1961)

Index

Absolute, presence of, in the
   aesthetic work 2, 4–5, 226–34,
   243
abstruseness, of the new music
   315–16
academicism 209
administered world 221–2
   see also authority; individual
Adorno, T.W.
   Aesthetic Theory 93
   Dialectic of Enlightenment (with
      Horkheimer) 42 n6
   Klangfiguren 249
   The Philosophy of Modern Music
      147–9, 284 n7
   Prisms 151 n7
aesthetic illusion
   Mahler's critique of 88, 93
   and musical meaning 5–6,
      316–17
   and the organic 163, 306–8
   and temporal succession 296–7
aesthetic work
   absolute negativity of 264–5
   ephemeral value of 223–4,
      242–3, 263–4
   ideal of, and eclecticism 113–14
   nature of causality in 293–4
   and representation of the
      Absolute 2, 4–5, 226–34, 243
   uniqueness of 12–13
aesthetics 5–6, 321

affirmation, principle of 4, 154,
   260–61
Aktion, Die 314
aleatory music 94, 290, 296, 308
alienation 161–2, 265
   see also reification
Apostel, Hans Erich 202
applause, meaning of 65–7
archaic survivals 27–9, 32–4
'areas', composition by 190
Art Nouveau 98, 118, 158
atonality, free
   and aesthetic necessity 294–5,
      309, 311
   and extended forms 181–2,
      186–200, 311
   in 1910s, and development of the
      new music 253–4, 273–5, 291
   and progressions in the bass
      214–15
   see also integral composition; the
      new music; tonality; twelve-
      note composition
audience, and the concert form
   65–7, 74–6
aura 35–6, 151 n7
Austria, and Mahler 82–3
   see also Vienna
authority, social
   and artistic autonomy 207,
      291–3
   and neo-Classicism 158

323

development, principle of, *see*
  thematic development
dilettantism 20
dissociation, principle of 218–19
dissonance
  enjoyment of, in popular music
    213
  in neo-Classicism 157
  neutralization of, in *Moses und
    Aron* 237–8
distantiation [*Verfremdung*] 146,
  169, 237–8, 265
doctors, in operetta 27
dome, the 76–8
Dostoevsky, Feodor 86, 144
dream-world, Wagnerian 29
  see also phantasmagoria
Dukas, Paul, *Ariane et Barbe Bleue*
  117
Dvorak, Anton, *Humoresque* 40–41
dynamism 14, 295–8

eating, in the theatre 75
eclecticism 111–15, 122
ego
  and God 22
  and pleasure 50–52
Ehrenfels, Christian van 300
Eimert, Herbert 284, 285, 287, 289,
  305
Einstein, Alfred, *Das neue
  Musiklexikon* 116
electronic music 258, 265–8
Ernst, Max, *Femme 100 Tetes* 156
eroticism 15–16
exchange-value 49
exoticism 22
experimental music, idea of 302–3
expert, the 20, 68, 72–3, 74
Expressionism 205, 234–6, 246,
  279, 280
expressiveness
  moderation of, in *Carmen* 59–60,
    64
  and music 1–6
  of orchestral sound, in Mahler
    101
  pictorial 230–2

and solitude of the individual
  234–6
and technique, in the new music
  12, 219, 220–1
see also inauthenticity

Fackel, Die 215
fashion, taboo on 223–4
Fate
  in *Carmen* 55–63
  in *Der Freischütz* 27
  in Rachmaninov 39–40
fetishism, musical 47–9
  see also commodification;
    reification
Fichte, J.G. 163
Flaubert, Gustave 149
  Madame Bovary 61
folklore, use of 19, 215–16
form, musical
  and atonality 310–12
  and Berg 181–200
  and Mahler 82, 83–97, 100–109
  in *Moses und Aron* 244–8
  and musical content 4–6
  and Stravinsky 164–6
  and subjectivity 87–8, 91–2, 93,
    162–6
  see also aesthetic totality; opera;
    sonata form
foyer, theatre 74–6
Franz Joseph, Emperor of
  Austria-Hungary 205, 206
free atonality, *see* atonality, free
freedom
  bourgeois, in Offenbach 26–7
  and coherence, antinomy of
    290–3
  commitment of music to 150–54
  compositional 24, 194–5
  and *musique informelle* 321–2
  and myth, in *Carmen* 62–4
  and opera 30
  and order, in Stravinsky 160–1
  paradoxes of 9
  and rationality 318–19
  see also autonomy; subjectivity
Freud, Sigmund 143, 204

Fuchs, Robert 116
functional characterization 94–5

gallery 67–9
genius, concept of 111–12, 127–8, 143, 242–3
George, Stefan 99, 235
  Die siebente Ring 135
  'Entrückung' 233 n5, 318
Goethe, J.W. von 102, 112 n1, 305 n18
  Faust 199
  Wilhelm Meister 199
  Wilhelm Meister's Apprenticeship 63 n7, 265 n11
Goetz, Hermann, *The Taming of the Shrew* 125
Gorki, Maxim, *The Lower Depths* 86 n4
Gounod, Charles
  Ave Maria 37–8
  Méditation sur le Prélude de Bach 37
Gundolf, Friedrich 103

Haba, Alois 274
Halévy, Jacques, *La Juive* 54
Handel, G.F. 25–6, 156
happiness
  caricature of, in commodity music 37–8, 49–52
  and musical meaning 92–3
  and sensual sonority, in Schoenberg 137–8
harmonic motifs, use of, by Berg 188–9
harmony, in Schreker 137
Hauff, Wilhelm, *The Singer* 31–2
Hausegger, Siegmund 251
Hegel, G.W.F. von 113, 228, 230, 235 n6
  The Phenomenology of Mind 144 n6
Heidegger, Martin 207 n4
Hindemith, Paul 252–3
Hoffman, E.T.A 31
Hoffmann, Joseph 213 n6
Hofmannsthal, Hugo von 119
Hölderlin, Friedrich 308
Holthusen, Hans Egon 150 n5

Homer, *The Odyssey* 156 n10
hope, 'cunning' of 109–10
Horkheimer, Max 169 n16
  Dialectic of Enlightenment (with Adorno) 42 n6
horses, archaicism of 29
humility, attitude of 21
Huxley, Aldous 242

ideology 51–2
images, prohibition on, and music 230–2
imagination, and the experimental 303–4
Impressionism 18, 137, 165
improvisation 67–9
  and thematic development 295–6
inauthenticity
  in Mahler's language 83–88
  of objectivity, in Stravinsky 146–7
individual
  commodification of 43–5
  impotence of, and musical form 97, 157, 161, 173, 283
  solitude of, and musical transcendence 234–6
instrumental timbre 19–20, 34–5, 135–6, 167–70, 220, 238–9
  control of, in electronic music 267–8
  see also orchestration; sound
integral composition
  and complexity 248
  and idea of totality 233–4, 288–90
  and postwar music 217–21
  and pre-rational form 212–13
  and Western tradition 205–6, 217, 236–42, 258–62
  see also atonality, free; serialism; twelve-note composition
intentionality, and music 2–6
International Society for Contemporary Music 249, 251
Internationale Gesellschaft für Neue Musik 249
interpretation, musical, significance of 3–4

totality, musical
  and integral composition 233–4,
    288–90, 311
  and integration of individual
    components 23–4, 86–8, 94–7,
    100–101, 107–8, 120–21, 182–5
  and musical expression 4–5, 62
  neo-Classical ideal of 111–12
  and theme, contradiction of 17
  see also aesthetic illusion; aesthetic
    work; organic, ideal of
tradition
  and Schoenberg 207–10, 236–42,
    273–4
  and the new music 258–62, 268
Trakl, George 204
transcendence
  absence of, in *Carmen* 62–4
  absence of, in Stravinsky 154–5
  as intrinsic to music 151
Trapp, Max 251
twelve-note composition
  and Berg 181
  and extended forms 181–2,
    186–7
  and free atonality 274–5, 294–5
  and organicism 309–11
  and reification 253–4, 283–95
  and simultaneous plenitude 194
  and Stravinsky 170–72
  and Zemlinsky 118
  see also integral composition;
    serialism

utopia
  and Mahler 103
  and maturity 199–200
  and negation 143
  and Schreker 138

Valéry, Paul 275
Varèse, Edgar 279
variation technique
  in Mahler 94–5
  in Zemlinsky 121–2
Vellinghausen, Albert Schulze 217
Verdi, Giuseppe
  Aida 54

Otello 34, 121
Rigoletto 61
Vienna, as birthplace of modernism
    201–24
violence
  and neo-Classicism 157
  and percussion 33–4
virtuosi 66

Wagner, Otto 213 n6
Wagner, Richard 30
  and Berg 197
  and Bizet 57, 61–2
  and chromaticism 306–7
  and eclecticism 113
  and Mahler 105
  and musical material 281
  and myth 29
  and Offenbach 24
  and Schoenberg 239, 240, 241,
    245
  and Schreker 132
  and Tchaikovsky 42
  theory of music 5, 261–2, 309
  and will to style 158
  and worldliness 222
  and Zemlinsky 117, 118, 123
  mentioned 17, 35, 252, 281
Wagner, Richard: Works
  Lohengrin 23
  Die Meistersingers 125
  Parsifal 239
  Ring cycle 29–30, 55, 239
  Tannhäuser 24
  Tristan und Isolde 306–7
Walter, Bruno 87
Weber, Carl Maria von
  Der Freischütz 27–9
  Preciosa 54
Webern, Anton
  aesthetic tension in 266, 271, 273,
    288–90
  asceticism of 128, 161–2, 169,
    193, 194, 283–4
  and Berg 182, 192
  influence of, on postwar
    composition 179–80, 217, 218,
    220

335